'This modern guide to living a good life by nurturing relationships, giving more to others, and resisting the self-imposed tyrannies of work, time, ambition and achievement, is entertaining and instructive.' *The Times*

'A guaranteed pick-me-up for the early days of January, and a book I'm going to be returning to for years.' *BBC Radio Scotland*

'History has the answers if we care to listen to them – a premise so simple it is surprising no one has highlighted it before. Krznaric selects some of the most telling, assembling them in a Wunderkammer or cabinet of curiosities.' *Independent*

'Roman Krznaric delves into the wonderbox of history ... and reveals how the past can prompt us to aim higher than we do.' *Metro*

'Krznaric is just what you'd want from a guide on a historical tour of the good life: knowledgable, congenial company, and passionate about his subject. A beguiling mixture of lightly-worn scholarship and unashamedly eclectic offerings, the book is driven by Krznaric's unshakable optimism about daily life's improvability.' *Jewish Chronicle*

'A great guide for the confused in love.' *Independent on Sunday*

'Taking one hefty theme per chapter – such as love, work or home – Krznaric serves up a fascinating series of accounts of how we got where we are now, sifting the valuable from the worthless with an impressive indifference to current fashions. After reading *The Wonderbox*, endlessly shopping for stuff you already have will seem distinctly strange.' *Reader's Digest*

'Inspiration for bold experiments in living.' *Oxford Times*

'A truly visionary guide that is delightfully quirky and immensely stimulating. Utterly indispensable.' *Good Book Guide*

'*The Wonderbox* is a treasury of history and philosophy that manages also to be ' ⟶n-Paul Flintoff,

D0993447

ROMAN KRZNARIC is a cultural historian and founding faculty member of The School of Life in London. He is an adviser to organisations including Oxfam and the United Nations, and previously taught sociology and politics at Cambridge and City University. He has been described by the *Observer* as one of Britain's leading lifestyle philosophers.

# THE WONDERBOX

Curious Histories of How to Live

**ROMAN KRZNARIC**

P

PROFILE BOOKS

This paperback edition published in 2012

First published in Great Britain in 2011 by
Profile Books Ltd
3A Exmouth House
Pine Street
Exmouth Market
London EC1R 0JH
*www.profilebooks.com*

1 3 5 7 9 10 8 6 4 2

Typeset in Palatino by MacGuru Ltd
*info@macguru.org.uk*
Printed and bound in Great Britain by
CPI Group (UK) Ltd, Croydon CR0 4YY

A CIP catalogue record for this book is available
from the British Library.

ISBN 978 1 84668 394 7
eISBN 978 1 84765 445 8

# Contents

Preface     ix

*Nurturing Relationships*
1. Love     3
2. Family     28
3. Empathy     53

*Making a Living*
4. Work     79
5. Time     101
6. Money     123

*Discovering the World*
7. Senses     151
8. Travel     176
9. Nature     204

*Breaking Conventions*
10. Belief     229
11. Creativity     253
12. Deathstyle     280

Epilogue     306

Bibliography     311
Notes     327
Illustration Credits     340
Acknowledgements     342
About the author     343
Index     344

*He who cannot draw on three thousand years is living from hand to mouth.*

Johann Wolfgang von Goethe

# Preface

How should we live? This ancient question has a modern urgency. In the affluent West, society is changing faster than we can adjust to it. Online culture has transformed how we fall in love and nurture our friendships. The demise of the job for life, and rising expectations of finding work that broadens our horizons as well as pays the bills, have increased our confusion about choosing the right career. Medical progress has given us longer lives than ever before, and we are left wondering how best to spend the precious extra years we have been granted. Ecological crises are posing new challenges for ethical living, from where we take our holidays to how we think about our children's future. Moreover, the quest for consumer pleasures and material wealth, which obsessed us during the twentieth century, has left many yearning for deeper forms of fulfilment and meaning. How to pursue the art of living has become the great quandary of our age.

There are many places to begin looking for answers. We can turn to the wisdom of philosophers who have grappled with the questions of life, the universe and everything. We might follow the teachings of religions and spiritual thinkers. Psychologists have developed a science of happiness, which offers clues for shaking us out of old habits and maintaining a positive outlook on life. Then there is the advice of self-help gurus, who often deftly wrap all these approaches into a five-point plan.

Yet there is one realm where few have sought inspiration for our dilemmas about how to live: history. I believe that the future of the art of living can be found by gazing into the past. If we explore how people have lived in other epochs and cultures, we can draw out lessons for the challenges and opportunities of everyday life. What secrets for living with passion lie in medieval attitudes towards death, or in the pin factories of the industrial revolution? How might an encounter with Ming-dynasty China, or Central African indigenous culture, change our views about bringing up our kids and caring for our parents? It is astonishing that, until now, we have made so little effort to unveil this wisdom from the past, which is based on how people have actually lived rather than utopian dreamings of what might be possible.

I think of history as a wonderbox, similar to the curiosity cabinets of the Renaissance – what the Germans called a *Wunderkammer*. Collectors used these cabinets to display an array of fascinating and unusual objects, each with a story to tell, such as a miniature Turkish abacus or a Japanese ivory carving. Passed down from one generation to another, they were repositories of family lore and learning, tastes and travels, a treasured inheritance. History, too, hands down to us intriguing stories and ideas from a cornucopia of cultures. It is our shared inheritance of curious, often fragmented artefacts that we can pick up at will and contemplate in wonder. There is much to learn about life by opening the wonderbox of history.

We will be guided on our journey by a host of famous and sometimes forgotten figures, from a seventeenth-century astronomer to a former leader of the Ku Klux Klan, from an early feminist firebrand to a Vietnamese monk who set himself on fire. They will escort us into unusual territory – the invention of the department store or the myth of the five senses. Their task will be to reveal the extraordinary variety of ways that human beings have approached crucial matters such as work, time, creativity and empathy. Our guides will help us question our current mode of living, and offer surprising and practical ideas for taking our lives in new directions.

'The principal and proper work of history,' wrote the seventeenth-century thinker Thomas Hobbes, is 'to instruct, and enable men by the knowledge of actions past to bear themselves prudently in the present and providently in the future'.[1]

Embracing this notion of 'applied history', I have delved into the writings of social, economic and cultural historians, anthropologists and sociologists, in search of the most enlightening ideas for dealing with the predicaments of living in the Western world today. While these scholarly studies have rarely been written with this pragmatic project in mind, they are bursting with insights for those who desire to lead a more adventurous and purposeful life. Just as the Renaissance rediscovered the lost knowledge of classical antiquity and revolutionised the arts and sciences as a result, we must unearth the hidden ideas for good living that have been buried for so long in the past, and create a revolution of self-understanding.

Learning from history is, on one level, about identifying the most compelling of our ancestors' ways of living and adopting them ourselves. Yet it is also about recognising the many ideas and attitudes that we have – often unwittingly – inherited from the past. Some of these are positive and should be welcomed into our lives, such as the view that immersion in the wilds of nature is essential to our wellbeing. But we have been bequeathed other cultural legacies that could be doing us enormous harm, yet which we scarcely spot or question, such as a work ethic in which we consider leisure time as 'time off' rather than 'time on', or the belief that the best way to use our talents is to become a specialist in a narrow field – a high achiever rather than a wide achiever. We need to trace the historical origins of these legacies which have quietly crept into our lives and surreptitiously shaped our worldviews. We may choose to accept them, understanding ourselves all the better for it, or we may reject them and cut ourselves free from an unwanted inheritance, ready to invent anew. That is the sublime power we wield when we have history in our hand.

All history is written through the eyes of the author, who filters the past by selection, omission and interpretation. This book is no exception. It does not cover the entire history of love, money or any other aspect of the art of living. Instead I draw on those episodes which seem best to illuminate the life struggles that many of us face on a daily basis. In the chapter on family, for instance, I concentrate on the history of the househusband and family conversation, partly because they give insights into difficulties I've had in my own life. My choices of historical focus are not, however, purely personal, and reflect a judgement of what may be most useful to people who feel perplexed – or just plain curious – about how to live, and who have the space and opportunity in their lives to make changes.

The following pages are a homage to Goethe's credo 'He who cannot draw on three thousand years is living from hand to mouth.' I examine the last three millennia of human history, from the ancient Greeks to the current day. While looking mainly at Europe and North America, I also turn to other areas of the globe for inspiring approaches to the good life, including Asia, the Middle East, and amongst indigenous peoples, whose contemporary cultures often reflect ancient ways of being.

This book seeks out the connections between the past and the present, creating a bridge of the imagination that can help us deepen our relationships, rethink how we make a living, and open us to new ways of exploring both the world and ourselves. It is time to lift the lid of the wonderbox and discover what history can reveal about how to live today.

# Nurturing Relationships

# 1

# Love

The man immortalised as St Valentine would be shocked to discover that he has become the patron saint of romantic love. His story is obscure, but he appears to have been a priest near Rome who was executed for his Christian beliefs in the third century. A feast in his name was first held in 496, and for most of the next millennium he was venerated for having the power to heal the sick and crippled. By the late Middle Ages, his fame rested on being the patron saint of epileptics, especially in Germany and Central Europe, where artworks from the period depict him curing children of their seizures. He had nothing to do with romance until 1382, when Chaucer wrote a poem describing Valentine's Day, celebrated each February, as a time when birds – and people – would choose their mates. From that moment on, his reputation as a healer started to fade, and his annual feast day turned into an occasion for lovers to send each other amorous verses, and village youths to play frolicsome love games. Valentine's Day was transformed again in the nineteenth century, when it became a commercial extravaganza fuelled by the birth of the greetings card industry and the arrival of mass marketing. A Valentine craze broke out in the United States in the 1840s: within just two decades retailers were annually selling close to 3 million cards, chapbooks and other love trinkets. Today, 141 million Valentine's Day cards are exchanged worldwide each year, and 11 per cent of courting couples in the US choose to get engaged on 14 February.[1]

The way that St Valentine has been converted from a herald

of charitable Christian love into a symbol of romantic passion raises the larger question of how our attitudes towards love have changed over the centuries. What did love mean in the ancient world, or during the chivalrous age of Chaucer? How did the ideal of romantic love develop and shape what we now expect from a relationship? These are the kinds of questions which would have intrigued the French nobleman François de La Rochefoucauld, who in the seventeenth century proclaimed, 'Few people would fall in love had they never heard about it.'[2] He understood that our ideas about love are, at least in part, inventions of culture and history.

Most of us have experienced both the pleasures and sorrows of love. We might remember the burning desire and shared rapture of a first affair, or have taken comfort in the security of a long-term relationship. Yet we may also have suffered from feelings of jealousy and the loneliness of rejection, or have struggled to make a marriage flourish and last.

We can navigate these difficulties of love – and enhance its joys – by grasping the significance of two great tragedies in the history of the emotions. The first is that we have lost knowledge of the different varieties of love that existed in the past, especially those familiar to the ancient Greeks, who knew love could be discovered not just with a sexual partner, but also in friendships, amongst strangers, and with themselves. The second tragedy is that over the last thousand years, these varieties have been incorporated into a mythical notion of romantic love, which compels us to believe that they can all be found in one person, a unique soulmate. We can escape the confines of this inheritance by looking for love outside the realm of romantic attachments, and cultivating its many forms. So how should we begin our journey into the history of love? With a cup of coffee, of course.

## The six varieties of love

Contemporary coffee culture has developed a sophisticated vocabulary to describe the many options for getting a daily caffeine fix – cappuccino, espresso, flat white, Americano, macchiato, mocha. The ancient Greeks were just as refined in the way they thought about love, distinguishing six different kinds.[3] This is the opposite of our approach today, where under a single, vague term we bundle an enormous range of emotions, relationships and ideals. A teenage boy can declare 'I am in love', but he is unlikely to mean the same thing as a sixty-year-old who says he is still in love with his wife after all their years together. We utter 'I love you' during intense romantic moments, while being able to casually sign an email 'lots of love'.

The inhabitants of classical Athens would have been surprised at the crudeness of our expression. Their approach to talking about love not only enlivened gossip in the market square, but allowed them to think about its place in their lives in ways that we can barely comprehend with our impoverished language of love, which in terms of coffee is the emotional equivalent of a mug of instant. We need to unveil the six types of love known to the Greeks and consider making them part of our everyday conversation. By doing so, we may be able to find relationships which better suit our personal tastes.

We have all seen those Valentine's cards with chubby little cupids fluttering around, shooting their arrows of love at unsuspecting people who instantly fall for one another. Cupid is the Roman version of Eros, the Greek god of love and fertility. For the ancient Greeks, *eros* was the idea of sexual passion and desire, and represented one of their most important varieties of love. But *eros* was far from the playful rascal we think of today. It was viewed as a dangerous, fiery and irrational form of love that could take hold of you and possess you. 'Desire doubled is love, love doubled is madness,' said Prodicus, a philosopher from the fifth century BC.[4] *Eros* involved a loss of control that frightened the Greeks, although losing control is precisely what many of us now seek in our relationships, believing that falling 'madly in love' is the hallmark of an ideal match.

In ancient texts *eros* is often associated with homosexuality, especially the love of older men for adolescents, a practice prevalent in fifth- and sixth-century Athens amongst the aristocracy. This was known as *paiderastia*, which in turn yielded one of the most exotic Greek verbs, *katapepaiderastēkenai* – 'to have squandered an estate through hopeless devotion to boys'.[5] Yet *eros* was not monopolised by all-male relationships. The Athenian statesman Pericles was compelled by *eros* to leave his wife in favour of the beautiful and brilliant Aspasia, who became his live-in mistress, while the poetess Sappho was renowned for her erotic odes to women, including those from her native island of Lesbos (hence our word 'lesbian').[6] The power of *eros* also appeared in Greek myths, in which the exploits of the promiscuous gods – notably the males – are revealing of the cultural norms of classical society. Zeus made a concerted effort to satisfy his sexual passions, transforming himself into a swan to seduce Leda, into a snow-white bull to rape Europa, and into a cloud to have his way with Io.[7] Even Polyphemus, the bestial Cyclops in the *Odyssey*, suffered from his unrequited *eros* for the sea-nymph Galatea, although his choice of chat-up lines hardly helped matters: 'White Galatea, why dost thou repulse my love? Oh, thou art whiter to see than curdled milk … brighter than a green grape!'[8] The most visually striking evidence of *eros* in daily life appeared in the bawdy 'satyr plays' that followed the performance of tragedies during the springtime theatrical festivals in Athens. The half-men half-goats romped around with enormous erect phalluses strapped to their waists, peppering their talk with lewd jokes.[9] The pains associated with *eros* could clearly be quelled with light comic relief.

Everyone can recount stories of having their soul pierced by *eros*. I was once lured by *eros* to move my whole life from Britain to the United States in rash – and ultimately failed – pursuit of a woman. Perhaps you were so infatuated with your first boyfriend that you had his name tattooed in Gothic script on your behind – and still bear the evidence. You might remember with mischievous delight making love in the open air of a Paris park on your honeymoon. Or you fell in love at first sight with your alcoholic English lecturer and embarked on a turbulent affair that ended in tears, or possibly children. Whether our memories of *eros* are full of sensual beauty or touched by tragedy, we can hardly imagine love without a strong dose of erotic passion and desire.

A second variety of love, *philia* – usually translated as 'friendship' – was considered far more virtuous than the base sexuality of *eros*. Philosophers such as Aristotle dedicated considerable brain power to dissecting the different forms of *philia*. There was the *philia* that existed within the family unit, for instance the closeness and affection displayed between a parent and a child, or the deep but non-sexual intimacy that could be felt between siblings or cousins tied together by the bond of blood. A utilitarian version of *philia* existed between people in relationships of mutual dependence such as business partners or political allies. If one person ceased being useful to the other, the *philia* could easily break down. We recognise such instrumental friendships in contemporary life, for example when people befriend influential work colleagues because it will aid their travels up the company ladder.

The *philia* most prized by the Greeks, however, was the profound friendship that developed between comrades who had fought side by side on the battlefield. These brothers-in-arms had seen one another suffer and often risked their lives to save their companions from being impaled by a Persian spear. They considered themselves as equals, and would not only share their personal worries but also display extreme loyalty, helping one another in times of need without expecting anything in return.[10] The model for this form of *philia* was the friendship between Achilles and Patroclus – who were allegedly also lovers – which is central to the story in Homer's *Illiad*. When Patroclus dies in combat, Achilles agonises over his body, smearing himself with ash and fasting, then returns to the battlefront to avenge the death of his comrade.

I remember in my early twenties sitting in a smoky Madrid bar with an old college mate, listening to him talk movingly about how much his friendships meant to him. And at that moment I had a revelation: I realised that I enjoyed little of the comradely *philia* that was such an important part of his life. I was rarely emotionally open with my apparently close friends – male or female – nor did I ever sacrifice much for them. My life was full of acquaintances but not many true friends. Since then I have made an effort to bring more *philia* into my relationships. How much philial love do you have in your life? That is an important question today, when so many people are proud of having hundreds of 'friends' on Facebook or 'followers' on Twitter, achievements that I doubt would have impressed the Greeks.

While *philia* could be a matter of great seriousness, there was a third type of love valued by the ancient Greeks, which was playful love. Following the Roman poet Ovid, scholars commonly use the Latin word *ludus* to describe this form of love, which concerns the playful affection between children or casual lovers.[11] We tend to associate playfulness with the early stages of a relationship, in which flirtation, teasing and light-hearted joking are ritualistic aspects of courtship. This ludic approach to love was developed into an art form amongst the aristocracy in eighteenth-century France. Love was a game, full of secret letters, titillating risqué humour and risky rendezvous at midnight.[12] We see *ludus* today when youngsters play 'spin the bottle', which provides the prospect of a first, nerve-wracking kiss. Our most exuberant ludic moments often take place on the dance floor, where physical proximity to others – often strangers – offers a playful sexualised encounter that acts as a substitute for sex itself. One of the reasons Latin American dances such as salsa and tango have become so popular in the West is that they are suffused with this ludic quality that many people feel lacking in their lives.

In his 1930s book *Homo Ludens*, the Dutch historian Johan Huizinga suggested that the instinct for play was a natural human trait evident in all cultures.[13] The implication of his thesis, which is reinforced by the growing psychology literature on the importance of play for personal wellbeing, is that we should seek to nurture *ludus* in a range of our relationships, not just with our lovers or on the dance floor, but also with friends, family and colleagues.[14] Simply sitting around in the pub bantering and laughing with friends is a way to cultivate *ludus*. Social norms that frown upon adult frivolity have allowed few of us to retain the playfulness we had as children, but it may be just what we need in our relationships to escape our everyday worries, nurture our creative selves and live with a greater lightness of being. Let *ludus* become part of our language of love.

Marriages in ancient Greece were rarely ludic. They were generally arranged by parents, and the wife was subordinate to her husband's wishes and expected to stay confined indoors.[15] Nevertheless, the Greeks managed to invent a fourth variety of love called *pragma*, or mature love, which referred to the deep understanding that could develop between long-married couples.[16] *Pragma* is about making a relationship work over time, compromising when necessary, showing patience and tolerance, and being realistic about what you should expect from your partner. It involves being supportive of each other's differing needs, and maintaining domestic stability so that your children have a nurturing atmosphere in which to grow up and the family's financial affairs are secure. Above all, *pragma* is about being committed to the other person and making an effort in your relationship on their behalf, turning love into an act of mutual reciprocity. In the 1950s, the psychologist Erich Fromm made a distinction between 'falling in love' and 'standing in love': he said we expend too much energy on the falling and should focus more on the standing, which is primarily about giving love rather than receiving it.[17] *Pragma* is at the core of this idea of standing in love. With around half of US and British marriages today ending in divorce, the ancient Greek notion of mature love is one we urgently need in order to revive our vision of life-long relationships.[18]

While *pragma* required giving to your partner, *agape*, or selfless love, was a much more radical ideal. This was an ancient Greek love defined by its lack of exclusiveness: it was to be extended altruistically to all human beings, whether they were a member of your family or a stranger from a distant city-state.[19] It was a love offered without obligation or expectation of return – a transcendent love based on human solidarity. *Agape* became one of the central concepts in Christian thought, and was the word used by early Christians to describe the divine love of God for man, a love which believers were expected to return to both God and other people. It can be found throughout the Gospels, for instance in Jesus's commandment to 'Love [agape] thy neigh-bour as thyself'. *Agape* was later translated into the Latin *caritas*, which is the basis for our word 'charity'; in the writings of the twentieth-century spiritual thinker and children's author C. S. Lewis, *agape*, or charity – which he also called 'gift love' – was upheld as the highest form of Christian love.[20]

The idea of an unlimited and selfless love did not arise in ancient Greece alone, and possesses a global resonance. Theravāda Buddhism advocates the cultivation of *mettā*, or 'universal loving kindness', which goes beyond humankind to embrace love and compassion for all sentient beings, and even sometimes plant life. In Confucian thought, the concept of *ren*, or 'benevolence', also refers to an all-encompassing selfless form of love. Yet while *agape* and *mettā* are undiscriminating, *ren* is a graduated love extending out from oneself in concentric circles, with the strongest love reserved for the inner circle of one's immediate family, and then progressively expanding to friends, the local community and humanity as a whole.[21] The power and beauty of inclusive loves such as *agape* is that they help balance our overwhelming desire to be loved, and instead ask us to engage in a life-affirming generosity of spirit. Unfortu-nately nobody has yet invented *agape* speed dating to help create a random kindness movement, nor can we find *agape* personal ads in the newspapers. Still, we can all easily perform acts of *agape*, such as paying the motorway toll fee for the stranger in the car behind us.

A final love known to the Greeks was *philautia*, or self-love, which at first glance seems the opposite of *agape* – a rival that would destroy it. The wise Greeks, however, noticed that it came in two forms. There was a negative kind of self-love, which was a selfish hunger to gain personal pleasures, money and public honours, far beyond your fair share. Its dangers were revealed in the myth of Narcissus, the irresistible youth who fell in love with his own reflection in a pool and, unable to draw himself away, perished there from starvation. The bad reputation of self-love has persisted in Western thought: in the sixteenth century the French theologian John Calvin described it as a 'pest' (by which he meant a plague), while Freud saw self-love as an unhealthy turning of the libido towards oneself, making us incapable of loving others.[22]

Luckily Aristotle had spotted a more positive version of self-love, one that enhanced our wider capacity to love. 'All friendly feelings for others,' he wrote, 'are extensions of a man's feelings for himself.' The message was that when you like yourself and feel secure in yourself, then you will have plenty of love to give. Similarly, if you know what makes you happy, then you will be in a stronger position to find a way of extending that happiness to those around you. If, on the other hand, you are uncomfortable with who you are, or harbour some self-loathing, then you will have little love to offer others. It seems we should learn to love ourselves in a way that does not transform into an entrancing gaze of self-obsession. That means, at the very least, accepting our imperfections and humbly acknowledging our individual gifts, rather than constantly looking at our failures and inadequacies.[23]

Armed with this knowledge of the varieties of love, you would no doubt have had plenty to talk about had you been invited to attend a philosophical discussion about the nature of love in classical Athens. The main reason to understand the six loves is not, however, to enhance the quality of your conversation, but to rethink the meaning of love in your own life. The most striking feature of the ancient Greeks' approach is that they recognised they had love in relationships with a wide range of people – with friends, family, spouses, strangers and even with themselves. As we shall shortly see, this is very different from how we approach love today, which usually involves a romantic focus on a single person who is supposed to satisfy all our loving needs. The Greeks are telling us to foster the many forms of love, rather than pursuing it in excessively narrow terms.

A virtue of thinking in this way is that if you are miserable in one part of your 'love life' – say you are failing to satisfy your *eros* because you have been rejected by someone – then you might focus your attentions instead on some other love. For instance, you could nurture your *philia* by spending time with your oldest friends, or expand your *ludus* by dancing through the night. Moreover, you may feel that you are suffering from an absence of love, but if you mapped out the extent to which all six forms were present in your life, you would probably discover that love is much more abundant than you had previously imagined.

One of the universal questions of emotional life has always been, 'What is love?' I believe that this is a misleading question, and one which has caught us in futile knots of confusion in an attempt to identify some definitive essence of 'true love'. The lesson from ancient Greece is that we must instead ask ourselves, 'How can I cultivate the different varieties of love in my life?' That is the ultimate question of love that we face today. But if we wish to nurture these varieties, we must first dispel the potent myth of romantic love which stands in the way.

## The myth of romantic love

The idea of passionate, romantic love that has emerged in the West over the past millennium is one of our most destructive cultural inheritances. This is because its main aspiration – the discovery of a soulmate – is virtually impossible to achieve in reality. We can spend years searching for that elusive person who will satisfy all our emotional needs and sexual desires, who will provide us with friendship and self-confidence, comfort and laughter, stimulate our minds and share our dreams. We imagine somebody out there in the amorous ether who is our missing other half, and who will make us feel complete if only we can fuse our being with theirs in the sublime union of romantic love. Our hopes are fed by an industry of Hollywood screen romances and an overload of pulp fiction peddling this mythology. The message is replicated by the worldwide army of consultants who advertise their ability to help you 'find your perfect match'. One of Britain's most popular online dating sites is called, unsurprisingly, Soulmates, and in a survey of single Americans in their twenties, 94 per cent agreed that 'when you marry you want your spouse to be your soul mate, first and foremost'.[24]

We take the possibility of romantic love for granted. But to understand why we have become so obsessed with it, and with the idea of a soulmate – a term that only emerged in the nineteenth century – we need to unveil how the concept of love has developed in the West over the course of the last thousand years. The unfortunate truth is that the myth of romantic love has gradually captured the varieties of love that existed in the past, absorbing them into a monolithic vision. This cultural calamity has evolved in five stages, beginning in the deserts of Arabia, where *eros* became the basis of romantic love. *Agape* was added to the romantic ideal in late medieval Europe, while *philia* and *pragma* were incorporated during a third stage in the seventeenth century. The Romantic movement deepened the importance of *eros* and, finally, *philautia* and *ludus* became part of our romantic hopes in the twentieth century. The consequence is that we are now burdened with the unfeasible and often dangerous expectation that all the varieties of love can and should be found in a single person.

Romantic love was born towards the end of the first millennium in the stories, poetry and music of early medieval Persia. Its central features can be found in *The Arabian Nights*, a collection of Middle Eastern folk tales dating from around the tenth century, told night after night by the Princess Scheherazade to her new husband, the hot-tempered sultan Shahryar, who had a nasty habit of executing his virgin brides. The tales were infamously translated into English in the 1880s by the explorer Sir Richard Burton, who made a point of emphasising their erotic content with copious footnotes on Persian sexual mores. You might remember 'Ali Baba and the Forty Thieves', but are probably less familiar with more sensual stories like 'Prince Behram and the Princess Al-Datma'. When the young prince first set eyes on the beautiful and graceful princess, whose face was 'more radiant than the moon', love immediately 'gripped his heart', and he cunningly dressed up as a decrepit old gardener to win her hand. Other stories, amongst them 'The Tale of the

First Eunuch, Bukhayt', were so sexually explicit they scandalised Victorian England.[25] What emerged in such tales was a new vision of love that combined the passion of *eros* with the fusion of lovers' souls.[26] These two elements are at the inner core of our contemporary notion of romantic love.

This Persian passion travelled west towards Europe, possibly with the help of the Crusades. But it also came across the Pyrenees from Al-Andalus, the Muslim kingdom that existed in southern Spain between the eighth and fifteenth centuries.[27] In 1022 the Cordoban philosopher and historian Ibn Hazm published his treatise on love, *The Ring of the Dove*, which echoed the developing romantic sensibilities in the Middle East. In the section entitled 'On Falling in Love at First Sight' he describes a typical case of bewildering love that makes complete sense to us today:

> The poet Yusuf Ibn Harun, better known as al-Ramadi, was one day passing the Gate of the Perfumers at Cordoba, a place where ladies were wont to congregate, when he espied a young girl who, as he said, 'entirely captured my heart, so that all my limbs were penetrated by the love of her'. He therefore turned aside from going to the mosque and set himself instead to following her … She accordingly went up to him and said, 'Why are you walking behind me?' He told her how sorely smitten he was with her, and she replied, 'Have done with that! Do not seek to expose me to shame; you have no prospect of achieving your purpose, and there is no way to your gratifying your desire.' … Recounting the story of his adventure [he said], 'I have frequented the Perfumers' Gate and al-Rabad the whole time from then till now, but I have never come upon any further news of her … and the feeling I have in my heart on her account is hotter than burning coals.'[28]

With a few minor adjustments, this could easily be the opening scene of a modern romantic film. Ibn Hazm's book was part of a wider Arab literature on love and sexuality, which popularised erotic practices such as the sensuous kiss on the mouth, hardly known in Europe during the Middle Ages. The author of the Tunisian sex manual *The Perfumed Garden* wisely advised that 'A moist kiss is better than a hasty coitus.'[29]

The troubadours of twelfth-century Provence transformed these Arabic-Andalucian ideals into what became the medieval European cult of *cortezia*, or courtly love – the second stage in the evolution of romantic love – which concerned the knightly love of a lady, and the etiquette or 'courtesy' that expressed it.[30] Amongst the champions of courtly love was the nobleman and wandering minstrel Arnaut Daniel, who sang out, 'I want neither the Roman Empire nor to be named its pope, if I am not to be brought back to her for whom my heart is ablaze and cleft in twain.'[31] The originality of courtly love was not so much that it was a bold reaction against Church disapproval of the bodily passions, but that it elevated heterosexual romantic love into an ideal of life. To live – and even die – for love became a new personal ambition, at least amongst the aristocracy.[32] The ideology of *cortezia* appeared in books such as *The Romance of the Rose*, a thirteenth-century French bestseller about a courtier attempting to woo his lady, which may be one of the sources of the custom of giving roses as a gift of love.

The courtly love tradition embodied two of the ancient Greek loves: *eros* and *agape*. *Eros* was present in the passion which the man directed towards his object of desire, who was typically a lady of noble blood. A peculiar rule of courtly love was that under no circumstances was this woman to be his wife. *Eros* was not yet part of the ideal of marriage, which was still considered an arrangement for the begetting of heirs and securing property. Hence the Countess Marie de Champagne declared that 'love cannot extend its domain over husband and wife', espousing a doctrine that may give comfort to today's adulterers.[33] How would you demonstrate allegiance to your lady love? Just as we display loyalty to a lover by wearing jewellery or clothing they have given us, a medieval European courtier showed loyalty by wearing his lady's veil – and sometimes even her dress – on top of his armour during a jousting contest.

An even greater peculiarity of *cortezia* was the presence of *agape*, a selfless Christian love for strangers. This was best illustrated by the legend of St George and the Dragon, which became popular in the thirteenth century. An evil, plague-infested dragon makes its nest at a spring that provides water for a nearby city. The king's daughter is offered as a sacrifice to the dragon so the citizens can access the spring. Suddenly along comes St George, who looks the dragon in the eye, makes the sign of the holy cross and charges towards the beast, giving it a near-fatal wound with his lance. Accompanied by the liberated princess, St George then leads the limping dragon back to the city on a leash, where he slaughters it before the eyes of the people. In honour of this heroic deed, the grateful citizens abandon their paganism and convert to Christianity. Such feats, in which knights rescued damsels in distress or were sent on dangerous quests to win the favours of a lady, were partly fuelled by erotic desire, but they were also frequently described with overtones of Christian sacrifice and virtue.[34] Familiar shows of gallantry today, such as a man opening a door for a woman or offering a seat, are faint echoes of courtly *agape*, indicating that the age of chivalry is not quite dead despite the fact that such actions may offend modern egalitarian sensibilities.[35]

Courtly love was often depicted as a chaste relationship. The lady was either unattainable because she came from a social station above the man's own, or was to be admired only from a distance. Yet it was precisely these barriers to sexual consummation underlying so much medieval romance that heightened the passion and eroticism.[36] This is clear from tragic stories that are suffused with frustrated desire, such as Tristan and Isolde, originally a Celtic folk tale before Wagner set it to music, Lancelot and Guinevere, who ends her days in a nunnery after her affair with King Arthur's chief knight, and the later doomed romance of Romeo and Juliet, which first appeared in fifteenth-century Siena.

The tragic tradition has left its mark today in the way that so many people seek lovers who are beyond reach or somehow inaccessible, for instance because they are already married or much younger than themselves. What seems like a perverse strategy in reality serves both to increase the sexual excitement – the thrill of the chase – and to satisfy an unconscious desire for suffering and risk.[37] As the psychologists put it, we often set ourselves up to fail.

The third stage in the story of romantic love, following the Middle Eastern and courtly traditions, surfaced in the Netherlands during the seventeenth century: the emergence of companionate marriage. The Dutch Golden Age is best known for Rembrandt and Vermeer, as well as the fabulous wealth gained from the world's first global trading empire, yet its greatest legacy may have been to transform marriage from a largely utilitarian contract into a passionate union of genuine companionship, or what was known as *gemeenschap*. The Dutch were 'pioneers on the frontier of friendly, loving marriages', argues the historian Simon Schama, and they helped replace the dominant practice of arranged marriage with the idea of marrying for love.[38] This all sounds like a good thing, but it also resulted in the varieties of love being further funnelled into a single relationship.

Unlike the knights and ladies of the courtly tradition, Dutch burghers believed that a marriage was a fit place for indulging in the pleasures of *eros*. The nuptial bed was not simply a convenient location for efficient procreation but a site to partake in the sensuality of 'fleshly conversation'. Although Dutch Calvinism has a pious image, seventeenth-century marriage manuals are quite explicit in their advice, suggesting that it is more fun to make love in the evenings than the mornings, and that it is probably best not to ejaculate more than four or five times a night in the interests of sexual health and enjoyment. Marriages were also expected to embody *pragma*, the mature love which involves sharing the responsibilities of having a family and maintaining a home. This was evident in the frequency of family feasts, the amount of time parents spent playing with their children, and in the curious practice of men publicly celebrating the birth of a child by wearing a quilted 'paternity bonnet' – a tradition which has unfortunately fallen out of fashion with the proud fathers of today.[39]

In addition to *eros* and *pragma*, the Dutch believed that married life should offer *philia*, the companionable friendship that was alien to the medieval concept of marriage, but which we now take for granted. More than at any other moment in the past, husband and wife were likely to consider themselves true partners and confidants. When a man had personal or financial worries, instead of seeking advice from his male friends, he may well have turned to his wife. Although men still dominated the household, deference was conditional on the reciprocal obligation to give the run of domestic affairs to the woman. Foreign visitors constantly remarked on the shows of tenderness and mutual affection between respectable Dutch couples, such as the way they would hold hands while promenading in the park, or kiss each other on the cheek in front of dinner guests.[40] This combination of intimacy and equality was reflected in a new kind of marriage portraiture. Instead of husband and wife being depicted in stiff poses surrounded by religious iconography in the Italian style, the Dutch masters such as Frans Hals created informal scenes of companionate bliss.

This quiet revolution in European marriage was led by the Dutch but began to spread to other countries. In seventeenth-century England, romantic marital love was increasingly appreciated as a source of personal fulfilment, and it was no longer considered strange for a man to develop a deep friendship with his wife. Couples revealed their intertwining love through the new fashion of being buried together with a shared headstone, so they were united even after death.[41] But it would be naïve to claim that gender equality was now the cultural norm across the continent, as patriarchal and chauvinist attitudes remained strong. Only towards the end of the nineteenth century, with the expansion of education for women, did it become common for husbands to treat their wives as equals worthy of intellectual as well as emotional friendship.

Soon after the appearance of companionate marriage, the history of love was set alight by a fourth development: the cultural explosion of the Romantic movement, which drew the emerging conception of Western love into a vortex of perilous

*Above, a seventeenth-century portrait of Ferdinand II of Tuscany and his wife Vittoria della Rovere by Justus Sustermans, which lacks any sense of intimacy. Compare this to* Married Couple in a Garden *(Isaac Massa and Beatrix van der Laen) by Frans Hals, 1622 (below). Notice the casual affection and spontaneity with which Beatrix drapes her arm over her husband's shoulder. A Renaissance garden of love fills out the background.*

passion dominated by the pursuit of *eros*. It began in 1774 with the publication of Johann Wolfgang von Goethe's scandalous novel, *The Sorrows of Young Werther*. In a loosely autobiographical tale, the sensitive artist Werther falls head over heels for Lotte, who is already engaged to Albert. Rejected by the woman he considers his true love, Werther eventually decides 'to drink the draught of death' and, with a pink ribbon Lotte gave him on his birthday tucked into his pocket, shoots himself. The three central themes – falling madly in love, unrequited love and a fatal end – were hardly original, but there was something in the unrestrained expression of emotion in Goethe's book that captured the European imagination.[42] 'Wertherism' became an instant cult, especially in Germany. Young men copied his dress, wearing blue coats and yellow breeches. You could buy Werther tea sets and Werther perfume. Contemplating suicide due to unrequited love 'became high fashion', writes one Goethe scholar, and the novel was said to have inspired over 2,000 copycat suicides.[43] Suffering from love-induced melancholia became the latest social malady, a theme that echoes through the work of Romantic poets such as Shelley, Keats and Coleridge. The overriding lesson of romanticism – which we continue to ignore today – is not that falling in love is a wonderful thing, but that an obsession with finding the mythical soulmate can cause immense personal anguish and wreak havoc upon your whole life.

Goethe's novel, and other romantic writings from the late eighteenth and early nineteenth centuries – such as Jane Austen's *Pride and Prejudice* – also helped spread the ideal of romantic love beyond the narrow confines of the European upper classes. Increasing rates of literacy, combined with the greater availability of cheap editions and the foundation of lending libraries, took the message far and wide, from provincial Prussian towns to the booming cities of the United States. These shifts prompted the historian Lawrence Stone to claim that the rise of marriage for love in the West 'was caused by the growing consumption of novels'. Stone may have stated his case a little too boldly given the Dutch precedent in the seventeenth century, but it is certainly true that in a world without radio, cinema or television, the written word transformed the emotional landscape of generations of men and women, offering a fresh vision of what one should expect from a relationship.[44]

The final layer of the romantic myth, additional to the legacies of Persia, courtly love, Dutch marriage and the Romantic movement, was the arrival of capitalist love in the twentieth century. Love became a commodity that could be bought and sold, with relationships tainted – even warped – by the ideology of the market. People have always bought sex, but buying love itself was a new development. Its clearest expression was in the diamond business. During the nineteenth century it had been highly unusual to buy expensive jewels for your lover unless you were a wealthy aristocrat. But from the 1930s, especially in the United States, mass advertising manufactured the belief that the gift of a diamond was the ultimate – and essential – expression of love for the woman in your life.

On behalf of South Africa's De Beers diamond cartel, the New York agency N. W. Ayer ran one of the most successful advertising campaigns in American history: to associate giving diamonds with romance. They placed glossy colour ads in magazines and offered diamonds to movie stars to wear in public, while also inventing the iconic slogan 'A Diamond Is Forever'. The result was a 55 per cent increase in US diamond sales between 1938 and 1941, with sales continuing to escalate in subsequent decades. A glittering diamond ring had become a symbol of love, and young men from all social backgrounds found themselves getting into huge debt to buy one for their fiancée, who now expected nothing less. N. W. Ayer were undoubtedly delighted with Marilyn Monroe's 1953 hit 'Diamonds Are a Girl's Best Friend', a song which would have made little sense a hundred years earlier. De Beers later hired the J. Walter Thompson agency to work the same magic in Japan, which they managed spectacularly: in 1967 only 5 per cent of Japanese women wore a diamond engagement ring but by 1981 this figure had risen to 60 per cent.[45] The practice of buying lavish gifts like diamonds has now been absorbed into the ideal of romantic attachment. It is worth remembering, when you next find yourself giving or receiving a diamond as a romantic offering, that it is not merely an expression of love but also an outcome of a clever sales strategy that has earned De Beers and others billions. And that goes for the whole range of luxury gifts, such as necklaces, earrings and watches, which we now use to buy a touch of romance.

An even more insidious effect of capitalist love is how we increasingly market ourselves as objects of desire.[46] Although human beings have been preening themselves with fine clothes and make-up since at least the time of the ancient Egyptians, it was in the twentieth century that they most fully became commodities, spending vast amounts on making themselves attractive to prospective partners. This began with a fashion for designer clothes in the economic boom years following the Second World War, and is now most apparent in the cosmetic surgery industry: around 10 million operations are performed in the United States each year, from breast enlargements and nose jobs to liposuction and abdominoplasty.[47]

The consumerist ethos infiltrating public culture also encouraged us to treat finding a lover as a form of shopping, a point first made in the 1950s when Erich Fromm wrote that two people 'fall in love when they have found the best object available on the market'.[48] We are now likely to tick off potential mates against a list of preferred traits, such as having a slim build or the right kind of job, as if we were buying ourselves a new car with all the accessories. Woody Allen was aware of this trend in his film *Husbands and Wives* (1992): 'Spencer was searching for a woman interested in golf, inorganic chemistry, outdoor sex and the music of Bach.' This has all been made easier by internet dating, where you fill out detailed profile questionnaires indicating likes and dislikes, and personal qualities and quirks. Combined with the all-important photograph (the choice of which is a matter for high anxiety), this allows potential partners to pick you off the soulmate supermarket shelves – just as you are able to do to them. Market efficiency is taking the place of serendipity.

But there is more than market efficiency at work. Just as it is common to upgrade a phone or even a car when a new model comes along, there can be a similar tendency to want to upgrade our lover if we see a better one on offer – somebody who ticks more of the necessary boxes. There is a danger, claim some psychologists, that we may seek to maximise the quality of our romantic purchases rather than accept imperfections, and end up treating our partners almost like material possessions that we can discard at will. The overall result is that we have become excessively focused on gaining individual satisfaction – gratifying our own desires – rather than on giving love to another person.[49] The Greeks would be sure to tell us that capitalist culture has gradually lured us into an unhealthy form of *philautia*, or self-love.

I do not wish to paint a completely dispiriting picture of twentieth-century relationships in the West. Alongside the expansion of self-interested *philautia* was a growth of *ludus*, or playful love, another variety of love that the romantic myth managed to appropriate from the ancient Greeks. This was in part spawned by the free love movement of the 1960s, which threw off inhibitions and feelings of guilt about sex, and was popularised by an erotic literature rejecting past prudery and arguing that sex could be fun. The essential text was Alex Comfort's manual *The Joy of Sex*, written in 1972, which has since sold more than 8 million copies. Comfort wrote that sex should be viewed as a 'deeply rewarding form of play', and is a matter of mutual enjoyment that 'involves letting both sexes take turns in controlling the game' (although he had little to say about same-sex relationships). He was particularly keen to promote having sex in odd places and under people's noses: 'this is childish, but if you haven't yet learned to be childish in your lovemaking you should go home and learn'.[50]

Unfortunately the well-meaning advice of Dr Comfort, and the thousands of sex guides that fill the shelves of bookshops, have made many people feel distinctly uncomfortable. The idea that you should be good at sex – a passionate and playful lover – has created severe bouts of performance anxiety. 'More than anything, I associate sex with anxiety, fear of failure ... being laughed at, compared, abandoned,' said one respondent in Shere Hite's classic report on male sexuality, first published in

1981.[51] Both men and women now worry that if they cannot offer their partner a potent combination of *eros* and bedtime *ludus*, they may suffer rejection and be cast back into the well of loneliness that so many of us fear.

Over the last millennium, from the Persian passion of the tenth century to the consumerist relationships of the twentieth and twenty-first, we have gradually come to believe that a single person – a soulmate – can provide all the diverse loves we need in our lives. This is, in historical terms, a radically new view that has few precedents in past civilisations. The idea of a passionate, romantic relationship has hijacked the varieties of love honoured by the ancient Greeks. We now search for a partner who can not only satisfy our sexual desires, but also provide the deep friendship of *philia*, the playfulness of ludic love, the security of *pragma*, and make the selfless sacrifices of *agape* on our behalf, all of which should be sustained by a substantial dose of *philautia*, or self-love.

The problem is that such demands raise expectations that are almost impossible to meet. Where can we find this extraordinary person who is able to give us everything? The answer is that they can usually only be found in our imaginations or on the cinema screen, where we are fed a reassuring diet of intoxicating romances with happy endings. The myth of romantic love has not only left millions harbouring fantasies that reality has failed to fulfil, but has also played a major role in causing the epidemic of divorce that has struck the Western world in the past half century, and the inexorable rise of unsatisfactory short-term relationships.[52]

So where does that leave us today – should we really give up on the possibility of romantic love? And if romance is not the answer, then what exactly should we be looking for in our relationships?

## Why kissing will never be enough

Our culturally inherited vision of perfect romantic love is symbolised by Constantin Brancusi's sculpture *The Kiss*. There is no doubt that it embodies the romantic ideal: the lovers see completely eye to eye, wrapped in an all-encompassing embrace. They are soulmates, united into an inseparable fused form. But *The Kiss* also embodies everything that is wrong about romantic love. These lovers are locked into a relationship that allows no breathing space between them. Their independence and uniqueness as individuals have disappeared, and they have turned their backs on the rest of the world, oblivious to the lives of others. They have become captives of their own love, trapped by an emotional myopia.

It is time to leave *The Kiss* and all it symbolises as a relic of the history of love. We can do so because we have an alternative: the varieties of love invented by the ancient Greeks. These are what we should be striving to cultivate, and with a range of people rather than just one person. I am not saying that you should get your *pragma* from a steady marriage but then satisfy your *eros* in a series of lustful affairs. That is bound to be a destructive strategy, for sexual jealousy is part of our natures and few people can tolerate open relationships. What I mean is that we ought to acknowledge that we may only be fulfilled in love if we can nurture it in a multitude of ways and tap into its many sources. So we should foster our *philia* through having profound friendships outside our main relationship, and make space for our lover to do the same without resenting the time they spend apart from us. We can seek the joys of *ludus* not just in sex but in other forms of play, from tango dancing and performing in amateur theatre to laughing with children around the family dining table. And we must recognise that being drawn too far into self-love, or limiting our love to only a small circle of people, will not be enough to meet our inner need to feel part of a larger whole. So we should all make a place for *agape* in our lives, and transform love into a gift for strangers. That is how we can reach a point where our lives feel abundant with love.

This still leaves the question of what we should seek in a

*Constantin Brancusi's* The Kiss *reveals the limits of romantic love.*

sexual partner, and how we can make the relationship thrive and last. The first lesson from history is to shift our expectations. We have to abandon the idea of perfection – of finding someone who meets all the criteria on our amorous wish list. It is too much to ask for another person to satisfy not only our desire for *eros* and *philia*, but for every other dimension of love as well. This does not mean that our relationships will be diminished, just that their depths will lie more in some types of love than in others. We may come to realise, for instance, that what really matters to us is not so much having a partner who makes us swoon every time we set eyes on them, as if Cupid has just shot us with his arrow, but forging a union with somebody with whom we can share the intimacies of friendship and the quiet pleasures of growing old together.

A second lesson is to understand that love has its own chronology, with the different varieties of love coming and going throughout the course of a relationship. It may all begin with the sexual excitement of *eros* and the flirtations of *ludus*. But once the euphoria of falling in love dies down, there is space for *philia* and the mature love of *pragma* to emerge. Eventually our love may express itself as *agape*, a form of giving to the other person or jointly giving to those around us, where their joys come to feel like our own. There is no set pattern for how these various loves show themselves. But we would be wise to tune into their shifting presence, gently letting go of those which have had their time, and nurturing those that are ready to bloom.

The challenge before us is to adopt a new vocabulary of love inspired by the ancient Greeks, and let our knowledge of its many forms permeate our minds, infuse our conversations and guide our actions. Only then will we be as sophisticated in the art of loving as we are when ordering a cup of coffee.

# 2

# Family

'Some fathers make good mothers, and I hope I was one of them.' After his wife died suddenly in 1964, the novelist J. G. Ballard was determined to bring up his three small children himself. Each morning he would get them breakfast, drive them to school, then at nine sit down at his desk and begin writing, with his first whisky of the day as company. In the afternoons he would help them with homework, play with them in the garden, then rustle up a favourite like sausages and mash for dinner. It was extremely rare to find a single father caring for his children in the 1960s, and he did it in his own style. 'I made a very slatternly mother, notably unkeen to do housework,' Ballard wrote in his autobiography, 'and too often to be found with a cigarette in one hand and a drink in the other.' Despite the lack of dusting, he was undoubtedly a loving and supportive parent. 'He was both daddy and mummy to me,' recalled his daughter Fay of her childhood in the London suburbs. 'I never felt that I couldn't talk to him about anything, be it boyfriends, clothes or make-up. He has no barriers at all. We have been a very close family, always the best of friends.'

The warmth and intimacy he sought to create for his children contrasted with his own youth, growing up in 1930s Shanghai. Ballard's parents spent most of their time downing Martinis at the country club with other British expatriates, and their home was a bastion of formality and conversational silences, as was common amongst the upper-middle classes. The little family life they had was disrupted between 1943 and 1945, when they were interned in a Japanese prisoner-of-war camp – an episode fictionalised in his novel *Empire of the Sun* (1984) – and once the war ended he was shipped off to boarding school in England, spending his teenage years deprived of parental care. These experiences formed the psychological backdrop to his devotion as a father. Ballard actively took part in the home births of his two daughters, 'almost shouldering the midwives aside', and wept throughout both deliveries. Family always came first, followed in the distance by his writing. 'Perhaps I belong to the first generation for whom the health and happiness of their families is a significant indicator of their mental wellbeing.'[1]

Ballard, who died in 2009, may have been an unusually dedicated father, but he was wrong to believe that his generation was historically unique in the value placed upon family life. Its importance echoes through millennia of mythology and storytelling, from the tale of Odysseus, who longs to return to his family in Ithaca, to Medieval Icelandic sagas, from the novels of Tolstoy to films like *The Godfather*. Negotiating the complexities of family relationships has been a constant challenge in the art of living. Whether dealing with neglectful parents, sibling conflict, generational divides or jealousy, being part of a family has never been easy, raising questions about how best to play out our roles in our personal family dramas.

Today Ballard appears a forerunner of the modern father who is not only at ease changing nappies or doing the ironing, but may even be a stay-at-home dad whose wife or partner goes into the office each day while he takes care of the kids. Despite their growing numbers, they remain an exotic species: in the United States full-time housewives outnumber househusbands by a ratio of forty to one, while in Britain only around one in twenty fathers is the main carer.[2] But in historical terms, such domestic dads are not nearly as rare as you might think: the househusband had a surprisingly prominent place in pre-industrial society. Understanding this forgotten history matters because it challenges the powerful and pervasive ideology, sometimes known as 'separate spheres', which assumes that a woman's natural place is the home, bringing up children and doing the household chores, while a man's natural place is as the main breadwinner for the family in the paid economy. In fact, there is nothing 'natural' about this arrangement at all.

The famine of conversation in Ballard's childhood home is familiar today, because in most families the art of conversation still fails to flourish. Parents can't get a word out of their teenage children. Couples spend more time watching television together – an average fifty-five minutes a day in Britain – than directly talking to one another.[3] The plague of divorce in the West is closely linked to the silences between couples, and in many families you can find relatives who refuse to talk to each other, often for days and sometimes for years. Conversation is the unseen thread that binds families together and it is time we took it more seriously. So after revealing the role that fathers once had in the home, we need to consider what we can learn from the past about making family conversation more nourishing.

## The lost history of the househusband

'So, are you getting any sleep?' This was the most frequent question I was asked by friends after my twins were born. Most young parents feel starved of time to sleep, time to relax, time to be alone. On top of this, however, is the issue of time inequality between women and men in running the typical family household. In Britain, women do twice as much cooking, cleaning and childcare as men, and in total perform two-thirds of all domestic work, on which they spend an average three hours a day. It's no wonder that many women complain that their husbands don't even know how to turn on the washing machine, or where the cot sheets are kept. Even in families with both parents working full-time, women are still doing at least a third more of the housework and childcare than men.[4] In other words, once they walk in the door from the office, they may face a 'second shift' in the home. This fundamental time imbalance can place a strain on any couple's relationship: my partner and I often bicker over my failure to do my 'fair share' of the housework. The issue is constantly raised in mothers' discussion forums on the internet.

The most popular British site, Mumsnet, recently contained the following message, which received scores of sympathetic responses:

> It has just dawned on me that my husband has absolutely no idea how hard I work looking after three kids under four whilst running my own business. I want to punch the useless twat!![5]

Time is not the only problem. There is also the question of responsibility. 'Let me take him off your hands for a while,' a father might say to his wife, trying to be helpful but unwittingly revealing that he thinks the ultimate responsibility for the child lies with her. She's the one who must make sure the baby has a good stock of winter clothing or gets immunised when due. He sees his main role as giving temporary relief, an extra hand. The secret fear of many young fathers is to be left completely alone with small children for a whole day, solely responsible for their wellbeing. They lack the confidence – and often the competence – to do it. Women are also faced by family-related career dilemmas. Around 70 per cent of women now work in the paid economy, so if they want to have children, they have to consider how doing so will affect their careers.[6] The stay-at-home dad may be on the rise, but it is still rare to find a man who has sacrificed his own career so his partner can quickly get back to work after the baby is born.

These kinds of tensions and challenges arise because having a family is like managing a small business. Although nobody is out to make a profit, there are services to provide, financial and time constraints to deal with, staff roles to negotiate, and some very demanding customers. Few of us have received appropriate training for the task: we may have to pass a test to drive a car, but not to have a child. So we could all do with some advice. An unexpected source of wisdom for understanding how men and women relate in the household economy is the history of the househusband, both in the European past and in indigenous societies. This neglected history offers rare insights into how couples today might rethink their domestic arrangements. It all starts in the jungles of the Western Congo Basin, home to the Aka Pygmies.

Aka men are the world's most dedicated fathers. For an estimated 47 per cent of each day, they are either holding their children or within arm's reach of them. Although women still do a majority of the childcare, the men are fully involved in almost every aspect of it and share most tasks with the mother. Fathers wash their babies and wipe their bottoms. When their children cry out in the night, it is often the men who will comfort them, even to the extent of offering a gentle suck on their nipples. Aka women preparing the evening meal do not carry their babies on their hips like women in many other hunter-gatherer societies, nor do they hand them over to older siblings; instead the father takes hold of them. When Aka men go out drinking palm wine with each other, they may take their children along. An anthropologist – and father of seven – who has spent two decades studying the Aka suggests that the high level of paternal involvement may be due to the peculiarities of their traditional subsistence activity, the net hunt, a year-long family venture to trap small animals. Both men and women take part, and the babies come too, with men having primary responsibility for carrying them over the long distances involved. The more childcare Aka men do, the more attached they become to their children, which reinforces their desire to care for them.[7]

Although the Aka are at the extreme end of the spectrum, they are not alone amongst indigenous cultures in their approach to child rearing. The Arapesh people of New Guinea and the Mbuti of the African Ituri forest are known for fathers' involvement in childcare, and when Europeans first arrived in Tahiti in the eighteenth century, they were shocked to find that women could become chiefs while men routinely did the cooking and looked after children. In around one in four cultures, men have historically played a nurturing and involved parenting role. That still leaves a clear majority of societies in which women bear most of the burdens of infant care, and in one-third of cultures, men barely lift a finger to help. The point, however, is the variety of parenting arrangements found in human societies. It is not biology that explains these variations, but context and culture. Men have been more likely to take on domestic responsibilities in societies where women are highly involved in food provision, where there is matrilineal descent and property rights for women, and where the men are not too busy being warriors – a constraint facing few men in the developed world today.[8]

Both men and women in the West frequently claim that the natural role of the mother is to take care of the child, while fathers are not genetically programmed for child rearing and that their natural role is to be a 'provider' for the family. In effect, to guard the cave entrance while the mother holds the baby. The courts reinforce this idea, disproportionately awarding children to mothers in custody disputes (although this practice is gradually declining). We must certainly acknowledge important biological differences: it is women, not men, who give birth and breastfeed, and this undoubtedly creates a special bond and intimacy between mother and child that a father does not enjoy. But once you know about the Aka and other paternally inclined peoples, it is no longer so obvious that it is 'natural' for fathers to remain at a distance from the practicalities of childcare.

One could try to counter this with evidence from the animal kingdom: 'What about all those male wildcats that sow their seed then disappear off to find another mate while the female has to raise the litter alone? Surely that's the natural way of things.' Not so. Like humans, non-human species are striking for the variety of their parenting systems. Many animals – butterflies, turtles, spiders – provide no parenting care whatsoever. Around 90 per cent of bird species, including owls, share parenting equally. Male marmosets and siamangs care for and carry their babies day and night. Parenting responsibilities can also shift: amongst kestrels and partridges, he hunts while she feeds, but if the mother dies the father takes complete care of the young – like J. G. Ballard.[9] Neither the natural world nor indigenous cultures provide easy justification for the doctrine of separate spheres.

It might seem difficult to translate the parenting approach

of the Aka and other indigenous peoples into your own family life. When was the last time you took your kids out on a jungle hunting expedition? That is why we also need to trace the history of household management in the West and discover how men's and women's roles have evolved. The great revelation is that today's hands-on fathers are reincarnations of fathers from our pre-industrial past. We have not always been as different from the Aka as we like to imagine, and the distribution of domestic work between men and women was once more balanced than it is in the present.

The first clues about the historical origins of the househusband lie in language. The term 'housewife' emerged in English in the thirteenth century, and 'housewifery' referred to the work traditionally done by women – cooking, laundering, sewing and nursing children. Less well known is that a 'husband' was originally a man whose work, like a housewife's, took place in and around the home. This is revealed in its linguistic roots: 'hus' is the old spelling of 'house' and 'band' refers to the house to which he was bonded – that he leased or owned. One of his main tasks was farm work, which used to be known as 'husbandry', a term still sometimes used today.[10]

This tells us something important. Before the industrial revolution, both economic life and family life in Europe and colonial North America were largely centred on the home, especially for independent agricultural families – the growing yeoman class. Men and women worked together in joint enterprise. While women cooked or sewed, men might be ploughing a nearby field they owned or rented. Men would also be chopping wood for the fire, making shoes, doing leatherwork, whittling spoons and occasionally going off to market to sell the family's produce. Household tasks were highly integrated: no cooking could be done without firewood, and while women tended infants, men built the cradles and cut the hay they lay on. Many household chores were done by both men and women – weaving, milking cows and carrying water. The practice of the man going off to work outside the home did not become widespread until the arrival of factories in the nineteenth century, which might explain why the word 'housework' did not emerge until then: all work had, to that point, been housework. And most husbands had been househusbands.[11]

Pre-industrial men were often directly involved in childcare. Since they were around the house much more than today, it is not surprising that they might have shared tasks such as caring for sick children. An eyewitness account from England in 1795 recorded that 'in the long winter evenings the husband cobbles shoes, mends the family clothes and attends the children while the wife spins'.[12] In the United States in the seventeenth and eighteenth centuries, as Mary Frances Berry writes, 'fathers had primary responsibility for child care beyond the early nursing period'.[13] They not only directed children's education and religious worship, but decided what clothes they would wear and hushed them to sleep when they woke at night. Men frequently became child carers due to force of circumstance, especially because so many women died in childbirth. Today one in twelve single-parent households in Britain are headed by men, but between 1599 and 1811, the figure was one in four. While men would tend to remarry or employ domestic help if they had the means, it is estimated that one-third of lone fathers in pre-industrial Britain had no live-in support from other adults. In the 1820s, when the journalist William Cobbett clopped on his horse through rural England, he noticed that many male labourers cared for their small children. 'There is nothing more amiable, nothing more delightful to behold, than a young man especially taking part in the work of nursing the children,' he remarked.[14]

But could fathers really have had so many domestic responsibilities? There is a widely held belief that we used to live in extended family households, in contrast with the nuclear families that abound today. We imagine the kitchens of old full of aunts and grandparents jiggling children on their knees or feeding them porridge, reducing the burdens on the mother and leaving the father to his craft or leisure. Few people realise, however, that this is a myth. In fact, the nuclear family has been the norm in Europe for hundreds of years. The average household size in

England has been remarkably constant, averaging 4.18 people in the seventeenth century, 4.57 in the eighteenth and 4.21 in the nineteenth. A study of England and North America between 1599 and 1984 showed that for most of this period – apart from a temporary increase in the late Victorian era – only around 8 per cent of homes contained members from the extended family.[15] While multi-generational households were not usual, relatives were often close at hand rather than in the same house, even until recent times. Interviews with 200 East Londoners in the 1950s revealed that between them they had 2,700 relatives living within a mile.[16] The strains of domestic life were also eased by the culture of hired help: even poor households might have had a servant or two. Nevertheless, the reality was that if the mother was ill or at the loom, the father was the most obvious alternative caretaker for the children.

I don't want to give the impression that pre-industrial fathers were all domestic goddesses doing most of the cooking, cleaning and childcare. Women were usually the main child carers and worked tirelessly to feed and clothe their families, even when they had maids working by their sides.[17] They also faced the extreme dangers of giving birth and were often on the receiving end of domestic violence. While some men spent considerable time with their children, others preferred the alehouse, while many were away for much of the year working as hired farm labourers, pedlars or soldiers. In the upper classes, men frequently had little contact with their offspring, since they were placed in the charge of nursemaids and governesses. Still, it should now be clear that the superdads of the twenty-first century had their predecessors – the generations of fathers who shared in the struggles and strains of domestic work and childcare as 'husbands', bonded to their homes.

So how did we end up with today's stark household inequalities between men and women? Why do young mothers so often feel guilty if they want to return to their careers, and fathers feel so inept at settling a crying child in the night? The immediate answer lies in the colossal economic and social changes of the industrial revolution in the eighteenth and nineteenth centuries.

A sharp decline in subsistence agriculture and home industry, and the invention of waged labour on the factory floor, forced a new separation between work in and out of the home. In the early industrial period both men and women could be found in the textiles mills and labouring in the mines, but soon men dominated the industrial workforce. Why was it men who became the designated 'breadwinners' – a term first used in the nineteenth century – while women became enveloped in a cult of domesticity which dictated that a 'good mother' rocks the baby and bakes cakes?

Patriarchy is one standard explanation. Men exerted their traditional power over women inside the family by taking the relatively high-status and skilled jobs available in the paid economy, leaving women with the Sisyphean domestic tasks of sweeping floors, preparing meals and boiling soiled nappies (women also often took on low-skilled, low-paid work to make ends meet). This division was sustained by an ideology of 'true womanhood' supported by male-dominated trade unions and other social institutions such as the Church, which promoted the belief that a woman's 'proper sphere' was the home. Such attitudes, it is argued, gradually became internalised by many women themselves – especially those from the expanding middle class – and seeped into everyday culture.[18] The bestselling *Mrs Beeton's Book of Household Management*, published in 1861, was addressed directly to women, not men. 'There is no more fruitful source of family discontent,' wrote the author, 'than a housewife's badly-cooked dinners and untidy ways.' Learning how to cook, clean and run the house are skills that 'particularly belong to the feminine character'.[19] The ideology of separate spheres became so ingrained that by the mid-twentieth century housework and childcare had come to be viewed as distinctly unmanly. In the 1955 film *Rebel Without a Cause*, when the hot-blooded James Dean bursts into the family home, he is disgusted to see his father wearing an apron over his suit and tie. There was nothing worse than an emasculated man.[20]

An alternative and equally plausible way of looking at the emergence of separate spheres has been offered by historians of domestic technology. They argue that fathers were 'deskilled' by the industrial revolution. The jobs they used to do around the home became obsolete due to technological change, while women's work was largely untouched, or became even more burdensome. The invention of the enclosed iron stove in the eighteenth century, for example, meant that men no longer had to spend so much time gathering and cutting firewood for cooking and heating. When coal replaced wood as the standard fuel, it then became necessary for them to go out and earn cash to buy enough of it. Other traditional male tasks, like making shoes, tools and furniture, were gradually taken over by the manufacturing industry – but there were no machines invented to nurse a wailing child. As men entered the paid workforce, the old household craft skills that they once passed on to their sons were lost, just as their previous role in looking after children became a distant memory.

While some new technologies, such as pulley-driven butter churns and egg beaters, reduced women's housework, other technologies conspired with the growth of consumer culture to expand it. In the pre-industrial era most people had few clothes and washed them infrequently, but with the introduction of manufactured cotton cloth, which was hard to clean, and the expectation that you should regularly change your shirt and own several sets of sheets, women were suddenly doing more laundry than ever. The institution of Monday 'wash day' did not exist until the nineteenth century, and the amount of time women spent on housework remained constant into the mid-twentieth century. Hence the popularity of the expression 'a woman's work is never done'.[21]

Ever since the birth of industrialisation, fathers have been only sporadically involved in housework. During the economic slump of the 1840s, an observer recorded that men who lost their jobs in Manchester and Bolton were 'taking care of the house and children, and busily engaged in washing, baking, nursing, and preparing the humble repast for the wife, who is wearing her life away toiling in the factory'.[22] But once the economy picked up, women went back to the double burden of industrial work and kitchen duties. In the early twentieth century, around a third of men in East Anglian fishing communities regularly did house-work, often because they might be at home for months at a time outside the fishing season. But such figures were untypical of most working-class communities, where men were usually less involved in household tasks.[23]

The second half of the twentieth century witnessed a challenge to the stereotypical division between men's and women's labour. The arrival of the Pill and feminism spurred more women into the professional workplace, and it started making financial sense for men to become the main carers if their earning power was comparatively lower. The exponential rise of divorce, with more and more fathers gaining custody of children, compelled a new generation of men to become domestically reskilled, a change depicted in the 1979 movie *Kramer Versus Kramer*, in which workaholic Dustin Hoffman is left by his wife and must care for his son. These shifts were reinforced by the historically unprecedented phenomenon of fathers being present at childbirth itself. Even up to the 1960s British men were banned from most hospital births, but by the 1990s nine out of ten saw their child being born, offering these fathers a new kind of emotional attachment.[24] The idea of the nurturing father slowly began to re-enter our cultural consciousness: the rugged cowboy image of Marlboro Man was eventually replaced by advertisements showing fathers confidently changing nappies and cooking tasty dinners. For all the hype, however, the stay-at-home dad remains a statistical anomaly, more talked about in the media than seen in reality. When I take my kids to their Monday morning playgroup, there are at most one or two other men in the room.

Having discovered the lost history of the househusband, we should consider how it might help us rethink our family roles. Could more men regain the domestic skills of their pre-industrial forebears, or even model themselves on Aka fathers?

The structural barriers to change remain formidable. Few Western countries offer fathers long-term paternity leave. Even if they wanted to spend more time at home after their children are born, they are unable to do so. You might be lucky enough to live in Sweden, which gives its fathers a year of unpaid paternity leave, although Swedish men still take only 14 per cent of the time allotted to them.[25] Financial factors also cast a long shadow. Women still tend to earn less than men, so when children arrive in a traditional two-parent household, if anybody is going to spend more time at home, it is likely to be the mother. The exorbitant cost of childcare contributes to this pattern. My partner, who works as a development economist for a major humanitarian aid agency, takes home just £30 a day after paying taxes and childcare costs for our twins – sometimes it hardly seems worth it from a financial point of view. Only the lucky few have regular free care from grandparents and other relatives.

Yet change begins as much with our own attitudes as with shifts in employment policy or pay structures. The most effective first step to erode the ideology of separate spheres, which remains pervasive despite decades of women's liberation, is simply to recognise that in other cultures, and other periods of history, family arrangements have been rather different. Yes, women have the wombs and breasts and always will. But there is no special female gene for sterilising bottles, buying Babygros, ironing a shirt or cooking mushy peas. History tells us that most childcare and housework can be done competently by both men and women. Men might embrace the fact that in becoming part-time househusbands they are entering a long and proud tradition of domestically engaged fathers. Women who do most of the child rearing and household chores could free themselves from the cultural expectation of being 'perfect homemakers' or 'superwomen' who hold down demanding jobs while also running the home.

Expanding a man's domestic role may also help him thrive as a human being. Although I don't believe that having children is necessary for a fulfilling and purposeful life, I do believe that most men who have joined the great chain of being by having children will benefit if they become more involved in their lives. I certainly have. Amongst other things, my responsibilities as a father have made me much more emotionally sensitive, so I feel sorrows more deeply but also joys more strongly – a change for which I am grateful. It is as if my emotional range has increased from a meagre octave to a full keyboard of human feelings. Do you want to know why Aka men want to look after their children, even when they keep them up at night? Because caring for them, holding them in their arms, breeds a love and attachment that adds meaning to their lives. Once they start, they don't want to stop.

## Why family conversation has been so difficult

'All happy families are alike but an unhappy family is unhappy after its own fashion,' Tolstoy famously wrote to open his novel *Anna Karenina*. For all the varieties of family friction – the jealousies, insecurities and clashes of personality and authority – a common underlying problem is the quality of family conversation. Conflicts can rarely be resolved unless people learn to talk to one another. Jealousies fester until they are voiced. I think of conversation as a dialogue that creates mutual understanding. It is different from superficial talk about the weather, a heated argument or a one-sided monologue. Conversation has the potential not only to forge family bonds, but to inspire new ways of thinking and living together.

In most families, however, the art of conversation remains in its infancy. The family dinner table can be a conversational battlefield, where simmering tensions, secrets and lies play themselves out in a combination of sharp words and even sharper silences. Teenagers often feel there is no point talking about personal problems with their parents, who spend more time trying to discipline them than understand their troubles, while the most frequent reason given for divorce in the Western world is women being frustrated that their husbands don't talk to them or listen to what they have to say.[26] Many of us dread family reunions, where old roles and wrangles so quickly resurface to blight the occasion. Moreover, while the traditional nuclear family has deep historical roots, an increasing number of step-parents, half-siblings and same-sex couples are adding new layers to the complexities of family life.

It would be comforting to look into the past and discover

a moment in history when family conversation was abundant, nourishing and brimming with mutual understanding. Indeed, the popular claim that the family meal is in sorry decline assumes that we all used to happily eat and talk together around the dining table – if only we could return to the good old days. But this nostalgic utopia never existed. Even in the 1920s – when we assume family dinners were the norm – a mother from a small town in Indiana lamented that 'meal-time as a family reunion time was taken for granted a generation ago' and there is growing desire to 'save meal-times, at least for the family'.[27] That such better times are largely in our imaginations becomes clear once we recognise the three historical barriers that have stood in the way of enriching family conversation: segregation, silence and emotional repression. The first of these can only be understood by returning to the origins of conversation itself.

If there was one individual responsible for the invention of conversation in the Western world, it was Socrates. The pug-faced philosopher had the habit of cornering both friends and strangers in the marketplaces of ancient Athens and asking them their opinions on every subject under the Greek sun, from justice and religion to love and metaphysics. His method was to inter-rogate their assumptions and question the consistency of their beliefs. At its worst this was a form of conversational bullying. But at its best, Socrates helped people rethink their approach to the art of living. One admirer, the politician and playboy Alcibiades, thanked him for 'turning all my beliefs upside down, with the disturbing realisation that my whole life is that of a slave'.[28] For Socrates, conversation was a dialectical process in which the dance of ideas could help people inch closer towards their own personal truth.

For all of Socrates' scintillating talk, there are no records of his conversations with his wife or parents. Typical of Greek men of his day, he seemed to save his verbal energies for his public promenades or display at a *symposium* – a conversational banquet at which supper was followed by a serious boozing session, with the words flowing as readily as the wine. At the most famous of these drinking parties, recorded by Plato in the fourth century BC, Socrates spent the evening with half a dozen male friends discussing the nature of love. While sipping from his terracotta cup and popping olives into his mouth, the playwright Aristophanes declared, 'Each of us is a mere fragment of a man; we've been split in two, like filleted plaice. We're all looking for our other half.' While this may have been an imaginative comment on the idea of the soulmate, it was quite clear where their other halves really were: the diners' wives were stuck at home with the slaves. The only women permitted at a *symposium* were flute players and dancing girls, who attended the men like Japanese geisha. While freeborn women in ancient Greece had their own feasts, usually connected with religious festivals, they were vigorously excluded from conversational dining with their menfolk, just as they were denied the right to political participation. Most of their lives were spent confined to the *gynaikeion*, the women's apartments in their home.[29]

This culture of segregation prevented the ancient Greeks from making any major advances in family conversation. The classical *symposium* anticipated the separate-spheres ideology of the nineteenth century, with women confined to work in the home while men stepped out into public life. But it also reflects a long tradition of segregated family dining in Western history. According to historian Beatrice Gottlieb, in Europe between the Black Death in the fourteenth century and the industrial revolution, 'sitting down together [as a family] for a formal meal may have been almost as rare as eating meat'.[30] In peasant households in nineteenth-century France, women would serve the men at table, but have their own dinner standing up or eat off their laps by the fireside, perhaps feeding a child at the same time. And in times of scarcity, who was most likely to sacrifice the food on her plate? The woman. Other historians report that in poor families, women and children would often eat at no special time and in no special place. In the upper-class dining rooms of Victorian England, it was not that children were 'seen but not heard'. They were frequently not even seen, since they ate their meals separately in the kitchen or with a nursemaid. Once the meal ended, men might stay to smoke a cigar, drink

The Family Meal *by the Le Nain brothers. In this seventeenth-century painting of a French peasant family, only the father has his meal at the table while mother and children hover around the edges, destined to eat after he has finished. Family dining was not yet in vogue.*

port and talk politics, while women were shooed out into the drawing room.[31]

Venturing beyond Western culture, it becomes apparent that family dining is far from the historical and social norm. The Nuer people in East Africa have traditionally associated eating – like excreting – with feelings of shame, so a husband will not dine with his wife for the first few years of their marriage. In Vanuatu, some men join ranked male societies, where members of each rank cook and eat with one another rather than with their families. Anthropologists have noticed that the Bakairi of the Amazon basin eat their meals alone, a practice also followed in some parts of Indonesia in homes which have no dining room. In many Muslim communities today, especially on religious occasions, women may eat in a separate room from the men – although some claim that such arrangements offer women the social space to discuss personal issues in privacy.[32]

Segregated meals are now, in the West at least, a relic of the past. This is good news, since it permits the dining table to become an arena where families can practise the art of conversation, without anybody being excluded because of their sex or age. Of course, there is no guarantee that we all use this historically unique opportunity granted to us. In fact, we don't. Nearly half of British families eat dinner in front of the TV, only one-third eat together regularly each evening, and the typical family spends more time in the car than at the dinner table. Figures are similar for the United States. When a family eats at a fast food outlet like McDonald's, the average meal lasts around ten minutes.[33] Yet we should beware those who tell us that the sacred ritual of the family meal is in rapid decline. Taking the historical long view, it never was ascendant.[34]

If you've ever experienced stony silences at a family dinner, you are in good historical company. Along with segregation, eating in silence has an established pedigree as a barrier to family conversation. For centuries, meals in European peasant households 'were silent occasions', argues Beatrice Gottlieb. Foreign visitors to Elizabethan England were particularly struck that there was little if any conversation at dinner, and Italian etiquette manuals advised that 'talk is not for the table, but for the piazza'.[35] At some level, this silence makes biological sense: my toddlers rarely talk during dinner simply because they are busy eating, stuffing themselves with the staff of life. But silent eating is also a cultural practice, with roots in early Christianity. The Rule of St Benedict, which has guided the life of Benedictine and other monks since the sixth century, asks its followers to 'avoid evil words' and spend much of the day, including meals, in silence. Dinner is a time for listening to readings from uplifting spiritual texts rather than having conversations, even about God. Such religious reverence for silence, which can also be found amongst Quakers and Buddhists, may help explain why medieval villagers spoke little while eating.[36]

On the other hand, silence is as much a matter of geography as religion. 'Scandinavians are of the opinion that you only

speak when you have something to say,' according to communication experts, and talkativeness is associated with being ego-
tistical and unreliable. So don't expect an exuberant discussion
if dining with a family in Finland – Europe's most conversationally reserved country – although they will probably listen to you
with unusual attention.[37]

Silence has certainly not ruled in all cultures, as anybody
who has sat down with a conversationally vigorous Neapoli-
tan family for Sunday lunch can testify. But whether we would
rather aspire to the kind of family meals that take place in Naples
or Helsinki, we still need to think about what happens to our
family conversations away from the dinner table, and what we
can do to improve their quality. For that, we must turn from
segregation and silence to a third historical barrier, emotional
repression, and trace its development over the last 300 years.

While the medieval period may be known for its silence, by
the eighteenth century conversation was being transformed into
an art form. London's flourishing coffee-house culture brought
together educated men to discourse on politics, business, art
and literature. Conversation clubs – the equivalent of the ancient
Greek *symposium* – sprang up around the city, amongst them
the Turk's Head Club in Gerrard Street, Soho, co-founded by Dr
Samuel Johnson, generally acknowledged as the most brilliant
talker of the Georgian era. Johnson deserves our praise because
he realised that conversation could be a pleasure rather than a
mere exchange of information. Yet, contrary to reputation, he was
actually one of history's most disastrous conversationalists, and
we have barely recovered from his legacy. 'None of the desires
dictated by vanity is more general, or less blameable, than that of
being distinguished for the arts of conversation,' he once said. In
doing so, he admitted that his preferred form of conversation was
largely about showing off, just as it was in the literary salons that
had begun to appear in France during the same period, where
you were expected to be au fait with the latest poetry or opera.
Johnson's own talk was full of clever quips and witty epigrams
which served to end conversations rather than open them out
and invigorate them. He taught us nothing about how families

might use conversation to ease the inevitable tensions and conflicts which arise from living together under the same roof.[38]

So the eighteenth century was the era of clever conversation. It was followed in the nineteenth by the era of hidden emotions. This began with the rise of the Romantic movement, which offered great conversational promise. Poets such as Coleridge and Keats willingly bared their tortured souls and unrequited love to the world. But they mostly did so on paper. The emotional sensitivity and popularity of romanticism was unable to permeate family conversation in reality. During the Victorian era a stark divide arose between how men and women expressed themselves, especially amongst the British middle and upper classes. Men came to prize cool rationality and emotional reserve, while women were more likely to display their inner thoughts and feelings – at least to each other – and showed a greater capacity for sympathetic listening. Just think of Mr Darcy in *Pride and Prejudice* (1813), who is unable to reveal his feelings for Elizabeth Bennet, held back by pride, social convention and emotional reticence. Virginia Woolf's father, the Victorian gent Sir Leslie Stephen, was known for his 'ineffable and impossible taciturnity'.[39] Family conversation became dominated by the stern paterfamilias who revered reason and distrusted passion. Under such conditions, conversation could be intellectually edifying but not emotionally sophisticated or empathic. Marriage guides advised wives not to burden their husbands with their personal troubles, while children were encouraged to repress their feelings and 'keep a stiff upper lip' – an idiom originating in a nineteenth-century nursery poem.

The psychological damage this could cause is evident in the case of the philosopher John Stuart Mill. Born in 1806, by the age of three his father had begun teaching him ancient Greek, and on their regular morning walks the precocious youngster was expected to give a detailed dissection of what he had read the previous day. Mill was trained to cultivate reason and sublimate his emotions, and there was little intimacy in their relationship. Recalling his father, Mill wrote:

The element which was chiefly deficient in his moral relation to his children, was that of tenderness. I do not believe
that this deficiency lay in his own nature. I believe him to
have had much more feeling than he habitually showed, and
much greater capacities of feeling than were ever developed.
He resembled most Englishmen in being ashamed of the
signs of feeling, and, by the absence of demonstration, starving the feelings themselves.[40]

Deprived of nurturing family conversation and suffering
under immense pressure from his father and himself to achieve
intellectually, at the age of twenty Mill had a mental breakdown.
'My father, to whom it would have been natural to me to have
recourse in any practical difficulties, was the last person to
whom, in such a case as this, I looked for help.'[41] He was only
cured of his emotional starvation several years later, when he fell
in love.

The barrier of emotional repression began to wither away in
the twentieth century, which became the era of intimate conversation. This great transformation originated in a new culture of
self-reflection in the West, first encouraged by the birth of psychoanalysis, and later by the therapy and self-help industries.
At last it was becoming acceptable – especially for men – to talk
openly about their emotions with friends and family. Following
the publication of Alfred Kinsey's reports on sexual behaviour
in 1948 and 1953, and the sexual revolution of the 1960s, couples
were also able to speak more freely about the touchy topic of sex,
which lay at the root of so many relationship difficulties.

The impact of these changes on family conversation was
uneven and often slow to materialise. When the actress Jane
Fonda was a teenager in the 1950s, she found it almost impossible to communicate with her father: 'I can remember long car
rides where not a word would be spoken. I would be so nervous
that my palms would be sweating from riding in absolute silence
with my own father.'[42] There are still plenty of parents who don't
know how to speak to their kids, just as there are couples who
are experts at avoiding discussing sexual problems or feelings

of jealousy. The idea of visiting a relationship therapist makes many modern men experience a wave of nausea. Nevertheless, by the end of the twentieth century a conversational revolution had occurred, with families being able to talk to each other in ways unimaginable in the Victorian era, mainly because men had become – emotionally speaking – a little more like women.

So family conversation had triumphed, overcoming the formidable barriers of segregation, silence and repression. But in the mid-twentieth century, just as conversation was starting to flourish in the home and around the dining table, another barrier arose that threatened to take the quality of family conversation back to the Middle Ages. This was the advent of new technologies, which brought other people's voices into our houses but cut short our own. George Orwell was one of the first to recognise the potential damage that technology could cause. Conversation is being replaced by the 'passive, drug-like pleasures of the cinema and radio', he wrote in 1943. A few years later, he detected a sinister development:

> In very many English homes the radio is literally never turned off, though it is manipulated from time to time so as to make sure that only light music will come out of it. I know people who will keep the radio playing all through a meal and at the same time continue talking just loudly enough for the voices and the music to cancel out. This is done with a definite purpose. The music prevents the conversation from becoming serious or even coherent.[43]

Just imagine what Orwell would have written had he lived to see the rise of television in the 1950s, when it began to colonise both the Western household and the Western mind. Within a generation, 99 per cent of US homes had one, and by the 1970s they were on for an average of six hours a day.[44] People in the US and Europe now give over most of their leisure time – on average four hours a day – to watching TV, which amounts to around nine years of continuous viewing by the age of sixty-five.[45]

Some media sociologists claim that it is a mistake to assume that television has eroded family conversation: not only can documentaries, soap operas and other programmes spark lively discussion amongst family members, but watching TV together is an important ritual that brings families into the same domestic space.[46] Such arguments miss the point about what a quality family conversation looks like. Can you really have a proper discussion with your spouse about whether she should leave her job if you are both half-watching the box? While television has potential to stimulate the mind and emotions, it is essentially a passive medium which draws us away from human interaction, whereas conversation is in essence an active form of engagement with others. Or, as the cultural critic Jerry Mander put it back in the 1970s, the effect of the television revolution is 'to have substituted secondary, mediated versions of experience for direct experience of the world'.[47]

Other technologies have been similarly winding back the conversational clock, or at least failing to advance it significantly. A US study showed that children aged eight to eighteen spend on average seven hours and thirty-eight minutes a day wired into digital media – video games, iPods, DVDs, social networking sites, email, as well as finger-happy texting.[48] There is no doubt that some of these technologies enable and expand 'communication' – that is, people staying regularly in touch with one another. They certainly help me keep in touch with my relatives in Australia. But again the quality of the interaction is an issue: how many of the billions of text messages sent between family members each year are nurturing and adventurous conversations?

We've come a long way in the history of family conversation and should try to preserve what we have gained, and expand its potential. The first obvious move may be to ration television time. My own attempt to do so involved keeping the TV in a cupboard at the top of the house. The thought of having to carry it down two flights of stairs was a good test of whether my partner and I felt a programme was really worth watching, and our weekly viewing hours fell substantially. Apart from a rationing regime, another option could be to put yourself on a digital diet while eating with others – turning the TV off and leaving mobile phones on silent in the hallway, just as polite medieval diners used to leave their weapons at the door.

While the family meal was not ubiquitous in the past, we can find inspiration in those cultures – such as Italian, Jewish and Chinese – which have maintained it as a regular ritual practice. But it may not be enough simply to decree that your flock must always gather for Sunday lunch. 'Conversation, like families, dies when it is in-bred,' writes the historian Theodore Zeldin. 'The family meal is made for stopping shop talk, and for mixing different kinds of talk.'[49] His advice is to invite stimulating strangers to your family meals, so the conversation can become a form of exploration. Ask your guitar teacher or new work colleague to come around. As W. S. Gilbert said, 'it isn't so much what's on the table that matters, as what's on the chairs.'

Breaking the silences in family life may require something even more personal than a communal meal. Simply spending time with your brother or stepmother doing something quietly pleasurable like taking a woodland walk is a way to allow your conversation to wander along new pathways – as long as nobody has to recite Greek verse like John Stuart Mill. But if you seek more invigorating conversational exercise, you could embark on a project like interviewing your parents or grandparents about their pasts and what they have learned about the art of living. When I did this with my father, over a period of seven years, I was not only preserving family memories for posterity. It was a way of bringing us closer together, since our conversation led to delicate subjects which rarely arose in our daily discourse, such as his relationship with my mother before she died. I also discovered what he believed about generosity, God and freedom. It is amazing how little we can know about people we have apparently known our whole lives.

The most important lesson from history may be to remember to take off our masks. Family conversation will never thrive until we become more open with our emotions, more intimate with our conversation. Suppressing thoughts and feelings is of course useful at times, both as a mechanism of self-preservation and to protect others. But we cannot allow ourselves to act like those Victorian men who starved themselves and their families of emotional life. Otherwise we may as well eat at segregated tables like the ancient Greeks or in silence like medieval monks.

If, after experimenting with these ideas, your family conversation still remains in the doldrums, there is only one more thing I can advise. Organise a family *symposium* whose subject of discussion is the curious lifestyle of the Aka Pygmies.

# 3

# Empathy

In 1206 Giovanni Bernardone, the 23-year-old son of a wealthy merchant, went on a pilgrimage to the Basilica of St Peter's in Rome. He could not help noticing the contrast between the opulence and lavishness within the basilica – the brilliant mosaics, the spiral columns – and the poverty of the beggars sitting outside its doors. He persuaded one of them to exchange clothes with him and spent the rest of the day in rags begging for alms.

Not long after, when Giovanni was out riding near his home town, he met a leper. Lepers were the outcasts of medieval society, and were both shunned and despised. Many were deformed and crippled, with missing noses and bleeding sores. They were forbidden from entering towns and drinking from wells or springs. Nobody would touch them for fear of contracting their dreaded disease. But Giovanni forced himself to stifle his immediate feeling of revulsion for lepers, which he had harboured since childhood. He dismounted from his horse, gave the leper a coin and kissed his hand. The leper kissed him in return.

These episodes were turning points in the young man's life. He soon founded a religious order whose brothers worked for the poor and in the leper houses, and who gave up their worldly goods to live in poverty, like those whom they served. Giovanni Bernardone, known to us now as St Francis of Assisi, is remembered for declaring, 'Give me the treasure of sublime poverty: permit the distinctive sign of our order to be that it does not possess anything of its own beneath the sun, for the glory of your name, and that it have no other patrimony than begging.'[1]

Empathy is the art of stepping into the shoes of another person and seeing the world from their perspective. It requires a leap of the imagination, so we are able to look through their eyes and understand the beliefs, experiences, hopes and fears that shape their worldview. Technically known to psychologists as 'cognitive empathy', it is not about feeling sorry for somebody – that is sympathy or pity – but rather about making an attempt to transport oneself into another's character and lived reality.[2] This is just what St Francis was doing when he swapped clothes with the beggar outside St Peter's: he wanted to know what it felt like to be a pauper.

Empathising comes naturally to us and we do it all the time, often without realising. When a friend tells us she has just been abandoned by her husband, we think about the anger and rejection she must be feeling, and try to be sensitive to her needs. If we have a colleague who is failing to meet his deadlines, we might decide not to pressure him to work late as we know his mother is descending into Alzheimer's and he is busy caring for her. Looking at life from another's point of view not only allows us to recognise their sorrows or joys, but can prompt us to take action on their behalf. 'Imagining what it is like to be someone other than yourself is at the core of our humanity,' writes the novelist Ian McEwan, 'it is the essence of compassion, and it is the beginning of morality.'[3]

Yet empathy matters not just because it makes you good, but because it is good for you. It has the power to heal broken relationships, erode our prejudices, expand our curiosity about strangers and make us rethink our ambitions. Ultimately empathy creates the human bonds that make life worth living. That is why so many lifestyle thinkers today believe that developing our empathy is a key to personal wellbeing. Happiness expert Richard Layard advocates 'deliberate cultivation of the primitive instinct of empathy' because 'if you care more about other people relative to yourself, you are more likely to be happy'. Mahatma Gandhi was already aware of this transformative potential of empathy half a century ago, embodied in what has become known as 'Gandhi's Talisman':

> Whenever you are in doubt, or when the self becomes too much with you, apply the following test. Recall the face of the poorest and the weakest man whom you may have seen, and ask yourself, if the step you contemplate is going to be of any use to him. Will he gain anything by it? Will it restore him to a control over his own life and destiny? In other words, will it lead to swaraj [freedom] for the hungry and spiritually starving millions? Then you will find your doubts and your self melt away.[4]

It is important when thinking about empathy to distinguish it from the so-called Golden Rule 'Do unto others as you would have them do unto you'.[5] Although a worthy notion, it is not empathy, since it involves considering how you – *with your own views* – would wish to be treated. Empathy is harder: it requires imagining others' views and then acting accordingly. George Bernard Shaw understood the difference when he remarked, 'Do not do unto others as you would have them do unto you – they may have different tastes.'

The challenge we face is that society suffers from what Barack Obama has called an 'empathy deficit'. How much effort do we make to put ourselves in the shoes of people living on the margins, like asylum seekers, the elderly, or subsistence farmers in developing countries? Do we really try hard to imagine and understand the realities of their lives? The deficit also appears in everyday relationships. When we are locked in an argument with a partner, sibling or parent, how often do we stop ourselves to consider their emotions, their needs, their perspectives?

We ought to find ways of nurturing and expanding our empathic selves, and tackling our personal empathy deficits. How can history help us do so? Our first task is to dispel the old-fashioned idea, rooted in seventeenth-century social thought, that human beings are primarily selfish creatures dedicated to individual gain. We will then turn to three strategies we can pursue to broaden our empathic imaginations: conversation, experience and social action. Our guides will be a one-time leader of the Ku Klux Klan, a literary Englishman who had the unusual habit of dressing as a tramp, and the revolutionary spirits behind the struggle against slavery in the eighteenth century. While empathy may not be a standard topic in discussions of how to live, taking this historical journey will reveal just why it should be: empathy can be not only a moral guide but an extreme sport for adventurous living in the twenty-first century.

## The serpent and the dove

Pick up a newspaper and it will undoubtedly seem that human beings are aggressive, cruel, self-seeking animals. There will be headlines about bombs being dropped on innocent civilians, about rapists and paedophiles, about murders and gang warfare, about terrorist training camps, about corrupt politicians stealing from the public purse, about companies pumping carbon into the sky and dumping toxic waste into rivers.

A little historical reflection will further confirm your views. Seventy million people were killed in the wars of the twentieth century. And then there were the Crusades and colonialism. The rule of empires and dictatorships. Slavery and the subjugation of women. Gulags and the use of torture. Genocide. You get the picture.

As well as possessing an extraordinary capacity for harming others, humans also display an ability to sit by passively and do nothing about suffering that they know is taking place. While we munch on our morning toast we can casually read news stories about droughts in Kenya or earthquakes in China without breaking down into sobs or bounding out of the door to do something about it all.

None of this really shocks us because for centuries we have been telling ourselves that human beings are, by nature, self-interested, self-preserving creatures with strong aggressive tendencies. This dark depiction of humankind was popularised by the seventeenth-century philosopher Thomas Hobbes. In his book *Leviathan*, he argued that we are bent on pursuing our own, individualistic ends, making the state of nature a 'war of all against all' where life is 'solitary, poor, nasty, brutish and short'. It is not surprising that he held such views. Hobbes wrote his book in the late 1640s, when England was embroiled in a bloody civil war. From his vantage point in exile in Paris, he came to believe that belligerent and self-serving conduct was an expression of our true selves, and that only authoritarian government could keep us safe from one another.[6] There was no room in this worldview for the idea that we are born with a strong empathic instinct. Hobbes's malign conception of human nature has become the cultural norm in the West, permeating the arts, media, politics and education. Take a course in economics today and you will typically be told to assume we are all rational, self-interested actors.

But there is an alternative narrative, another way of understanding what it means to be human. This is the idea that we are *homo empathicus* – that we have a natural capacity to empathise which is just as strong as our selfish inner drives.[7] There is nothing new about this notion. In fact, in the eighteenth century it was commonplace to believe that empathy was an innate characteristic of human beings which gave us our ethical sensitivity and could spur us to treat people with greater consideration. Unfortunately this powerful strand in the history of ideas has been overshadowed by the legacy of Thomas Hobbes.

The most renowned proponent of *homo empathicus* was a professor of moral philosophy at the University of Glasgow named Adam Smith. Today he is remembered as the father of capitalism for his book *The Wealth of Nations*, published in 1776. Economists generally assume that Smith, like Hobbes, believed that human beings invariably pursue their self-interest. How wrong they are. Seventeen years earlier Smith wrote another, now largely forgotten book – *The Theory of Moral Sentiments* – which offered a far more sophisticated approach to human motivation than Hobbes's *Leviathan*, and was in part a direct riposte to it.[8] This is clear from the opening lines: 'How selfish soever man may be supposed, there are evidently some principles in his nature, which interest him in the fortune of others, and render their happiness necessary to him, though he derives nothing from it, except pleasure of seeing it.' What followed was the world's first fully developed theory of empathy – at the time known as 'sympathy' – in which Smith argued that 'our fellow-feeling for the misery of others' is based on our imaginative capacity for 'changing places in fancy with the sufferer'. He gave countless examples of the way we naturally step into the shoes of other people, without intending to benefit ourselves:

> When I condole with you for the loss of your only son, in order to enter your grief, I do not consider what I, a person of such a character and profession, should suffer, if I had a son, and if that son was unfortunately to die; but I consider what I should suffer if I was really you; and I not only change circumstances with you, but I change persons and characters. My grief, therefore, is entirely upon your account, and not in the least upon my own. It is not, therefore, in the least selfish.[9]

Smith only had to look around him to see his empathic view of human nature expressed in reality. Although the eighteenth century is associated with the emergence of profit-hungry, competitive capitalism, it also saw the birth of the first organisations to combat child neglect, slavery and cruelty to animals.[10]

Adam Smith's ideas about our capacity for empathy are scarcely known today, having been eclipsed by his more famous writings on political economy, but over the past century they have been confirmed by a growing accumulation of evidence in the fields of psychology, evolutionary biology and neuroscience. In the 1940s the Swiss psychologist Jean Piaget presented a group of children with a three-dimensional model of a mountain scene, then asked them to choose which of several pictures depicted what a doll would see from different positions around the model. Those aged under four tended to choose their own perspective of viewing the model, rather than that of the doll, whereas the older children were able to step into the doll's shoes. His conclusion was that from the age of four we are able to imagine the perspectives of other people. The current consensus is that children as young as two have this ability, and can act upon it. An eighteen-month-old child, for instance, might try to comfort a crying friend by offering her own teddy bear. Six months older, she may have realised her teddy is no use – her friend's teddy must be found and offered instead. This is the cognitive leap of empathy.[11]

Evolutionary biology has now turned against the old Darwinian idea of the competitive struggle for existence, and instead emphasises the role of cooperation and mutual aid as an evolutionary force. Primatologists like Frans de Waal argue that the extraordinary amount of caring and cooperation evident amongst apes, dolphins, elephants and human beings, for example – such as the way mothers care for their young, or how they issue warning signals for others when predators approach – is due to a natural capacity to empathise which has developed to ensure community survival.[12]

Neuroscientists are also convinced that empathy is wired into us. When we imagine our finger being pinched in a door, one part of our brain is active, but when we think about the same thing happening to another person, different areas – the empathic spots – are switched on. If such core brain areas are damaged, for instance in a car accident, we can lose our ability to empathise.[13] Recent research by Simon Baron-Cohen suggests that our brains have ten interconnected regions that comprise an 'empathy circuit', and that people with low levels of empathy show less neural activity in these regions. They may have smaller than average amygdalas, have a lack of binding of neurotransmitters to one of the serotonin receptors and relatively limited neural responsiveness in the orbital front cortex and the temporal cortex. In his view, our empathy circuitry is genetically inherited and formed in early childhood, but it can also be consciously developed in later life.[14]

The science of empathy has now reached a stage where we can free ourselves of the conventional idea that human beings are essentially self-seeking. We can discard this Hobbesian notion of human nature that has been a spectre haunting our minds for over 300 years. The scientific evidence points towards embracing Smith's view that our egoistic desires coexist with our more benevolent, empathic natures. Or as his Scottish contemporary David Hume put it, there is in each of us 'some particle of the dove, kneaded into our frame, along with the elements of the wolf and the serpent'.

The question that remains is what to do with what we've got. How can we expand our empathy in a way that broadens our personal horizons and contributes to the art of living? Unfortunately psychology, evolutionary biology and neuroscience provide few answers. To stir our imaginations we must turn to the example of real historical figures, to individuals who practised and mastered the three approaches to an empathic life: conversation, experience and social action.

## How to leave the Ku Klux Klan

Most of us live in a small world of friends, families and colleagues, surrounded by strangers about whom we know little. How much do you know about the life of the woman who delivers your post, or the quiet librarian who lives across the street? Then there are all those people we may be sitting next to on the train or standing behind in the supermarket queue, whose ideas and ways of living might be radically different from ours and have the power to inspire us, yet we rarely find the courage to talk to them beyond a few brief comments about the weather. We are stranded from each other on a networked planet. Conversation is one of the most effective ways to access the thoughts, experiences and wisdom that lie hidden inside other people's heads. It enables us to discover the extraordinary diversity of humankind, and to gain an empathic understanding of how others view themselves and the world.

Conversation is also a means by which we can move beyond the labels we habitually use to identify people. Terms like 'Islamic fundamentalist', 'rich banker' and 'single mother' are often suffused with assumptions and prejudices. We lump people together, prejudging them on the basis of hearsay or media stereotypes, and thereby denigrate their individuality. Conversation allows us to dispel the myths perpetuated by such labels. Through hearing people's personal stories and struggles, we come to recognise their uniqueness and start to treat them as human beings. We open ourselves to finding commonalities as well as differences. This is the beginning of an empathic connection, a human bond to the lives of others.

What does empathic conversation look like? How can it break down the barriers between people and alter the landscape of their minds and lives? One of the most remarkable instances can be found within the history of US race relations. It took place in the city of Durham, North Carolina, in 1971, and led to one of the most unlikely friendships of the twentieth century.

Claiborne Paul Ellis – known as C.P. to his friends – was born into a poor white family in Durham in 1927. When C.P. left school, he went to work in a petrol station to support his mother and sister, then eventually had a family of his own. One of his four children was born blind and mentally impaired. 'He's never spoken a word,' C.P. recalled in an interview with the oral historian Studs Terkel.[15] 'I hug his neck. I talk to him, tell him I love him. I don't know whether he knows me or not, but I know he's well taken care of.'

C.P. worked all day, seven days a week, and every hour of overtime he could. But with low pay and high rents, the family could barely survive financially. He became bitter. 'I began to blame it on black people. I had to hate somebody. Hatin' America is hard to do because you can't see it to hate it. The natural person for me to hate would be black people, because my father before me was a member of the Klan. As far as he was concerned, it was the saviour of the white people. So I began to admire the Klan.'

He joined the Ku Klux Klan, taking the traditional oath to uphold the purity of the white race, to fight communism and to protect white womanhood. Most members were low-income whites who, in the 1960s, were actively opposing and intimidating the growing civil rights movement. C.P. and his friends celebrated in 1968 when they heard that Martin Luther King had been assassinated. 'We just had a real party at the service station. Really rejoicin' cause that sonofabitch was dead.' Over the years he progressed from being a regular member to the top position of Exalted Cyclops, president of the Durham chapter of the KKK.

The turning point in his life came in 1971. As a well-known and outspoken figure in Durham, C.P. was invited to a ten-day community meeting to help solve racial problems in schools. He took a machine gun with him in the back of his car. He stood up in front of the assembly of black activists, liberals and conservatives, and let loose, declaring, 'If we didn't have niggers in the schools, we wouldn't have the problems we got today.' Amongst the crowd he spotted a black civil rights campaigner whom he had despised for years. 'I will never forget some black lady I hated with a purple passion, Ann Atwater. How I hated – pardon the expression, I don't use it now – how I just hated that black nigger. Big, fat heavy woman.' To his astonishment, on the third night of the meeting, a black man suggested that he and Ann Atwater be joint chairs of the main committee. He accepted, even though he feared it would be impossible to work with her.

C.P.'s friends in the Klan immediately turned against him, telling him that he was selling out the white race by working with Ann Atwater, that he had become a nigger-lover. At the same time, she was being chastised for cooperating with a known Klansman. After several days trying unsuccessfully to recruit people to their committee, C.P. remembered how they sat down together to reflect: 'Ann said, "My daughter came home cryin' every day. She said her teacher was makin' fun of her in front of the other kids." I said, "Boy, same thing happened to my kid. White liberal teacher was makin' fun of Tim Ellis's father, the Klansman, in front of other peoples." At this point I begin to see, here we are, two people from the far ends of the fence, havin' identical problems, except her bein' black and me bein' white. From that moment on, I tell ya, that gal and I worked together good. I begin to love the girl, really. Up to that point we didn't know each other. We didn't know we had things in common.' He and Ann found that they shared the oppression of poverty. He was then working as a janitor at Duke University, she as a domestic servant, and both were struggling to get by.

Working on the race committee with Ann Atwater and other black activists was a conversational revolution that exploded his prejudices. 'The whole world was openin' up. I was learnin' new truths that I had never learned before. I was beginning to look at a black person, shake hands with him, and see him as a human bein'. I hadn't got rid of all this stuff. I've still got a little bit of it. But somethin' was happening to me. It was almost like bein' born again.'

On the final night of the community meeting, he stood at the microphone in front of a thousand people and tore up his Klan membership card.

Ann Atwater was herself transformed by the experience of the race committee. She was originally surprised by everything they had in common: 'When I first met C.P., he told me he wasn't educated. I wasn't either. Neither one of us had nothing no more than what we had to work hard to get. He was cleanin' commodes and I was cleanin' babies, baby-sittin'. We was cleanin' the same thing.' Her attitude to whites fundamentally shifted as a result of their conversations. 'There's been a change in me like the change in C.P.,' she said several years after meeting him. 'I used not talk to any white people, now I talk to any of them. I would pass them on the street, they would speak at me and I wouldn't say a word. I don't know if I was afraid 'cause I was taught that white was superior. But after I learned, the change was there. Where before, if a white person would tell me today is Tuesday, I'd say no, it's not. I didn't believe 'em. I'd look on the calendar to make sure this is Tuesday. Now I can call 'em up and talk. I have several white friends I can call on right now. That's the same thing with C.P. He trusts blacks … The other thing is – C.P. would never shake my hand. Now we don't shake hands. We hug and embrace.'

C. P. Ellis later became a civil rights campaigner and labour

*Former Ku Klux Klan leader C. P. Ellis talking to his friend Ann Atwater.*

organiser for a union whose membership was 70 per cent black. Most of his old KKK associates avoided him for the next thirty years, but Ann Atwater became a steadfast friend. When C.P. got Alzheimer's disease in his seventies, Ann was a regular visitor to the nursing home. He died there in 2005.

If you look back over your own life, you will probably be able to identify conversations which shattered your assumptions about people and challenged stereotypes you may have carried around for years. These are moments of empathy in action, when you get behind the facade and start to recognise the individuality of another person. They are also moments of self-understanding, offering personal insights which can shift our beliefs and open out a world of potential relationships.

I have never forgotten the time I met Alan Human. I used to see him walking up and down East Oxford's Cowley Road, picking up cigarette butts, jabbering away to himself and shuffling along in an assortment of filthy coats. Then one day, through my involvement in a local community project, we sat down together for a conversation. Beforehand I had been told he was a paranoid schizophrenic with a history of violence, who had spent years living on the streets and had been locked up seventeen times under the Mental Health Act. Having hardly ever spoken to anybody who was mentally ill or homeless, I arrived at our meeting replete with assumptions and prejudices. Many of them were immediately confirmed. He described his experiences of seeing fairies and unborn children in outer space, and I could barely understand his high-speed mutterings. Alan was, it seemed, completely mad, and I couldn't imagine there would be much connection between us.

But when I met Alan for a second time, we got on to the subject of philosophy. He turned out to be a devotee of Nietzsche and Marx, and to have a brilliant philosophical mind. He then revealed that in the 1970s he had done a degree in Philosophy, Politics and Economics at Oxford University, before becoming a milkman and later dropping out of conventional society. I was astonished, because it seemed unbelievable to me that a fifty-something Oxford graduate was trawling the streets in search of half-smoked cigarettes. Alan and I subsequently developed a friendship based on our mutual interest in moral philosophy and pepperoni pizzas. My ideas about people with mental illnesses have never been the same since, and I now find myself stopping more readily to talk to strangers – old or young, seemingly rich or poor – knowing that each of them may possess a secret history like Alan Human.[16]

The world is filled with conversations like these which are just waiting to happen. We can bring them to life by cultivating curiosity about strangers. You might make a particular effort to have a conversation with the person sitting next to you on the bus, or the guy at the corner shop who sells you a newspaper every day, or the new employee who eats his lunch alone in the office cafeteria. You will need courage to get beyond idle chit-chat and find out how they see the world – what are their views on family life, politics, creativity, death? And be ready to share your own thoughts, to make it a mutual empathic exchange.

C. P. Ellis would probably suggest that we go even further than this, and turn our conversational attention towards the kinds of people we might be intolerant of, or whose way of life seems alien or immoral to us. Indeed, anybody with whom we might have an empathy deficit. If you suspect that very wealthy business people lack compassion – an opinion I held for years – test your belief by talking to an oil company executive or a hedge fund manager about their philosophy of life. I remember how shocked I was to discover that the rich Guatemalan industrialists and coffee plantation owners whom I interviewed for my doctoral dissertation were not simply the racist, heartless oligarchs I had assumed them to be, but often had a caring side and some sense of social justice. If you think Jehovah's Witnesses are religious fanatics or that all women who wear burkas are oppressed, embark on a conversational odyssey with one of them. By doing so you may, like C. P. Ellis and Ann Atwater, be surprised not only by what you hear but also by what you share, and be transformed by the encounter.

## How to become a tramp

Aside from conversation, challenging ourselves with new experiences is a second and possibly more demanding approach to expanding our empathy. Yet its rewards may be even greater, and the adventure more thrilling. Journeying into the world of someone whose daily life is very different from our own can etch empathy onto our skin and memories in a way we are unlikely ever to forget. In Western history, there is one person who did more than almost any other to transform this experiential form of empathy into an extreme sport: George Orwell.

Best known for his novels *Animal Farm* (1945) and *Nineteen Eighty-Four* (1949), Orwell also cultivated himself as an empathist, making temporary sojourns into other people's lives that inspired his writing and fundamentally changed the way he viewed the world. After a privileged upbringing in the British upper-middle classes and an elite education at Eton, in the early 1920s he spent five years in Burma as a colonial police officer. Orwell developed a creeping distaste for imperialism, and a growing self-disgust for his own part in it.

As for the job I was doing, I hated it more bitterly than I can perhaps make clear. In a job like that you see the dirty work of Empire at close quarters. The wretched prisoners huddling in the stinking cages of the lock-ups, the grey, cowed faces of the long-term convicts, the scarred buttocks of the men who had been flogged with bamboos – all these oppressed me with an intolerable sense of guilt.[17]

If Burma was his apprenticeship as an empathist, Orwell's formative training took place in London in the late 1920s and early 1930s. Determined to be a writer, he came up with a plan that would give him both a literary and a moral education: to conduct a radical experiment in experiencing poverty. He wanted to know what it was really like to be downtrodden, to exist on the margins of society, to be short of food, money and hope. Reading about it was not enough – his aim was to *live* it. As he later wrote of his intentions:

I felt that I had got to escape not merely from imperialism but from every form of man's dominion over man. I wanted to submerge myself, to get right down among the oppressed; to be one of them and on their side against the tyrants.

So, for several years, Orwell regularly dressed as a tramp in shabby clothes and shoes, and ventured out virtually penniless to frequent the 'spikes' – hostels for the homeless – and doss-houses of the East End of London, wandering the streets with beggars and other destitutes. He would stay for anything from a few days to several weeks. At all times he did so without concessions or compromise, without carrying spare money for an emergency or wearing extra layers of clothes against the winter cold.

On one occasion, in 1931, determined to find out what it would be like to spend Christmas in prison, Orwell donned his tramping clothes, went to a pub on the Mile End Road and got himself thoroughly drunk. This was all part of his cunning plan, for later he was arrested while reeling along the pavements of Whitechapel. He was looking forward to being sentenced since he could not afford the six-shilling fine, but to his annoyance was released the same day as the police seemed to have a better use for their cell. It is not always easy being an empathist.[18]

Orwell was not so naive as to believe that he had gained a complete understanding of life on the edge in the East End, for he knew that he was only dipping into the lives of the poor, and could always step out of his guise and return to the comfort of his parental home in Suffolk. In *Down and Out in Paris and London* (1933), he admits to having only seen the fringes of poverty, but still spells out some clear lessons he learned:

> I shall never again think that all tramps are drunken scoundrels, nor expect a beggar to be grateful when I give him a penny, nor be surprised if men out of work lack energy, nor subscribe to the Salvation Army, nor pawn my clothes, nor refuse a handbill, nor enjoy a meal at a smart restaurant. That is a beginning.[19]

Orwell's empathic adventures as a tramp in London did not transform him into a perfect moral being. He had a healthy malicious streak and happily expressed contempt for some of his fellow writers, such as Jean-Paul Sartre, of whom he ungenerously wrote, 'I think Sartre is a bag of wind and I am going to give him a good boot.' He chose to empathise with those he considered to be shunned by society. Orwell's empathy grew out of an attempt to liberate himself from his elite background and the imperialism of which he had been a foot soldier. But he also wanted to touch injustice with his own hands rather than be just another clever intellectual who pitied the poor from a comfortable distance. And in this he undoubtedly succeeded.

He also succeeded in showing how empathy was about far more than ethics. His tramping excursions certainly challenged his prejudices and shifted his moral values, but they also gained him new friendships, nurtured his curiosity, expanded his ability to talk to people from different social backgrounds and provided him with a rich seam of literary materials which would last him for years. For a young man who had once worn a top hat at Eton, his experiments in living down and out were an intense, exhilarating and often challenging lesson in life itself, catapulting him out of the narrowness of his privileged past. Trying to survive on the streets of East London was the greatest travel experience he would ever have.

Few of us would go to such extremes to gain first-hand knowledge of how other people live and look at the world. But most of us can recognise the impact that stepping into someone else's shoes, even for a limited time, might have on us. In my own case, I once worked in a refugee community in the Guatemalan jungle, living in a straw hut with no electricity or running water. This gave me a brief glimpse into the realities of poverty that I have never forgotten, and which inspired me to work in human rights for many years. Closer to home, upon leaving university I had several jobs in telesales, all of which I hated – the verbal abuse from people I called, the supervisors shouting at us to close the sale. Now when I receive an unsolicited sales call while trying to cook dinner for my kids, I try to be polite and friendly, knowing from my own experience what a disheartening job it can be. This is empathy doing its quiet work to forge human relationships.

How might we go about pursuing experiential empathy in everyday life? If you happen to be devoutly religious, you might decide to attend the services of religions other than your own, or a meeting of Humanists. You could try doing a job swap with a friend whose profession is very different from yours – you could spend a day with them to gain a taste of being a gardener or an accountant, for example, and they in turn could shadow you for a day. If there are few elderly people in your life, could you volunteer in an old people's home for a day each month? Or if you are intent on travelling to Thailand, instead of lying on a beach, might it be possible to contact an educational charity that could arrange for you to be a volunteer English teacher in a rural primary school? Inspired by George Orwell and St Francis of

Assisi, you might want to give yourself a 'deprivation trip', discovering what life is like on the social margins. One option might be to sleep rough for a night, or to help serve food in a homeless shelter. But unless you do this with the frequency and dedication of Orwell, there is a danger of it being a form of poverty voyeurism – like those foreign tourists who cruise through the slums of Rio or Soweto for a couple of hours without emerging from their air-conditioned SUVs. However you decide to nurture your empathic curiosity, you will probably come to understand the wisdom of the Native American proverb 'Walk a mile in another man's moccasins before you criticise him'.

The idea of empathy has distinct moral overtones and is often associated with 'being good'. But experiential empathy should really be regarded as an unusual and stimulating form of travel. George Orwell would tell us to forget spending our next holiday at an exotic resort or visiting museums. It is far more interesting to expand our minds by taking journeys into other people's lives – and allowing them to see ours. Rather than asking ourselves, 'Where can I go next?', the question on our lips should be, 'Whose shoes can I stand in next?'

## Mass empathy and social change

We usually think of empathising as something that happens at the individual level, between two people: I come to see the world from your perspective and may, as a result, start to treat you with greater sensitivity. But empathy can also be a mass phenomenon, with the potential to bring about fundamental social change. Many of the most important shifts in history have taken place not when there has been a change of government, laws or economic systems, but when there has been a flowering of collective empathy for strangers, which has served to create new kinds of mutual understanding and bridge social divides.

Although these moments from the past may seem to be a subject for historians, they are also relevant to the art of living. Why? Because participating in mass empathic movements can help us escape the straitjacket of our individualism and make us feel connected to something larger than ourselves. We find meaning and fulfilment in life not only in pursuit of private ambitions, but through social action in which we join with others to achieve common goals. One instance of such a movement, which illustrates how empathy has altered the contours of human history, is the British struggle against slavery and the slave trade at the end of the eighteenth century.

In the early 1780s slavery was an accepted social institution throughout Europe. Britain presided over the international slave trade and some half a million African slaves were being worked to death growing sugar cane in British colonies in the West Indies. On a plantation owned by the Church of England, the word SOCIETY was branded onto the chests of the slaves with a red-hot iron, a sign that they belonged to the Society for the Propagation of the Gospel in Foreign Parts, on whose board sat the Archbishop of Canterbury. This was a nation – and church – with blood on its hands.

But within two decades something extraordinary happened. A mass social movement rose up that turned large sectors of the British population against slavery, leading to the abolition of the trade by Parliament in 1807, and the end of slavery itself throughout the British Empire in 1838. How and why did this profound and unexpected change take place?

Open a typical school history textbook and you will be told about the heroic efforts of the British parliamentarian William Wilberforce to end slavery. There may also be a paragraph or two about the role of slave revolts on the plantations. But few of them will mention empathy. Yet the most recent research puts empathy at the centre of this apparently familiar story. According to the historian Adam Hochschild, the success of the anti-slavery movement was based on the fact that 'The abolitionists placed their hope not in sacred texts but in human empathy.'[20]

The brilliant campaign against slavery led by the Anglican deacon Thomas Clarkson and a group of Quaker businessmen used empathy as its main strategic tool: they planned to rouse the public to action by exposing them to the traumas and sufferings experienced by slaves on a daily basis, so people could step into their shoes and begin to imagine the realities of their lives. The abolitionists printed a famous poster of the *Brookes* slave ship, illustrating how 482 slaves could be squeezed on board, head to toe, down in the dark and airless hull. Nearly 10,000 copies were made and it was pinned on walls in pubs and homes around the country, a reminder that there was nothing innocent about the lumps of sugar that sweetened the nation's cups of tea.

Clarkson also went to a shop in Liverpool that sold essential gear for slave traders, and purchased handcuffs, thumbscrews, leg shackles and a scissor-like instrument for prying open slaves' mouths for force-feeding, which he showed to horrified audiences in public talks and courtrooms. With his colleagues he produced a damning report, *Abstract of the Evidence*, containing unforgettable accounts of the suffering of slaves. Soon newspapers were printing extracts such as this:

When [slaves] are flogged on the wharves … [they] have their arms tied to the hooks of the crane, and weights of fifty-six pounds applied to their feet. In this situation the crane is wound up, so that it lifts them nearly from the ground and keeps them in a stretched posture, when the whip or cowskin is used. After this they are again whipped, but with ebony bushes, (which are more prickly than the thorn bushes in this country), in order to let out the congealed blood.

The campaign had remarkable results. Tens of thousands of members of the British public attended meetings, formed local committees, signed petitions, boycotted sugar from the plantations and made demands on the government. It was the most powerful human rights movement that the world had ever seen. Thanks to the upswell of empathy, writes Hochschild, 'it was the first time a large number of people became outraged, and stayed outraged for many years, over someone else's rights'.

But why was there such a huge public response to the issue in Britain, whereas no mass movement against slavery arose in other European countries? Empathy again provides an answer. Hochschild pinpoints something that set Britain apart:

People are more likely to care about the suffering of others in a distant place if that misfortune evokes a fear of their own. And late-eighteenth-century Britons were in the midst of widespread first-hand experience with a kind of kidnapping and enslavement that stood in dramatic contradiction to everything about citizens' rights enshrined in British law. It was arbitrary, violent, and sometimes fatal ... It was the practice of naval impressment.

Since the 1600s the Royal Navy had 'pressed' tens of thousands of British men into service at sea. This involved press gangs of armed sailors patrolling around the nation's ports and further inland, forcibly taking any sturdy men they could find in the pubs, the fields or the street and instantly enlisting them in the navy. Press victims, who were often – although not exclusively – from the working class, could find themselves effectively enslaved for several years, robbed of their fundamental freedoms. Campaigners against the slave trade drew direct parallels with this practice of impressment: the British public had an empathic understanding, often from personal or family experience, of what it meant to be enslaved and to have their basic liberties denied. Hence they could clearly recognise the cruel injustice of slavery on the sugar plantations. More than a century of social struggle against impressment, says Hochschild, 'psychologically set the national stage for the much larger battle over slavery'.

The parallels went further. British factory workers saw similarities between their own exploitation and that of the slaves, with some marching under banners calling for ending slavery 'both at home and abroad'. Anti-slavery ideas also spread rapidly in Ireland, where there was a shared understanding of what it felt like to be oppressed by the British. These were the roots of a new kind of solidarity that was able to cross the Atlantic Ocean.

In the light of such evidence we have no choice but to rewrite the annals of slavery and give empathy its own chapter. The power of empathy helps explain the rise of the mass movement,

*A press gang at work, around 1780.*

the strength of public opinion and the legislation that resulted in abolition. It was during the struggle against slavery that empathy came of age as a force for shifting the course of history.

If we wanted to rewrite history from the perspective of empathy, we would have to include further examples of collective empathic flowering, such as the efforts of Danes, Bulgarians and others during the Second World War to prevent Jews being sent to the Nazi death camps, and the overwhelming public response to the Asian tsunami in 2004. We would also need to document historic tragedies of collective empathic failure, such as colonialism in Latin America and the Rwandan genocide. By doing so, we would gradually come to view history not just through the lens of the rise and fall of nations, or the emergence of new religions or technologies, but through the periodic revolutions of human relationships in which mass outbreaks of empathy – or a lack of them – have altered people's lives.

Since the publication of Samuel Smiles's *Self Help* in 1859, most self-help books and lifestyle advice has been unashamedly individualistic, encouraging people to reach their personal goals or improve the quality of their own lives. But when we look at people like Thomas Clarkson, or others who dedicated themselves to empathic social movements, such as Emmeline Pankhurst and Martin Luther King, we start to realise that we, like them, might also find purpose and satisfaction in life through engaging in shared struggles on behalf of others.

So the challenge we each face is to take the art of living out of the private sphere and into the public realm. We can do so by participating in social movements that help to create a more empathic world. You may wish to play a role in tackling child poverty in your own community or human rights abuses abroad. Perhaps you feel inspired to join an organisation campaigning to generate empathy for future generations who may be affected by the ecological destruction we are bequeathing them. These are the kinds of communal adventures in which we might take part, leaving an indelible mark of humanity on history.

## The invisible threads of empathy

'Know thyself,' advised Socrates. Following this credo requires more than gazing, like Narcissus, at our own reflections. We must balance introspective searching with a more 'outrospective' attitude to life. To discover ourselves, we must step outside ourselves and find out how other people think, live and look at the world. Empathy is one of our greatest hopes for doing so.

But cultivating empathy can be a challenge, whether through conversation, experience or social action. Having a conversation with your new neighbours may at first be awkward or embarrassing. A volunteering holiday could put you under physical or emotional strain. Attending community meetings might take up your precious Friday nights. But in time you are likely to become accustomed to your empathic exertions, and gradually it may seem odd or even dissatisfying *not* to make the imaginative leap into other minds in everyday life. Slowly, as the barriers between yourself and other people begin to dissolve, you will come to appreciate how empathy is changing who you are.

One day you may wake to find the world looks different. When you walk into a room full of people you will no longer focus on the individuals, but on the relationships between them. You will notice where empathic bonds are strong and where they remain latent. Your vision will be filled with invisible threads of human connection – both real and potential – that hold the world together in a tapestry of mutual understanding. And you will be able to see the design in the tapestry, and whether the pattern woven by your own actions is adding to its beauty.

# Making a Living

# 4

# Work

Anybody who has visited a careers fair or flicked through a standard career guide has probably begun with a sense of hope but quickly become dazed and confused by the array of possibilities. Should you train as an accountant or try finding work in a children's charity? Is it best to opt for a steady job in local government, or risk opening that yoga café you've always dreamed about? We often forget that the difficulties of choosing a career are a modern dilemma. For centuries, human beings had little choice about the work they undertook. The way they earned their daily bread was largely a matter of fate or necessity. Understanding the stages in the historical shift from fate to choice is an ideal starting point for thinking about the future of our own working lives.

If you were born in medieval Europe, it is unlikely that you would have been one of the knights or ladies that appear in tales of courtly love, or a monk bent over an illuminated manuscript. The vast majority of people were serfs, tied to rural estates and the whims of their lords in a system of feudal servitude.[1] The industrial revolution and urbanisation in the eighteenth and nineteenth centuries offered an ambiguous liberation from the largely static social order of feudalism. Yes, you were emancipated from serfdom and the fetters of the guilds, but now you were a guest of the bourgeois order, a 'vampire that sucks … blood and brains and throws them into the alchemist's cauldron of capital', as Karl Marx so delicately put it. With the freedom to sell your wage labour to whoever you wished, your opportunities were largely limited to the monotony and exploitation of a factory job – or maybe independent employment in the vibrant urban economy as a 'pure finder' (collecting dog dung for tanneries) or street-seller of pickled whelks.[2]

Standard history texts will tell you that the nineteenth century saw the beginnings of a new era of choice for Europe's workers, primarily due to the invention of meritocracy – rewarding people on the basis of their skills or aptitude – and the growth of public education. Certainly Napoleon deserves praise for his idea of 'careers open to talent' (*la carrière ouverte aux talents*), which meant that you could rise up the military ranks simply by being a good soldier rather than through patronage and nepotism.[3] And the birth of competitive examinations for the French and British civil services, although centuries behind the Chinese, boosted equality of opportunity. Yet the beneficiaries of these developments were usually well-educated men.

Only in the twentieth century, when education became more widespread, did it become plausible to claim that the majority of people born in the West would have a wide variety of career choices and the chance for social mobility. Women were increasingly accepted into the paid economy, a reward partly resulting from their struggle for the vote and factory work during two world wars, and the arrival of the Pill in the 1960s gave women significant control over when or if they would have a family so they could more easily pursue their chosen careers. Immigrant workers gradually defied prejudice and discrimination, with their children finding jobs in professions previously dominated by native citizens.

Despite the general evolution over the centuries from fate and necessity to freedom and choice in the work we do, there remain considerable barriers facing some of those who wish to pursue their passions and use their talents. How easy is it for a woman to become chair of a multinational corporation, or maintain a successful career while doing most of the childcare? What prejudices face a man of Turkish descent hoping to rise in one of Germany's state police forces? Moreover, poverty ensures that there are permanent underclasses whose work choices are limited to tedious McJobs in the service sector.

Many people today, however, feel overwhelmed by the career choices that confront them. All those handbooks and websites listing hundreds of professions can leave us crippled with uncertainty and anxiety. The freedom we have gained has, unexpectedly, become a burden. This is one of the least recognised misfortunes of Western history. The problem has been exacerbated by the erosion of the 'job for life' over the past three decades due to the rise of downsizing, short-term contracts and temping, under the guise of labour market 'flexibility'. Today the average job lasts just four years, forcing us to make difficult choices throughout our working lives.[4] Professional career advice, which dates back to the first 'Vocation Bureau' established in Boston in 1908, has the potential to help us confront the paradox of choice. Yet most career counsellors are much better at identifying why your current job isn't suitable for you than they are at pinpointing better alternatives. This is in part due to the limitations of some of the tools at their disposal, such as personality tests like the popular Myers-Briggs Type Indicator, which aim to match your apparent character traits with particular jobs. Unfortunately there is little empirical evidence to suggest that these tests are any more likely to lead you to a satisfying career than getting some advice from a good friend.[5]

So I want to explore how we should negotiate the quagmire of deciding what work to do and which career path to follow. The difficulties are compounded by the irony that, despite the extraordinary historical revolution of choice, so many people still find their jobs unrewarding and dull. Surveys by the Work Foundation and others repeatedly show that two-thirds of workers in Europe today are unsatisfied with their jobs and feel that their current career falls short of their aspirations.[6] How did it get to be this way? And what insights from the past can inspire us to find a career that better suits who we are and who we want to be? On our search we will be meeting with organists, gardeners, ballet dancers and death camp survivors. But first, we must reach into our pockets and take out our wallets.

## Escaping the pin factory

It is astounding that the main culprit responsible for the toils of modern work has, since the late 1990s, been celebrated on the twenty-pound note. A portrait of the romantic composer Edward Elgar was replaced by the eighteenth-century philosopher and political economist Adam Smith staring dispassionately at workers grafting away in a pin factory. The caption on the note reads: 'The division of labour in pin manufacturing (and the great increase in the quantity of work that results)'.

Smith argued that the best way to increase industrial productivity and economic growth was to divide complex tasks into tiny segments. In a famous example in his book *The Wealth of Nations* (1776), he described how there are eighteen separate stages to making a pin. If one worker tried to do all of them himself, he 'could scarce, perhaps, with his utmost industry, make one pin in a day'. But if the process was split into separate operations, with each worker doing just one or two tasks, they could each make, on average, nearly 5,000 pins in a day.

The apparent miracle of the division of labour became a mantra of capitalist economics and was swiftly put into practice throughout the industrial world. It also ushered in the era of monotonous work. Smith's account of the pin factory was hardly a vision of utopia:

> One man draws out the wire, another straights it, a third cuts it, a fourth points it, a fifth grinds it at the top for receiving the head; to make the head requires two or three distinct operations; to put it on, is a peculiar business, to whiten the pins is another; it is even a trade by itself to put them into the paper.[7]

Buried in the final pages of *The Wealth of Nations*, Smith revealed his empathic side by admitting that the result of jobs like straightening pin wire all day was not just greater national income but 'torpor of the mind' and a loss of 'tender sentiment'. He conceded that 'the man whose life is spent in performing a few simple operations ... has no occasion to exert his understanding, or to exercise his invention.'[8]

*Political economist Adam Smith keeps an eye on workers toiling in a pin factory.*

Many people today know just what Smith was talking about. We are the inheritors of the division of labour, the most deadening legacy of our industrial history. Whether we are employed in factories or offices, the chances are that we are charged with performing a small number of specialised and repetitive tasks. Did any of us, as spirited children, dream of growing up to spend our days doing nothing but copy-editing magazine articles, drafting legal contracts or marketing pharmaceuticals? Few get to draw on their diverse skills and take a job from start to finish. We are denied the satisfactions of a chair maker who might cut down the tree, strip the bark, shape the rungs, steam the legs, bore the mortises, clamp the pieces, weave the seat and finally polish the wood with beeswax.

'Work,' wrote Mark Twain, 'is a necessary evil to be avoided.' Indeed, there was an age, up until only a few decades ago, when it was widely accepted that work was inevitably destined to be dreary. But this is no longer the case. One of the major cultural shifts of our time has been a rising expectation for work more personally fulfilling than anything Adam Smith could have imagined. Today we search for jobs that are not only pleasurable but life-enhancing. We want our careers to widen our horizons, express our ideals, offer opportunities for learning, excite our curiosity, and provide friendship and even love.[9] A major reason for this attitudinal change has been material prosperity in the West since the end of the Second World War. Now that so many people have their basic needs met, there is an appetite for deeper forms of individual satisfaction. Sociologists have referred to this as the emergence of 'post-material values', such as the desire for personal improvement and ethical living, leading many to seek work that nurtures their souls as well as finances the mortgage.[10] This trend has been bolstered by more recent changes in the balance between work and leisure, with working hours gradually on the rise across Europe and North America. The fact that in the last two decades our jobs have been taking up more and more of our time means that if we cannot make our work fulfilling, then there are few remaining hours left in the day to live the good life.

Unfortunately our great expectations leave us with a new quandary: how can we satisfy our hunger for more meaningful work when we are still burdened by the inheritance of the pin factory? A common answer is to find meaning and motivation through the pursuit of money. Work is approached as a means to an end rather than something intrinsically valuable, and we opt to tolerate the tedium and stresses of our jobs as a necessary cost. Money, it is believed, can be used not just to pay the bills, but to purchase our quality of life.

The desire for money, and other forms of wealth such as property, is a long-established ambition. In 1504, when the Spanish conquistador Hernán Cortés arrived in the Americas, he declared, 'I came to get gold, not to till the soil like a peasant.' Soon the invaders became obsessed with finding El Dorado, a legendary kingdom in the Amazon that was reputedly ruled by a tribal chief who covered himself in gold dust. Over the course of two centuries, hundreds of adventurers died of disease and hunger in their vain search for the golden city. The quest for El Dorado has come to symbolise the reckless desire for wealth prevalent in contemporary society.

Few people interested in earning substantial sums would go to the same lengths, but anybody who feels that the main point of work is to make money should beware that having lots of it is rarely an effective way of achieving personal fulfilment. In the past half-century real incomes have risen substantially in industrialised nations, but levels of 'life satisfaction' or 'well-being' have been almost entirely flat in North America and most European countries. A major study at Johns Hopkins University showed that lawyers – the highest-paid professionals in the US economy – have the greatest incidence of depression of any occupational group, being more than three times as likely to suffer from depression than the average worker.[11]

It is no surprise, then, that many people eventually seek jobs that provide a more profound sense of purpose; work which is an end in itself rather than a means to an end, and which helps them feel that they're not wasting their lives. What are the most important forms of purpose that have motivated human beings? Four stand out in the history of work: being driven by our values; pursuing meaningful goals; obtaining respect; and using the full array of our talents. All of these can help overcome the drudgery we have inherited from the division of labour, and considering which of them we are drawn towards is a guide for navigating our way through the confusion of job choices.

## Values: being true to your beliefs

Albert Schweitzer was one of the most accomplished polymaths of his generation. Born in 1875 in Alsace-Lorraine, he obtained doctorates in philosophy, theology and music, wrote a major biography of Johann Sebastian Bach and a groundbreaking book on the life of Jesus, and also managed to be one of the finest organists in Europe. Most of this he achieved in his twenties. But at thirty, Schweitzer decided on a major change in direction, giving up his music and brilliant academic career to retrain as a doctor. In 1913 he left for French Equatorial Africa, where he established a hospital for lepers, and in 1952 received the Nobel Peace Prize for his decades of pioneering medical work in the African jungle. Schweitzer was motivated by the desire to give service, and contribute to what he called 'the great humanitarian task' of taking medical knowledge to the colonies. He felt a duty, an obligation, to work for the benefit of others. 'Even if it's a little

*Albert Schweitzer, one of Europe's greatest organists, switched careers and opened a hospital in Africa. He took his moustache with him.*

thing,' he said, 'do something for those who have need of man's help, something for which you get no pay but the privilege of doing it.'[12]

The classic route to a purposeful career is working for a cause that embodies our values, something which transcends our own desires and makes a difference to other people or the world around us. Service has been one of the most powerful motivating values in Western history, and is rooted in the medieval Christian idea of giving service to God through good works. Europe's first hospitals, which began emerging in cities such as Paris, Florence and London in the twelfth century, were religious foundations established to serve the Almighty as much as the destitute and sick – an attitude reflected in the old French term for hospital, *hôtel-Dieu*, 'hostel of God'. Around the same period, Christian crusading orders like the Knights of St John of Jerusalem and the Knights Templar – best known for their slaughter of non-believers – also built hospitals throughout the Mediterranean and German-speaking lands as a matter of sacred service.[13] Albert Schweitzer was propelled by this Christian ethic of service, as were the nineteenth-century founders of the modern nursing profession, such as Florence Nightingale and Clara Barton. The ideal of giving service spread beyond religious boundaries in the twentieth century, so that those who work today for the civil service – whether as front-line social workers or statisticians in the education department – often do so not just because they may be offered a steady income or promotion prospects, but because they feel their work contributes to the public good.

The values that drive so much human activity are often responses to the needs and ideas of the time. The French Revolution popularised 'the rights of man' as a reaction to the absolutism of monarchical rule. In the nineteenth century, equality and social justice also emerged as central values as the horrendous inequalities resulting from industrialisation became glaringly clear. Yet at that time, unless you were employed by the Church – for instance as a nun working in an almshouse – finding a job where you could be true to your beliefs was far from easy. You might have dedicated yourself to the growing trade union movement or the incipient cause of women's suffrage, but it was unlikely anybody would pay you for your efforts. This only began to change towards the end of the century as new value-based sectors of the economy developed, such as independent charitable institutions. By 1905, Dr Barnardo's homes for orphans and destitute children were caring for more than 8,000 young people in nearly a hundred locations, and needed a range of staff including teachers, nurses and administrators. Another growing sector – particularly in Britain, Denmark and Germany – was the cooperative movement, which at the turn of the century employed hundreds of thousands in retail and wholesale operations, most of whom benefited from the egalitarian profit-sharing ethos.

The possibilities for living out your social and political values in everyday work grew exponentially following the Second World War. Across Western Europe, and also in North America, there was a boom in charities, or what we now call the 'third sector' (to distinguish it from the private and public sectors). Oxfam and CARE USA were founded in the 1940s, World Vision in 1950, Amnesty International in 1961, and Médecins Sans Frontières a decade later, offering job opportunities for those motivated to tackle human rights abuses and poverty in developing countries. Animal rights and ecology organisations also became increasingly prominent, and by 2007 around half a million British workers were employed full-time in the third sector. Alongside them were tens of thousands of professionals drawn to making a difference by working in the public sector, for instance as teachers in state education or doctors and mental health workers in government clinics.

In the past, you would have had to take holy vows if you wanted your values and work to coincide. No longer. Values have always been with us, but only in the last fifty years has it become realistic to express them in your career. Although we may not want to make the same personal sacrifices as Albert Schweitzer, who was still working at his jungle hospital when he died at the age of ninety, the satisfaction of being true to your beliefs and principles is a genuine and inspiring option.

## Goals: a concrete assignment

During the Middle Ages it was generally accepted that work was an arduous burden rather than a path to fulfilment. Christian doctrine stressed that labour was a punishment for Adam's sins, while the classical Greek tradition saw virtue in a life of leisure rather than the sweat of manual work. But all this changed with the Protestant Reformation in the sixteenth and seventeenth centuries. Theologians such as Martin Luther and John Calvin promoted the idea that hard work – even as a lowly cobbler – was a worthy activity and a religious duty which brought you closer to God. Sloth was viewed as a terrible sin and, in the words of the historian R. H. Tawney, 'mundane toil' became 'itself a kind of sacrament'.[14]

This so-called 'Protestant ethic' has a bad press today, being frequently blamed as the root cause of our culture of excessive work, especially in Northern Europe and North America, and as the reason why we so often feel guilty for taking an extra half-hour at lunch on a sunny afternoon before returning to the office. Yet the veneration of hard work was only one element of the new ideology. A second strand of Protestant thought was the idea of a 'calling'. For Luther, this referred to a decisive event that led a person to give their life to God, for instance as a pastor. But for later Puritan thinkers, it represented the view that each person should follow a vocation they feel drawn towards – say as a carpenter or cloth merchant – and which contributes to public welfare. In this sense, it resembled the ethic of Christian service discussed above. Monastic contemplation was no longer the ideal. 'This monkish kind of living is damnable,' wrote the Puritan clergyman William Perkins in the late sixteenth century, for 'every man must have a particular and personal calling, that he may be a good and profitable member of some society.'[15]

Following your calling was supposedly good for your spiritual health, but its more practical benefit was to give you a clear goal and direction in life. This may be why 'having a calling' still seems such an appealing prospect today, although the concept has now been secularised to describe how we can be inextricably attracted to a particular occupation which completely absorbs us. Typically a calling includes a specific goal that provides both a deep sense of meaning and a definite path to pursue, and may or may not be driven by our ethical beliefs. Thus we might feel a calling or 'mission' to devote our lives to doing research on the causes of autism, to being a stone sculptor or to keeping the family business alive – even if we might not always find it easy to explain why.

The most profound modern formulation of the notion of a calling appears in the writings of the Austrian psychotherapist Victor Frankl. In *Man's Search for Meaning* (1946), based on his experiences in Nazi concentration camps, Frankl seeks to explain 'the apparent paradox that some prisoners of a less hardy make-up often seemed to survive the camp life better than those of a robust nature'. He noticed that the survivors were those who had some future goal beyond mere survival, which gave a spiritual depth to their lives and a 'will to meaning'. Frankl cites one case of a scientist who had not yet completed writing the series of books he had begun before the war intervened; he realised that nobody else could complete his work, so he had to stay alive to finish it. A second case was a man who wanted to commit suicide, but was kept alive by the thought that he might be reunited with his son, whom he adored and who he knew was still alive. Such camp inmates had an inner strength that reflected Nietzsche's saying 'He who has a *why* to live for can bear with almost any *how*'.

Frankl realised that it was crucial to have a why to live for, a compelling future objective which he referred to as a 'concrete assignment', although it echoes the older idea of a calling: 'What man actually needs is not a tension-less state but rather the striving and struggling for some goal worthy of him … One should not search for an abstract meaning of life. Everyone has his own specific vocation or mission in life to carry out a concrete assignment which demands fulfilment.'[16]

We can each ask ourselves: do I have a concrete assignment? Perhaps yours will be working as a marine biologist to save the Great Barrier Reef, or reinventing children's playgrounds in the inner cities. But the challenge is how to discover what your calling might be. In reality, very few people have a flashing insight or epiphany that miraculously reveals their life's mission. If they find a calling at all, it often creeps up on them after they have been working in a field for some years, or becomes clear only after experimenting with many different careers. Consider the example of Vincent Van Gogh. He started out as an art dealer, worked as a schoolteacher in England, tried life as a bookseller, and then suddenly realised his true vocation was to be a Protestant pastor. So after a period of theological study, he worked for two years as a missionary amongst poor Belgian coal miners. It was only after recognising that preaching was not the dream job he had imagined that he began to draw seriously. Finally, in his late twenties, it dawned on him that he wanted to dedicate himself to painting, which he did with absolute intensity, amidst bouts of mental illness, until his death in 1890, aged thirty-seven.

While Van Gogh's life was extraordinary, his experience of a calling was in many ways typical. It came to him after much trial and error, and was more about using his talents and expressing his personality than about trying to 'do good' in the world. Moreover, like many people who obey a calling, the journey was often far from pleasurable. Van Gogh's artistic pursuits forced him to live in poverty and isolation. Few people appreciated his work, and he sold only one painting during his lifetime.

Those who pursue a calling, like Van Gogh, also find that their work merges with the rest of their life. Due to their single-minded commitment, they may have few hobbies outside their work, their friendships are found through their jobs, they don't live for the weekends and often work right through them. To follow a calling is to question the ideology of 'work-life balance' – a term first used in the 1970s – which assumes that your professional activities and your 'real life' are somehow distinct. When so much meaning derives from your work, the need to seek balance can seem less important, even a distraction.

Although it may be hard to discover a calling, if you are able to do so and turn it into a career, you will gain a sense of purpose that carries you through the years, and which provides far more than the monotony and mental torpor of a job in a pin factory.

## Respect: the search for recognition

Throughout the history of work, the desire for recognition – to have others acknowledge our existence and show appreciation of our worth – has rivalled money as a primary ambition. One of the most sought-after forms of recognition is status: attaining a lofty position or rank in a social hierarchy. In China, for over a thousand years, the highest status was accorded to the literati, an educated elite known as *puo che*, or 'living libraries', who were rewarded with positions as government officials. In pre-modern Europe, those who received the greatest honour were not normally the rich, but rather individuals who stood out as fine warriors, pious clerics, or men (and occasionally women) of great learning. Today, while there is a much closer association between wealth and status than in the past, there are still professions – such as being a barrister or surgeon

– whose degree of social prestige cannot be reduced simply to their earning power.

There has always been something hollow about the recognition gained through status. We might be revered for work that we don't find personally compelling or socially valuable, or we might feel admired for the image we represent – 'leading entrepreneur' or 'top diplomat' – rather than for our individuality. In the end, we may find that how society rates us is not as important as how we are perceived by family, friends and colleagues. There is also the problem that the desire for status can all too easily transform into a craving for fame, where we become obsessed with the breadth of our public renown. Yet it is well known that the very famous are often extremely miserable, trapped in public lives and superficial relationships, and holding themselves together with a rich cocktail of antidepressants and other drugs. This is what prompted Louis Armstrong to say, 'You don't have no fun at all if you get too famous.' In any case, the possibility of achieving genuine renown is so limited. How many people can become a famous pop star, footballer or TV chef?

Over the last hundred years an alternative form of recognition has been increasingly coveted: respect.[17] This differs from status in that it concerns being treated with consideration and humanity, and being valued for our personal contributions, rather than occupying a particular position in a hierarchy. One profession in which respect has been conspicuous by its absence is gardening.

Until the mid-twentieth century, garden labourers were usually treated as domestic servants, with little if any respect. In the 1830s, the garden designer John Loudon noted that the wages of even experienced estate gardeners who had studied botany were half that of illiterate bricklayers, and that 'there is no class of gentlemen's servants so badly lodged as gardeners generally are.'[18] Horses were often given better accommodation than gardeners, who would freeze during the winter months in makeshift shacks. Throughout the nineteenth century, destitute gardeners could be found begging on the streets of London with a rake in hand. Left out on the streets, they were also left out of the history books, which refer to the great landscaped gardens of Capability Brown and other designers, without mention of the hundreds of skilled plantsmen who created the beautiful vistas, ha-has and herbaceous beds. The English have always loved their gardens, but clearly not respected their gardeners.

The situation has hardly changed today, as I can attest to from my own experience of working as a gardener at an Oxford college. Like the other assistant gardeners I was paid just over six pounds an hour – not much above the national minimum wage – despite the fact that we all had professional horticultural qualifications. But more striking than the low pay was the way we were treated. As I crouched on the ground weeding, college fellows and students would usually walk straight past without even a friendly 'hello'. For all our efforts to create beauty in the grounds, rarely did anybody give us thanks for our work. At lunchtime we were permitted to eat the same food as the lecturers, but we were not allowed to sit with them at 'high table': we were relegated to a staff table that was both physically and symbolically lower down, as if we were still in the age of feudalism. Over time, the early pride I had in my work was eroded by this lack of respect, and without this my self-respect began to dissolve. Feeling that my presence did not matter was doing subtle damage to my soul. That is when I decided to leave. Looking back, I might have gained greater respect working as a gardener somewhere less hierarchical and more community-orientated, such as on a horticultural therapy project.

Respect is a necessary condition for a purposeful, nurturing working life. So where, and how, can we find it? Respect tends to flower where there is a space for genuine human relationships to develop – where you have direct contact with colleagues and clients rather than being stuck behind a computer all day, and where you do not feel like an anonymous cog in the machine. The problem is that the general trend over the past century has been towards increasingly large organisations that are designed to foster efficiency, not respect. When Henry Ford established his huge Highland Park car factory in Michigan in 1910, he argued that worries about the quality of the assembly-line jobs were 'mere moonshine' and that his employees would be happy to tolerate the repetitiveness as long as wages were high enough. In effect, his workers were treated not as human beings deserving of respect but as an economic resource, an input into the production process, just like the steel and bolts for the car doors.

The good news is that even large, bureaucratic organisations can sometimes offer their employees respect. My father, who worked for IBM for fifty years, almost always felt appreciated for the contribution he made, supported by his colleagues, and part of a community of 'IBMers'. It was only in his final years, when many of his old friends retired and the company started to treat its workers in a more expendable fashion, that he felt the community spirit and respect dissolve. Equally, it is worth recognising that small organisations might have the potential for generating respect, since everyone knows your name, but they can easily be ruled by tyrants who have little interest in treating employees with humanity. In the end, respect is more a function of organisational culture than it is of size. Why is the drinks company Innocent regularly voted as one of the best places to work in the UK, and why does it have such low turn-over amongst its 200 employees? The answer is not so much in high salaries, as in high respect. It has a reputation for treating its workers as human beings, offering them extensive consultation in decision making, adventurous nature weekends, extra holidays if they are going on honeymoon, free beers on Friday afternoons, and personal development scholarships so they can pursue their interests outside work. Staff are often spotted playing with hula hoops in the car park.

Respect can also emerge in the most unusual professions. I know of someone who shifted from being a refrigeration mechanic to becoming an embalmer in a funeral parlour. The reason he loves his job is because he receives so much genuine appreciation from people for making their deceased loved ones look peaceful, dignified and even beautiful. 'I have a folder full of thank-you letters from family members,' he told me.

## Talents: high achiever – or wide achiever?

Having a job that expresses our values, has meaningful goals and offers respect may not be enough if there is limited scope to use and explore our talents. Most of us would like to look back on our working lives and see that we have cultivated our gifts and fulfilled our individual potential. This raises one of the great questions of modern work, which is whether we should aspire to be specialists, channelling our talents towards a single profession, or aim to be generalists who develop them across a broad range of fields. In other words, should we seek to be high achievers or wide achievers?

The choice matters because, over the past century, both education and work have encouraged us towards increasing specialisation, and the prevalent ideal is to be an expert who excels in a narrow area. Why has this become the accepted ideal? First, due to the legacy of the division of labour: Adam Smith's pin factory created work that was not only tediously repetitive, but highly specific in the skills required, so now we usually only do part of a task – for example designing a logo or creating a marketing plan – rather than the whole task from beginning to end, as a craftsperson might do.

A second reason is that academic learning has become extraordinarily specialised, leading to the veneration of those who know a lot about a very precise and often obscure subject. This is clearly the case with the PhD, a nineteenth-century German invention that quickly spread across Europe and North America. I should know, having spent seven years writing a doctoral dissertation on the political and social thought of the Guatemalan oligarchy in the 1990s. Subject areas have also been split into multiple subfields. Two hundred years ago science was a single field known as 'natural philosophy', but today experts in inorganic chemistry and molecular biology each have a knowledge and technical language so specific that they have difficulty talking to one another.

A third explanation for the cult of specialisation is that the amount of information in the world has grown so vast that it is impossible to gain deep understanding across a range of subjects or professions, leaving us with little choice but to become an expert in a single area. In the seventeenth century René Descartes made major contributions to philosophy, theology, mathematics and physics, while also dabbling in anatomy and music theory. Mastering such diverse fields would be unfeasible today. There is simply too much to read and too much to know.[19]

So should we just follow the trend? There are, undoubtedly, benefits to being a specialist. Working as an aeronautical engineer may give us superb opportunities to use our mathematical talents, while also being a socially useful profession: we would hardly want aircraft wings to be designed by sushi chefs or curious laymen who were model plane fanatics. Yet we should beware the possibility that becoming an expert might make work limited and uninteresting. Excessive specialisation may be a trap that prevents us from fully fostering the range of our abilities. Theodore Zeldin writes that 'an increasing proportion of those searching for a career feel they have talents which no single profession can nurture and develop.'[20] We need to consider whether our job is allowing us to explore the various sides of who we are.

My own approach has been to follow the route of the generalist; I aspire to be a wide achiever. That is why I have worked not only as a gardener and university lecturer, but also as a human rights monitor, carpenter, journalist, book editor, community worker, real tennis coach, and consultant on empathy and international development. This apparently wayward career path means that I am sometimes looked upon as a jack of all trades and master of none.

Yet being a generalist should not be dismissed too quickly. During the Italian Renaissance it was considered the ultimate human ideal. One of the most famous polymaths of the era was Leon Battista Alberti (1404–72), an author, artist, architect, poet, linguist, cryptographer, philosopher and musician. He was apparently a gymnast too: with his feet together, he could spring over a man's head. And he wrote a solemn funeral oration for his dog. Alberti was feted as one of the great 'many-sided men', as they were known, and certainly lived up to his belief that 'men can do all things if they will'.[21] He was accompanied by others such as Leonardo da Vinci, Dante and Michelangelo, who popularised the notion of expressing your individuality by putting your full range of talents to use.

I believe that, in our era dominated by specialisation, we need to rediscover the Renaissance ideal of the generalist. We are not all as multi-talented as Alberti or Leonardo, yet we can be inspired by the three different ways people in the past have approached the art of being a generalist.

First, we can join professions that require mastery of numerous skills or areas of knowledge. Teaching has, historically, been one of the most popular outlets for the generalist. Aristotle, whose students included Alexander the Great and Ptolemy, taught his charges a huge range of subjects, including physics, metaphysics, poetry, theatre, music, politics, ethics, biology and zoology. A modern equivalent is the primary school teacher, who is typically required to know about a variety of subjects such as science, history and language acquisition; to possess an ability to sing, tell stories and draw pictures; to have the sensitivity to offer emotional support to children; and to be an imaginative thinker who can put curriculum guidelines into practice and keep the inspectors happy. The finest primary school teachers are consummate generalists who rival Aristotle and Alberti for their breadth of knowledge, understanding and experience.

A second approach to being a generalist is to pursue several careers at the same time. This was the path followed in the twelfth century by the almost impossibly talented German abbess Hildegard of Bingen. As well as founding Benedictine monasteries and being a revered Christian mystic, she was also a naturalist, herbalist, linguist, philosopher, playwright, poet and composer whose liturgical music is still performed. Hildegard's approach was close to Karl Marx's ideal vision of work, which was to 'hunt in the morning, fish in the afternoon, rear cattle in the evening, criticise after dinner, without ever becoming hunter, fisherman, shepherd or critic'. Today this is known as following a 'portfolio' career, where the idea is to work freelance and possibly in several fields rather than commit oneself to a single employer or profession. So you might be an accountant three days a week and spend two days starting up a landscape design business. For all the freedoms gained, you may well find yourself working more hours than you ever planned and becoming stressed by the insecurity of not having a guaranteed pay cheque at the end of the month. Instead you could follow a variant of the portfolio career, which is to pursue several different careers in succession: to become, in effect, a 'serial specialist'. I once met a man who began life as a dancer in the Royal Ballet, then became a top music executive at EMI and followed this with a career as a sculptor – his works can be found in the National Portrait Gallery – while managing all the while to keep up a regular column in *International Sheep Dog News*. They say you only live once, but it may be possible to live many working lives, one after another.

A final option is to bring the thinking of other professions and disciplines into your own, so you become a generalist without having to change jobs. In 1931, Harry Beck, an engineering draughtsman working at the London Underground Signals Office, noticed that the Tube map was incredibly confusing, like a plate of spaghetti. In his spare time, he used his knowledge of electrical circuit diagrams to redesign it in a simplified, schematic format. The result was the iconic map still used today – a classic of graphic design – where the position of the Tube stops and intersections is extremely clear, although not geographically accurate. This teaches us that it may be worth learning to wear the hats of different professions in order to stimulate us to ask new questions or challenge our assumptions and conventional thinking. So if you are a musician you may spend time talking to an engineer, and see if it helps you rethink how to play the piano or compose a sonata. This approach to being a generalist was already perfected by Leonardo da Vinci in the fifteenth century: although an expert in many intellectual fields, he was also a virtuoso at taking his understanding from one area and applying it in another. For example, his studies of anatomy influenced the way he approached painting, and his investigations of bird and bat flight directly impacted on his designs for flying machines.[22]

The life of a generalist is increasingly attractive in this age where we desire work that nurtures the multiplicity of our talents, interests and aspirations. Scaling the heights of a single profession may come to be seen as an old-fashioned career goal, and career counsellors might one day be trained to provide the advice you need to become a wide achiever. But until this occurs, you will have to find your own way to pursue the art of the generalist, and transform a Renaissance ideal into a personal reality.

## Is your job big enough for your spirit?

If Adam Smith were alive today, I believe he would have the humility to be ashamed of his presence on the twenty-pound note. The division of labour may have led to a 'great increase in the quantity of work', but it has done little to benefit the quality of our working lives. From the textile sweatshops of Dhaka to the telephone call centres of Dublin, many jobs remain conditioned by the everyday burdens of the division of labour. Yet we need not accept this inheritance without a struggle. Even for those whose opportunities are restricted, and even in difficult economic times, there are usually many more choices available than we realise, more cracks in the world of work through which we can peer to glimpse something more rewarding.

Navigating our way through the possibilities may seem a daunting task. We can be guided and inspired by thinking hard about what a purposeful job would really look like – one that makes us feel fully alive, and provides more than the shallow pleasures of wealth or status. We no longer face the strictures of feudalism that kept us firmly in our place, and the history of work suggests we can find careers that not only embody our values, but that have meaningful goals, give us a sense of respect and use our talents. Some, if not all of these, may be within your reach, offering you a job that is big enough for your spirit.

For these possibilities to become realities, we need to find ways of overcoming our fears and lack of self-confidence, which may be holding us back from taking action. What if I make the wrong choice? Do I really have the skills to be successful? Can

I take the financial risk of changing jobs? Won't I be wasting all those years I spent getting to where I am now? There are many ways to approach such fears and begin on a pathway towards change. You might, for instance, start with conversational research, seeing what you can learn from talking to people who have made the kind of career change which you are contemplating. Or you could embark on trial 'branching projects': rather than taking the drastic measure of jettisoning your old job completely, first try your hand as a massage therapist in the evenings or on the weekend, to see if it really does provide that spark that seems to be missing from your life. Whatever strategies we try, we should endeavour to treat our working lives as experiments in the art of living, heeding the words of the nineteenth-century writer Ralph Waldo Emerson: 'Do not be too timid and squeamish about your actions. All life is an experiment. The more experiments you make the better. What if they are a little coarse, and you may get your coat soiled or torn? What if you do fail, and get fairly rolled in the dirt once or twice. Up again, you shall never be so afraid of a tumble.'[23]

# 5

# Time

My first watch was a present from my father, brought back from a business trip to Japan. I was thrilled that it counted not only seconds but tenths of seconds, and that I could see each moment running into the future in flickering black digits. I remember proudly showing off the watch to my friends and being able to record how quickly I could cycle to school. Eight minutes, forty seconds. After my mother died, when I was ten, I developed a compulsive and superstitious habit during tennis matches of glancing at this watch after I hit every shot. I knew it was distracting me from the rally but I just had to look, for the briefest instant. What had initially been a gift had become a dependency.

Knowing the time is a drug, and most of us are addicted to it. If you accidentally leave your watch at home you may begin to notice how often you glance at your wrist throughout the day, almost as if you have a nervous tic. Not knowing the time can make us feel anxious and frustrated. Are we running late? Will we finish on time? But luckily our addiction can be satisfied, because we live in a world full of clocks: on mobile phones, in the bottom corner of our computer screens, on the microwave oven in the office kitchen, on car dashboards, on the facades of church towers, in shops and train stations.

An alien anthropologist visiting the earth would probably conclude that amongst this strange species, clocks were idols for religious veneration or perhaps talismans to ward off evil. This is precisely what the Lilliputians thought when they noticed Gulliver looking at his watch so often. He assured them that he seldom did anything without consulting it. They took it off for examination, remarking, 'We conjecture that it is either some unknown animal, or the god that he worships; but we are more inclined to the latter opinion.'

Our obsession has deepened as people in the Western world confront an ever-worsening famine of time. As working hours rise, traffic jams lengthen and email in-boxes overload, we just don't seem to have enough of the stuff. Around a quarter of Americans 'always feel rushed' according to a national survey, a figure which rises to over 40 per cent for working mothers. In Britain 20 per cent of workers say they don't have time for a lunch break, while the siesta has almost disappeared from Spanish life: only 7 per cent now indulge in the traditional afternoon nap.[1] We yearn for more time but have devised no way of extending a day beyond twenty-four hours. We are constantly rushing to save time but there are no banks in which to deposit our savings. Feeling that we are always trying to beat the clock can not only leave us stressed and give us ulcers, but also strain our relationships, cloud our judgement, curtail our pastimes and deaden our curiosity and senses.

But there is hope. Humanity managed to survive for centuries without this fixation on time, without being able to divide the days into tiny, precise portions. Socrates invented Western philosophy without knowing if it was ten past three or actually ten to. Hildegard of Bingen revolutionised medieval music never having heard of minutes or seconds. Leonardo da Vinci was not checking his watch as he painted the Last Supper, nor did he enjoy the benefits of an electronic calendar to organise his time.

We have created our obsession with time, and we are shackled by chains of our own making. This means we also have the power to reinvent our culture of time. But how? We need to understand how three aspects of its history have shaped our current quandaries: the measurement of time since the Middle Ages, its manipulation since the industrial revolution and the growing cult of speed from the nineteenth century. Only then will we be in a position to rethink our personal approaches to time, and consider how we might develop a more gentle and meaningful relationship with the passing moments of our lives.

## The tyranny of the clock

Each morning we break the silence of sleep with artificial bleeps and rings which shock our bodies into wakefulness. Timetables summon us onto trains, clocks send us off to meetings, call us back from lunch and prevent us from going home even if we are ill or being unproductive. It is as if we have all been to obedience classes and trained to be submissive to time. How have we become so subject to the tyranny of the clock?

The first civilisations to take a serious interest in time were the Babylonians and ancient Egyptians. Living as they did in agricultural societies, their main concern was to measure the passing of the seasons: they needed to know when to plant crops or irrigate their fields. So they created calendars to reflect the cycles and movements of the moon, sun and other stars. The Babylonians, for instance, lived by the lunar month, but since moon cycles didn't fit neatly into the solar year, in 432 BC they devised a nineteen-year calendar where some years had twelve months and others thirteen, which turned out to be far too complicated for everyday use. Jews and Muslims still live by similar lunar calendars; hence the fasting month of Ramadan has no fixed date, shifting back around eleven days each year.[2] With their eyes and mathematical prowess focused on the heavens, the Babylonians and Egyptians had little interest in finding accurate ways to segment the days. Most of the devices used in the ancient world for doing so were inexact and unreliable. The Romans had thirteen kinds of sundial, but none of them was much help on a cloudy day or at night. The water clocks found everywhere from Egypt to the Chinese imperial court suffered from the difficulty of maintaining the speed of flow at a constant rate.

The invention of the mechanical clock in Europe in the thirteenth century – nobody knows exactly where or by whom – was the greatest revolution in the history of time and an event which changed human consciousness for ever. From around 1330 the day was divided into twenty-four equal periods, with the hourly chimes introducing a new kind of regularity and regimentation into everyday affairs. The earliest clocks, which could be found in monasteries, were designed to tell monks exactly when to shuffle along to prayer services such as vespers and matins. By the late fourteenth century they were becoming popular in towns. Merchants opened and closed their shops in accordance with the local clock, which also came to determine when meals would take place and when lovers would have their secret liaisons. In 1370 a public clock was erected in the German city of Cologne: within four years a statute was passed that fixed the start and end of the work day for labourers, and – a sinister sign of things to come – limited their lunch breaks to 'one hour and no longer'. These early clocks did not segment the hours into small portions: at their most accurate they struck every quarter of an hour. Nor did they usually have dials, so were heard rather than seen, creating a new soundscape as their tolling bells reverberated across the landscape.[3] Those that did have faces, such as the astronomical clock constructed in Prague in 1410 – which is still mounted on the southern wall of the Old Town City Hall – typically retained the ancient interest in the heavens, depicting seasonal movements of the sun, moon and zodiacal ring.

It was not until the seventeenth century, following the invention of the pendulum by Galileo, that most clocks had minute hands, and another hundred years before the second hand appeared regularly on the faces of long-case clocks. Fewer and fewer clocks had any astronomical indicators. By the eighteenth century, showing the phases of the moon was thought to be less interesting than slicing time into smaller and smaller divisions which had little if anything to do with the natural world. A manufactured culture of chronological precision was taking hold of our minds. By the nineteenth century the pocket watch, previously a luxury item, had become cheap enough even for labourers to carry their own signifiers of time around with them, chained to their clothing – although it was unclear who was chained to whom. Wristwatches only appeared in the 1880s,

The United States of North America (1861) by Yoshikazu. This Japanese print depicts an American man proudly showing off his pocket watch to his wife. The text describes how American people are 'patriotic and, moreover, quite clever'.

when they were first produced for German naval officers under the orders of Kaiser Wilhelm I. At last the voluntary handcuff had arrived.[4]

This increasingly accurate measurement of time initially appeared to be a positive development. People could make sure they weren't late for Sunday lunch with their ageing uncle, and managed to catch the last steam train home. Wasn't it useful to know when a grocery shop would close and exactly how long to keep the roast beef in the oven? Yet as the industrial revolution progressed, more negative consequences gradually became apparent: time evolved into a form of social control and economic exploitation.

Most antique collectors today who appreciate the fine craftsmanship of Wedgwood pottery are unaware that the founder of the firm, Josiah Wedgwood, was a strict disciplinarian who bears considerable responsibility for the way time has come to dominate our lives. The factory he founded in 1769 in Staffordshire, in the north of England, was not only the first in the country to use steam power, but also introduced the first recorded system of clocking in. If his potters were late, they forfeited a portion of their daily wages. The timesheet soon became a ubiquitous feature not just in pottery workshops, but also in textile mills and other industries.[5] In his 1854 novel *Hard Times*, Charles Dickens critiqued this growing culture of utilitarian efficiency with his character Mr Gradgrind, whose office contained 'a deadly statistical clock in it, which measured every second with a beat like a rap upon a coffin-lid'.

Controlling time was so rewarding for businessmen that they manipulated it wherever they could. The anonymous author of *Chapters in the Life of a Dundee Factory Boy* (1850) remembered how:

> ... in reality there were no regular hours: masters and managers did with us as they liked. The clocks at the factories were often put forward in the morning and back at night, and instead of being instruments for the measurement of time, they were used as cloaks for cheatery and oppression.

Though this was known amongst the hands, all were afraid to speak, and a workman then was afraid to carry a watch, as it was no uncommon event to dismiss any one who presumed to know too much about the science of horology.[6]

A new language evolved to reflect the changing culture of time. People began talking about 'lengths' of time, as if they were speaking about lengths of cloth. Time was now something that could be 'saved' and 'spent' like money. Workers sold their labour time to factory owners, transforming it into a commodity. By the nineteenth century, 'time is money', a phrase supposedly first uttered by Benjamin Franklin in 1740, had become a mantra of the capitalist system, and the ideal worker was 'regular as clockwork'. Punctuality was elevated into a supreme virtue, while 'wasting time' was a sin.[7]

Towards the end of the nineteenth century, tasks on the production line, initially measured in minutes, were coming to be measured in seconds. Slow labourers were sacked. Workers protested against the new forms of regimentation by 'going slow'. By the early twentieth century the industrial world was subject to 'time-and-motion' studies. Their intellectual architect was Frederick Taylor, whose 1911 book *Scientific Management* explained how workers could be made more efficient by studying the speed at which they performed each task, and then simplifying the tasks and demanding they were done more rapidly. Two years later Henry Ford, advised by Taylor, installed the world's first large-scale moving assembly line at his car factory in Detroit. Production immediately doubled. In 1920 the husband-and-wife team of Frank and Lillian Gilbreth noticed that bricklayers used eighteen separate movements to cement in a brick. By looking at film footage, they discovered how these movements could be reduced to just five, thereby increasing the number of bricks laid each day from 1,000 to 2,700. These fanatical timekeepers even filmed their own children washing up to improve their efficiency. Time-and-motion studies may have boosted productivity, but for the employees who had to work faster and faster, they represented a dangerous alliance between

*Henry Ford's first moving assembly line, installed in 1913, which used Frederick Taylor's techniques of 'scientific management' to increase the pace of car production.*

the clock and the capitalist.[8] Such developments prompted the historian and philosopher Lewis Mumford to conclude that 'the clock, not the steam engine, is the key machine of the modern industrial age'.[9]

Most of us today are unlikely to have time-and-motion experts peering over our shoulders, or to have our wages docked for arriving late to work. We may even be allowed to work flexitime and occasionally from home. But the culture of controlled time persists nonetheless. We can't arrive late to the office with the excuse that it was such a beautiful morning we decided to go out for a stroll. We are sent on 'time management' courses to make us more efficient, and are expected to meet countless 'deadlines' – a term originally referring to a line around a US military prison, which if crossed by inmates would result in them being shot.

As you read these lines, the tyranny of the clock is operating not just in every school, where children are taught obedience to it through the incessant ringing of bells, but in the sweatshops of the developing world. The women who sew the shirts we are wearing keep their jobs only if they keep to time. We are controlled by the clock, but we are also complicit in its regimental domination over others.

The increasingly precise measurement of time, and its emergence as a means of social control, have been accompanied by a third historical development: the cult of speed. We have all experienced living in a high-velocity society, in a perpetual state of fast forward. We hurry to work, we eat fast food, we search for love by speed dating and try to fit in power naps. We want fast-growing plants for our gardens, and pack as much as possible into our diaries as if a blank space is damning evidence that we are missing out on life. The advertising industry tells us that faster is better: faster computers, faster cars. Live life in the fast lane. We are now unlikely to say, 'Slow and steady wins the race': the tortoise, we believe, will never catch the hare.

The cult of speed has infiltrated our lives in three ways, the first of which is through transport. There may be nothing which altered the pace of daily life more than the coming of the steam train in the 1830s. These beasts of smoke and iron traversed the landscape at a speed nobody had ever before experienced. Just imagine a world in which nothing happened at more than around ten miles an hour suddenly being swept aside by machines that could travel three times as fast, easily outrunning a stagecoach.[10] In the 1840s, J. M. W. Turner painted an oncoming train cutting through the misty rain in a golden, rustic scene. *Rain, Steam and Speed* not only depicts the intrusion of the industrial revolution into the English countryside, but also conveys how Turner sensed that the future was now hurtling towards Victorian society. Too much, too fast. At that time, people were frightened by the speed of steam trains: it was obvious to most observers that their velocity was unnatural and even dangerous. A renowned scientist of the day feared that 'rail travel at high speeds is not possible because passengers, unable to breathe, would die of asphyxia.' But soon society became accustomed to the culture of speed, which was later fed by the arrival of the motor car and the aeroplane. Today few us would be content to take a horse-drawn carriage from London to a business meeting in Edinburgh; we want to get there fast, and are incensed when the train is late or our plane delayed.

If the steam train enabled our bodies to travel faster than ever, the invention of electrical communication – particularly the telegraph – allowed our ideas to travel at an even greater pace. One of the first public demonstrations of the telegraph took place in 1844, when Samuel Morse sent the following message from Washington to Baltimore: 'What hath God wrought'. It could hardly have been more appropriate, because this new technology was set to transform economic and social life, shrinking the world more radically than the internet did 150 years later. Just think what it would have been like living in Australia before the telegraph link-up to England in 1872. A letter you sent from Sydney to your sister in Liverpool would take 110 days to arrive by ship; at best you would receive a reply seven months after writing to her. In the 1850s Australians were anxious for news of the Crimean War, but they only heard about events three months after they had happened. The country's farmers exported their wool to Europe having no idea of current commodity prices. Once Australia was connected to England by telegraph cable – a monumental technological feat that took decades to complete – information could travel back and forth almost instantaneously in Morse code. As the historian Henry Adams wrote in 1909, the speed of the telegraph had 'annihilated both space and time'.[11]

Communication innovations such as the telegraph, the telephone and the internet have continually raised the tempo of daily life. Where are we left today? Twenty-four-hour financial markets. Work colleagues who get annoyed if we don't respond to emails within a couple of hours. Social network sites that beckon for constant checking. An overload of online information at our fingertips, which we must somehow find the time to sift and process. And through an insidious ratchet effect, we get used to the increased speed of the latest technology – such as the speed of our internet connection or computer – and can get frustrated with anything slower. We have become hooked on rapid communication and the hyper-connectivity it has enabled. The result: when the server goes down or we lose our mobile phones, we feel electronically and existentially marooned, much like those first Australian settlers in the days before the telegraph.

A third area of everyday life to fall to the gods of speed was eating. The founding fathers of fast food were two brothers, Richard and Maurice McDonald, who emigrated from New Hampshire to Southern California during the Depression. After working as set builders at Columbia Film Studios, in 1937 they founded one of the first drive-in restaurants, a new industry that fed on the boom in private cars. They made a fortune having waitresses – called 'carhops' – serve hot dogs and burgers directly through car windows. But in 1948 they came up with an idea that would increase the speed of service, lower prices and boost the volume of sales: the McDonald's Speedee Service System. The brothers fired their carhops and built a new restaurant in San Bernardino, at the end of Route 66, where customers would have to get out of their cars and queue up to order food. The old menu was cut by two-thirds, including anything that required cutlery, so the only sandwiches available were hamburgers or cheeseburgers, and every burger was sold with the same condiments – onions, mustard, ketchup and two pickles. They replaced the crockery with throwaway paper plates and paper cups, and food was prepared on a production line, so workers only had to perform a simple task like shovelling fries. The McDonald brothers – and subsequent owner Ray Kroc, who bought the firm in 1961 – had found a way of making food as efficiently as Henry Ford manufactured his automobiles, and eating has never been the same since. Today McDonald's serves 58 million customers a day, each of whom, as noted earlier, finishes their meal, on average, in a little over ten minutes.[12]

Not everyone has succumbed to fast food. There is a global

Slow Food movement that began in Italy in the 1980s, which now has 100,000 members. Launched by food writer Carlo Petrini in response to the opening of a McDonald's right by the Spanish Steps in Rome, it is the opposite of the speedy culture of McDonald's and other fast food outlets, advocating leisurely dining with friends and family, using fresh, local and seasonal produce, developing sustainable food production, and of course taking pleasure in culinary delights.[13] Slow Food – whose symbol is a snail – remains a minority pursuit in a world geared towards quick and convenient eating. But we should remain hopeful. Just as Italy gave birth to new approaches to the arts of painting and sculpture during the Renaissance, it may well be doing the same today for the art of eating.

We can no longer think of time as a natural phenomenon, an invisible thread that stitches one moment to the next, an expression of the immutable laws of an infinite universe. We have captured time and rendered it artificial, dicing it up into tiny portions, using it to control our fellow human beings, and increasing its velocity. Time, as we now know it, is a social invention. How can we forge a new relationship with it?

Effective time management. That, at least, is the most common solution offered today. You can read books on how to 'make every second count' and take corporate courses which leave you with lists of ideas to bring time under control. There is plenty of useful advice out there, such as only checking your emails once a day, learning to prioritise your tasks and becoming better at delegating them. But these techniques seldom go deep enough into dealing with our difficulties. Time management is, in effect, an ideology that teaches us to do things faster and more efficiently, so we can squeeze more and more into our days – thus resembling Frederick Taylor's theory of 'scientific management', which aimed to make us more productive. It deals with the symptoms not the underlying causes of our dilemmas, and rarely encourages us to think about time in fundamentally new ways.

We need to do much more than 'manage' time. History offers

a quartet of ideas that might help us resist the tyranny of the clock. They involve changing how we talk about time, celebrating everyday slowness, learning from alternative cultures of time, and immersing ourselves in a long-term outlook.

## Metaphors we live by

Metaphors help us to think and express ourselves, and we often use them without realising. You might, for instance, say, 'She attacked my argument', 'I demolished her position', 'Your claims are indefensible', 'He's entrenched in his views' or 'I really dug in and refused to budge on that issue'. All these expressions use the language of warfare. The underlying metaphor is 'argument is war'.

Our concept of time is similarly structured by metaphors, and we need to become aware of the subtle ways they work on our minds.[14] One of the most prevalent metaphors already mentioned, which emerged during the industrial revolution, is of time as a commodity: spending time, buying time, wasting time, saving time, 'time is money', 'living on borrowed time'. Another dating from the same period is time as a possession: 'my time is my own', 'give me a moment of your time'. These two metaphors, in tandem, constitute the psycholinguistic roots of our problems with time. If our time is like private property, it becomes possible not only for it to be freely granted to others, but possibly owned by them or appropriated at an unfair price against our wishes.

One manifestation of the 'time as a commodity and possession' metaphor is when we talk about taking 'time off' from work. This expression is essentially saying that we have given our employer ownership of our time, just as Josiah Wedgwood would have wished it. Each year the firm will give us back a little of our time, usually no more than a few weeks. This holiday period is usually referred to as 'time off'; it is their gift to us, a temporary pause in the regular pattern, in which being at work is, by implication, 'time on'.

But imagine if we thought of our leisure time as 'time on';

113

could it not alter the way we approach our work? A few years ago, my partner started doing exactly this, reversing the accepted language. She wanted to give her holidays and weekends more value, so began referring to them as her 'time on'. In her view, she still owns her days, and grants some to her employer for forty-seven weeks each year. This change has had tangible results. She no longer feels so guilty when not at work, whether on vacation or because of illness. She is far less likely to bring home work at the weekends: why should she be handing over more of her precious 'time on' to her employer? Moreover, she has become more dedicated to her passions outside work, such as photography, which she has ceased to think of as a hobby in her 'time off', a temporary respite from work. When offered a pay rise, she was prompted by her new thinking to ask instead for more holiday time, requesting a 'day review' rather than a 'pay review'.

Recognising how we use such metaphors, putting them under scrutiny, and experimenting with new ones, represents the beginnings of developing a different relationship with time. We need to become detectives of the metaphors we live by, noticing when we use expressions like 'time off' or 'saving time', and asking ourselves whether they really are appropriate. Should we talk about 'spending time' with a friend, or would simply 'being' with them be truer to our desires? As we heighten our level of metaphorical awareness, those nineteenth-century ideas about time as a commodity and possession will no longer have such a hold over us, and time may gradually become more of our own making.

## The art of slow living

'There is more to life than increasing its speed,' said Gandhi. Most of us understand the virtues of slowing down, of taking more time to visit our friends, play with our children, watch a beautiful sunset, eat a delicious meal or think through an argument. But we find it extraordinarily difficult to do. Our high-velocity culture of deadlines, instant messaging and speed snacking hardly allows it. We have even developed the unusual habit of equating being 'busy' – short of time – with being successful. People sometimes greet each other not with the question 'How are you?' but with 'Are you busy these days?'. It is customary to reply something like, 'Yes, I'm rushed off my feet.' To respond 'No, not particularly' is considered to be self-disparaging and evidence of failure.

Slowing down, it seems, has become a luxury primarily reserved for the idle rich or those who live in countries like Mexico or Indonesia, where the pace of life is far slower, where it is standard practice to arrive an hour later for lunch and then to linger over it leisurely until a mid-afternoon departure for a snooze. When I spent a few months in a remote jungle village in Guatemala, I was surprised to discover there was no timetable for the bus to the nearest frontier town. It came when it came, and it was quite normal to wait four or five hours for its arrival. I thought that Guatemala had taught me patience, but after a few weeks back in London, like everyone else I was harrumphing and tapping my foot on the ground when I heard that the next train was held up. There was no escape from the culture of speed.

Why do we find it so difficult to slow down? We may, in part, be the inheritors of a Protestant ethic which encourages us to believe that time must be used 'productively' and 'efficiently'. We feel we should be getting things done, ticking them off a list. But it could be that many of us are driven by fear. We are so afraid of having longer, emptier hours that we fill them with distractions, we strive to stay occupied. How often do we sit quietly on the sofa for half an hour without switching on the television, picking up a magazine or making a phone call, and instead just thinking? Within minutes we find ourselves channel-surfing and multitasking. What exactly are we afraid of? On some level we fear boredom. A deeper explanation is that we are afraid that an extended pause would give us the time to realise that our lives are not as meaningful and fulfilled as we would like them to be. The time for contemplation has become an object of fear, a demon.

Taking aspects of daily life more slowly is, after challenging our metaphors, a second way to develop a new relationship with time, and the most obvious means of countering our inheritance of speed. Unfortunately we have no museums dedicated to those who have been icons of slow living. But if we did, who would be honoured? There should, at the very least, be a display devoted to the nineteenth-century French writer Gustave Flaubert, who said, 'Anything becomes interesting if you look at it long enough.' With his novelist's eye he took in the world slowly, absorbing its many meanings. This no doubt influenced his fastidious approach to writing itself: while most of his rivals, like Émile Zola, were turning out a novel a year, it took Flaubert five years to complete *Madame Bovary*. But Flaubert was positively speedy compared with the Austrian novelist Robert Musil, who began his modernist masterpiece *The Man Without Qualities* in 1921 and hadn't finished it by the time he died in 1942, despite working on it almost every day for over two decades. He too deserves a corner in the museum.

So much for inspiration. But what practical steps could we take to decelerate our own approaches to the art of living? My personal efforts began around fifteen years ago when I stopped wearing a watch, as an act of symbolic protest against half a millennium of excessively zealous measurement of time. But the results were more than symbolic. Liberated from a childhood obsession with my digital watch, I discovered the pleasures of ignoring and disobeying time. I was now less likely to interrupt a conversation or a thought with a glance at my wrist that would send me scuttling to some new task. I stopped wolfing down sandwiches and developed a love of long, meandering walks. Contrary to what you might expect, I did not suddenly start turning up late for everything. Hiding your watch in a shoebox for a week is a worthwhile experiment.

Mobile phones make this tactic of slowing down less effective, since we can so easily check the time, which automatically appears on most displays. When I eventually got one for myself, the first thing I did was turn off the time function. But the struggle does not end there. Clocks have become part of the furniture of our homes, sitting on the mantelpiece or dominating the hallway, evil eyes watching our every move. In response, I have banished such timekeepers from my house, except those that are built into appliances. To deal with the latter, I have made a little flap to hide the fluorescent green of the digital clock on the cooker. Having children who wake at dawn means I do not need an alarm clock.

My adventures with time are not simply a rejection of the clock, but an embrace of absorbing the world at a more gentle pace. When I go to an art gallery, I try to visit only two or three paintings. Each morning I walk in the garden and search for something that has changed – perhaps a bud that has opened or a new spiderweb – which helps bring a stillness to the beginning of the day. I attempt to eat slowly, savouring the flavours. Almost everybody laughs at my tiny diary, which gives each day a space half the length of my little finger. As it is so easily filled, it helps keep down my number of appointments. Artificial? Absolutely. But it works for me. The best way I know to have more time, to feel less rushed, and appreciate life to the fullest, is to plan fewer activities.

Despite these efforts, the art of slow living continues to defy me in many ways. I put myself under enormous work pressure, constantly setting myself tight deadlines. My two-year-olds do not allow me time to linger in bookshops. I would like to emulate nineteenth-century French peasants who, in an effort to preserve food and energy, effectively hibernated through the long, dark winter months, staying indoors and sleeping, only occasionally rising to eat a hunk of bread, feed the pigs or keep the fire going.[15] Most of our employers would hardly allow us the luxury of hibernation. But we should still consider how we might alter our pace throughout the year, keeping closer to the rhythm of the seasons. Though perhaps it would be just as good to cultivate one of Winston Churchill's exemplary habits, which he followed even during the Second World War: 'You must sleep sometime between lunch and dinner, and no halfway measures. Take off your clothes and get into bed. That's what I always do.'[16]

## The arrow, the wheel and the step out of time

Western culture is dominated by a linear notion of time, the arrow of time that travels from the past, through the present and into the future. Positioned on this pathway, we find ourselves worrying about what happened yesterday and what will happen tomorrow, and have a distinct inability to be in the present, to experience the now. Our imaginations and conversations are in a perpetual state of fluttering back and forth in time. There are, however, cultures that offer enticing ways to expand our repertoire of approaches to time, and to discover a route to the here and now. One is the Balinese idea of time as a wheel, and another the Zen Buddhist practice of stepping out of time.

On the island of Bali, a unique fusion of Hinduism and animism has helped to create a cyclical conception of time which has been a subject of curiosity for European visitors since the seventeenth century. The calendar, called the Pawukon, comprises a series of wheels within wheels, where the major repeated cycles of five, six and seven days together help constitute the 210-day annual cycle. Conjunctions of the various wheels determine which days are of particular ritual significance. So the main purpose of the calendar is not to tell you how much time has passed (e.g. since some previous event) or the amount of time that remains (e.g. to complete a project), but to designate the position in the cycle of days. The cycles do not indicate what time it is, they tell you what *kind of time* it is.

One result is that Balinese time falls broadly into two types: 'full days', when something of importance happens, such as a temple ritual or a local market; or 'empty days', when nothing much happens. In this system, the linear passage of time is blunted, and time becomes more punctual than durational, as it is in the West. Time 'pulses' rather than shoots forward like an arrow. When you ask a Balinese when they were born, they may well answer with something equivalent to 'Thursday the ninth'. The moment in the cycle is more significant than the year.[17]

The idea of cyclical time is not completely foreign to us. We are aware of the recurrent passing of the seasons, and many women's bodies are in sync with the moon. Most religions are structured by cyclical rituals. There is the annual fasting for Lent and Ramadan, and the weekly Sabbath – Saturday for Jews and Sunday for the majority of Christians – which is supposed to be a day of religious observance and abstinence from work and play. 'Sabbath' itself comes from the Hebrew word for 'rest'. People of a more secular inclination might consider adopting their own regular Sabbath or Balinese-style division between full and empty days. Freelancers could experiment with having several full days, where they work with incredible intensity, followed by an empty day, where they put up their feet and practise idleness. Or we might try to resist filling the weekend with activity, and instead ring-fence part of it as 'empty time', when we intentionally and studiously do nothing very much. This may well be a perfect description of your Sunday mornings lying in bed and reading the paper, punctuated by intermittent dozing. Perhaps the spirit of cyclical rest already lies within us all.

An alternative to cyclical thinking about time is the approach found in Zen Buddhism, which is to step out of time by abandoning the past and future, and living completely in the present. The classic way of entering this different world is through meditation. As the Zen monk Thich Nhat Hanh playfully put it, 'Don't just do something; sit there.'[18] Typical meditation techniques involve concentrating on your breathing, or sensations in a particular part of the body, as a means of arriving in the now. The flurry of thoughts about the past and future that regularly invade your mind should start to settle, to be replaced by a picture of mental clarity and spiritual presence. This might be possible to achieve on a meditation retreat in rural Wales, but harder to do every morning when your children are watching television downstairs. And perhaps it is only a master monk who is able to maintain a state of meditative composure while sitting in an office surrounded by frantic colleagues, ringing phones and clunking photocopiers.

Despite the challenges, it is important to recognise that the growing popularity of Eastern meditation in the West over the past half-century has been a major event in the history of the art of living. It is astonishing that several million Westerners from California to Catalonia are engaged in Buddhist meditation practices that date back to first-century India, and that the British government is being pressured by doctors to offer meditation under the National Health Service, to help patients suffering from depression. We need to thank pioneering figures like the Japanese Zen teacher Daisetz Teitaro Suzuki, who from the 1890s until his death in 1966 regularly visited the United States, encouraging people to grapple with those tricky Zen koans like 'What is the sound of one hand clapping?' whose contemplation could lead to *satori* or enlightenment. Of equal importance were the enterprising Europeans and North Americans who conveyed their personal experiences of Buddhism in the East to an uninitiated audience, such as the German philosopher Eugene Herrigel. In the 1920s he spent six years studying Zen archery and meditation in Tokyo, out of which emerged his classic *Zen in the Art of Archery*.[19] This book inspired a whole genre imitating his title, most notably the 1970s bestseller *Zen and the Art of Motorcycle Maintenance*.

Through practices like Buddhist meditation we have an opportunity to escape the legacy of linear time and our temporal one-track minds. Speed can be replaced by stillness, busyness by being. I once bumped into the Tibetan monk who runs the meditation centre around the corner from my house and asked him, 'How are you doing?' He smiled and replied, to my delight, 'Nothing doing.'

## Time and responsibility

Altering our metaphors, cultivating slowness and learning from non-Western traditions are all ways to renegotiate our personal relationship with time, and stand up to the tyranny of the clock. There is one further approach, which matters not just for our individual lives, but for society as a whole: to liberate ourselves from the habit of short-term thinking. Modern civilisation has developed a pathologically short attention span. Politicians can't see beyond the next election, while market-driven economics takes little heed of long-term consequences, as recurrent stock market bubbles and bursts clearly demonstrate. Combined with the high speed of daily life and rapid technological change, our whole culture has become obsessed with the immediate and blind to the long view. Time has been compressed and no longer stretches into the distance. Deep, geological time means almost nothing to us, and we can barely think ahead even a generation or two.

This inability to take a long-term perspective has bred a culture of social irresponsibility. We squander planetary resources without considering the impact on future generations, to whom we are bequeathing an altered climate, depleted biodiversity and ecological fragility. We are yet to find safe methods for dealing with the radioactive waste produced by nuclear power stations, which will remain dangerous for thousands of years. We get excited about genetic engineering and biotechnology, but have we really thought hard enough about how developments like human cloning might affect societies to come? The future is a place that increasingly exists only in the imaginings of science fiction novels and feature films.

We must find ways to feel the presence of the future in everyday life, and forge a new unity between time and responsibility. We might imagine ourselves as Viking warriors, who not only sensed their ancestors gazing down at them from the halls of Valhalla, but envisioned their long line of descendants casting judgement on their deeds. Or, like the Tewa Indians of the American Southwest, we could say, 'Pin peyeh obe' – 'Look to the mountain' – which reminded them to view life as if from a mountain top, noticing themselves as only one of many generations passing by below, who will inhabit the same landscape for countless centuries.

Another powerful antidote to short-term thinking is to reconsider the meaning of the present. We have an extraordinarily narrow conception of what constitutes the 'now'. We think of now as being today, or maybe this week, but never a year or a millennium. When someone asks you for the time, you say four o'clock, not 2012. But just imagine expanding our idea of the present into a 'long now', where the now encompasses thousands of years.

This is precisely the aim of a visionary project called 'The Clock of the Long Now', conceived by, amongst others, the writer Stuart Brand and the avant-garde musician Brian Eno. They are behind the construction of a slow-time clock in a limestone mountain in the Nevada desert which ticks only once each year and will last 10,000 years. It represents the opposite of the clocks we have inherited from the industrial revolution, with their obsessive minutes and seconds. When they made a prototype in 1999, as the second millennium arrived it bonged very slowly, twice – once for each thousand years. 'In a world of hurry,' says Brand, 'the Clock is a patience machine'.[20] The designers believe that the desert clock will encourage long-term thinking and a more responsible attitude towards our ravaged environment. Their hope is that a new mythology of time will arise, where the now is not only in the present, but also in the distant future, where next millennium begins to feel like next week. What might happen if we all began to live by the rhythm of the Clock of the Long Now?

# 6

# Money

Every Saturday morning, for as long as I can remember, my parents have gone up the street to the local newsagent to buy a ticket for the Big One, Australia's multi-million-dollar national lottery draw. They also get themselves a few 'scratchies' – little cards which offer instant cash prizes if the silver boxes you scratch off are matching. When I lived in lottery-obsessed Spain, on almost every street corner there was a blind man or woman selling tickets, and the nation stopped on 22 December to hear the winning numbers for El Gordo, the Fat One, the biggest lottery on the planet. Such rituals have occurred all over the world since the invention of public lotteries in the Netherlands in the fifteenth century, where they became grand civic occasions to raise funds for building mental asylums and old-age homes.[1] We have long lived in hope that the ancient goddess Fortuna will spin her Wheel of Fortune in our favour and deliver not love, friendship or job satisfaction, but something possibly more alluring: money.

Why do we care so much about it? Clearly because it can be used to satisfy our basic needs – food, clothing, shelter – in an age when few of us are self-sufficient or live off the grid of modern society. But money is also attractive because of a unique quality: it is frozen desire.[2] It possesses a versatile ability to transform itself into our myriad wants and cravings. Money can be used for anything from purchasing an antique hunting gun to buying sex from a prostitute, from having a tummy tuck to investing in private education for our children. The dreams of every lottery-ticket holder are built on the belief that wish fulfilment is a financial affair.

Despite being universally coveted, money has often had a bad reputation. Aristotle was convinced that the pursuit of money was not a route to the good life, a point he illustrated with the fable of King Midas of Phrygia, who was granted his wish of having everything he touched turn to gold. In one version of the story he starves after trying to eat and drink. In another he touches his daughter and she turns into a statue. Greed for wealth can indeed have a deadly effect on our relationships. Every major faith warns against excessive riches. 'It is easier for a camel to go through the eye of a needle, than for a rich man to enter the kingdom of God,' declares the Bible – although this does not prevent popes from living in palaces or property tycoons being devout believers. In Dante's *Divine Comedy*, written in the fourteenth century, the usurers were cast deep into Hell alongside the sodomites. Many think today's banking bosses deserve a similar fate. While the lust for money has always been present, almost every culture has given birth to sects and movements which have rejected the material values associated with money, and extolled the virtues of living more simply and sharing wealth more equally.

These persistent doubts about money explain why we are unsurprised to read news articles about lottery winners whose lives have been wrecked by their good fortune. There are stories of marriages falling apart, vicious inheritance battles, friends suddenly having dollar signs in their eyes, drug addiction. A life of promised luxury often turns out to be stressful, boring or lonely. And we admire those winners who give all their windfall away to charity or who endeavour to maintain their old habits and values, like the British woman who kept up her job selling household products door-to-door despite having become a millionaire. 'People think I'm crazy to still do my job, but the truth is I love it,' she said. 'It's all about people. Money doesn't make you happy, people do.'[3]

The contrasting views of money as a source of personal fulfilment or as a road to misery and sin raise questions about what kind of relationship we should have with it. How much money do we really need to live wisely and well? How does it shape the way we work, our ethical priorities and our sense of who we are? How can we feel more in control of money, and less dependent on it? Unravelling these issues calls for exploring two mirror-image aspects of the history of money: how consumerism became the dominant ideology of our age, and whether we can thrive on frugality by becoming experts at simple living. Our starting point is the origins of one of the most overrated inventions of Western civilisation: shopping.

## How we became consumed by shopping

For the first time in history, shopping has become a form of leisure. In Britain it ranks just behind television as one of the top leisure pursuits. But if indulging in a little retail therapy sounds like a harmless activity, consider that almost one in ten Westerners are addicted to shopping – when they are feeling down or stressed, they go on shopping sprees at their favourite store to help boost their spirits or self-esteem.[4] Although we may not enjoy wandering around shopping malls on a Saturday afternoon, most people desire the comforts, conveniences and aesthetics of consumerism. Even if we already own a television, we might be tempted to upgrade to a widescreen TV. We treat ourselves to the latest miniature iGadget. A promotion at work? Maybe it's time for a new car. Because, as the ads say, we're worth it. Each year ends with a shopping orgy that would have impressed the gluttonous Romans. We call it Christmas, a commercial festival that gets the average adult spending around £500 on presents and entertainment, while the average child under four receives gifts costing over £120.[5]

In a consumer society, the most obvious way to express who we are is through what we buy: I shop, therefore I am. Why do so many people – from a range of income groups – own more than a dozen different handbags, sweaters or pairs of shoes? Why might we spend a thousand pounds on a leather sofa when we could buy a perfectly comfortable and sturdy one second-hand for under a tenth of the price? Why do we buy a new shirt rather than repair the old one, and pay so much for haircuts? Though few people openly admit to it, most of us want to be seen as fashionable, and care what others think about our looks, homes and what car we drive. Across social classes, people forge their identities through their purchases. We want to fit in with the crowd, but also sometimes stand out from it, in both cases judging ourselves through the eyes of others. If we felt that nobody could see us, our consumer spending would plummet and we would spend much more time slouching around in our Sunday morning tracksuits. Many people claim their purchases reflect purely individual tastes and that they are not influenced by what is in vogue. But such personal preferences – whether for glossy high heels or a zen-like living space – are often remarkably similar to prevalent fashions. It becomes quite clear when you notice – as I did – that you have the same Habitat sofa as three of your friends. And all of it costs money, even if we avoid the most exclusive brands or pride ourselves on getting bargains.

This consumer culture is a recent development. The idea of shopping as a leisure activity or therapy cure would have made little sense in pre-industrial Europe. Naturally, people bought what they needed for daily life, but shopping itself was not considered a route to personal fulfilment or self-realisation. In fact, until the middle of the eighteenth century the word 'consumer' was a pejorative term meaning a waster or squanderer, just as 'consumption' was a disease which wasted away the body.[6] It is only since the early twentieth century, writes William Leach, a historian of shopping, that we have become 'a society preoccupied with consumption, with comfort and bodily wellbeing, with luxury, spending and acquisition, with more goods this year than last, more next year than this'.[7] The result is that we confuse the good life with a life of goods. There may be no greater cause of life dissatisfaction amongst the affluent citizens of the Western world. How this happened is one of the most important episodes in the history of our relationship with money.

The rise of shopping can be traced to new attitudes to wealth that emerged in the early modern period, between the sixteenth and eighteenth centuries.[8] Prior to this time, the vast majority of people were far more preoccupied with avoiding poverty than getting rich, and those who sought to accumulate wealth were often viewed with suspicion or hostility. Gradually, however, acquiring wealth became a widespread personal ambition. In 1720 Daniel Defoe visited Norfolk and found every man 'busy on the main affair of life, that is to say getting money'.[9]

One reason for this cultural change may have been the appearance of the Protestant ethic in the sixteenth century, which taught that going into business was a perfectly godly career move. More important was a seismic shift in economic thought in the seventeenth century, when economic and philosophical writers increasingly claimed that human beings naturally seek to maximise their material self-interest, and that by doing so society in general would benefit – the economic pie would get larger for everyone.[10] A century later these ideas, central to the capitalist ethic, became the building blocks of Adam Smith's *The Wealth of Nations*.

This new model of economic man, which was supported and spread by interested parties such as merchants, socially legitimised the pursuit of riches and was the engine of a consumer society. As credit became more readily available and the bank accounts of the elite burgher class grew, they had the disposable incomes to buy more and more luxury goods. Shopping as we know it was born. By around 1700 the traditional town markets were giving way to a flood of shops – individual retail outlets with their own premises, which were open most of the week rather than only operating at intervals like the markets. You could walk into a store in London or Paris and be spellbound by the elaborate display of exotic teas from China, sumptuous upholstered furniture and looking glasses with bone handles. Wander around the streets near the Plaza Mayor in Madrid, and you would find fine cloths being sold on the Calle Nueva and jewellery merchants running along the Calle Mayor. Travel to Venice and you could head straight for the opulent shops of the Marzaria, a narrow lane between Piazza San Marco and the Rialto, which is still home to ostentatious retailers like Gucci and MaxMara.

The consumer revolution was even open to craftworkers, tradesmen and farmers, who might be able to afford small luxuries like pottery, needles, gloves and linen. They started imitating the incipient bourgeoisie by dividing their homes in two. Half was filled with 'front-stage' goods including pewter jugs and soft furniture to impress visitors, while 'back-stage' goods were used for everyday living. Today some people retain this practice by having a separate sitting room used only for guests or special occasions.

The result of these changes, writes the historian Keith Thomas, was a new culture of 'limitless desire' in which being a consumer was increasingly considered a way of life. More than this, social status was undergoing a fundamental shift. Honour and reputation were no longer primarily based on having noble blood or being a fine swordsman. Instead, status became fused with the display of wealth. Being conspicuous with your consumption – parading around in your fashionable hat or using special crockery for visitors – was developing into a way of feeling good about yourself.[11] Important though these changes were, by the end of the eighteenth century consumerism was still not nearly as culturally dominant as it is in our own time. To understand how it became so, we must explore the next phase in the history of shopping: the rise of department stores.

On 9 September 1869, Aristide Boucicaut, the son of a Norman hatter, stood at the junctions of the sixth and seventh arrondissements in Paris. Unnoticed by most passers-by, he bent down and laid the foundation stone of what would soon be hailed as the greatest department store in the world, the Bon Marché. In that single act, he launched a new era in which consumerism became such a powerful social force that it radically altered our conception of the good life.

The invention of the department store in the nineteenth century transformed shopping. Through the use of sophisticated marketing techniques that had been absent in the pre-industrial period, shopping became the all-embracing wrap-around entertainment experience that we know today. With its panoply of products in a single immense building, the department store created a fantasy land away from the filthy streets, where the virgin culture of limitless desire could run rampant. Bon Marché was the largest and most fantastic of them all. It was bigger than Macy's or Wanamaker's in the United States, and dwarfed British efforts such as Whiteleys and Harrods. When Émile Zola decided to write a novel about this extraordinary new form of retailing to represent what he ironically called 'the poetry of modern activity', he based the story on Bon Marché.

Boucicaut, the founder of the store, was born in 1810. After working his way up the ladder in several Parisian retail outlets, in 1863 he became owner of an inconspicuous Left-Bank shop named Bon Marché – which roughly translates as 'the good deal'. But he soon realised that his growing operation needed new premises, so in 1869 he commissioned a grand building whose colossal structure was masterminded by an upcoming young engineer, Gustave Eiffel, who two decades later would design a landmark tower for Paris to mark the 1889 Universal Exposition.

What made Bon Marché such a phenomenal success and one of the most innovative capitalist enterprises in Western history? Like other department stores in the nineteenth century, its ambition was to democratise luxury – to use the advantages of bulk purchasing and mass manufacturing to keep prices affordable so that consumer items which had previously only been available to the elite could be bought by the expanding middle classes. Boucicaut's genius was using clever salesmanship and marketing to make shopping not just convenient, but a form of pleasure.

According to Michael Miller, the historian of Bon Marché, the store was 'part opera, part theatre, part museum'.[12] The shopping experience began with the architecture. Visitors were stunned by Eiffel's ornate iron columns and vast panels of glass. There were sweeping staircases leading up to balconies where you could become a spectator watching the stage set below. Under superb lighting, sumptuous merchandise was displayed for all the world to see. Oriental silks cascaded from the walls, Turkish rugs were draped over the bannisters. Shoppers were lured into the store with bargain counters just inside the door. By squeezing them through narrow passageways, Boucicaut created the illusion of frenzied crowds clambering for his goods. Tens of thousands came for the famous White Sale in early February, when white sheets, towels, curtains and flowers filled every display. Combined with the summer fashion sale in April and the furniture sale each September, Bon Marché created a new calendar for Parisians, just as the revolutionary government had done in 1793 by giving the months new names such as Brumaire, Germinal and Thermidor. If you've ever been to a January clearance sale, you can thank Monsieur Boucicaut for the privilege.

Bon Marché was not just a shop. It was a leisure complex. There was a reading room where you could peruse the latest journals and newspapers, a Grand Hall containing free art exhibitions, classical music performances where up to seven thousand people could come to see the city's opera stars, and a huge restaurant bustling with liveried waiters. People made a day trip out of visiting the store, buying, eating, drinking and meeting friends. For many bourgeois women, Bon Marché became the centre of their social lives, an escape from the confines of the domestic household. Shopping had never been so easy or enjoyable. Unlike small local shops in Paris where you were expected to haggle over the price, Bon Marché had fixed prices and you could wander its magnificent halls without being accosted by sales assistants. To help people absorb the opulence, there was a guided tour of the premises each afternoon at three. And to ram home the message that Bon Marché was as much a public monument as Notre Dame or the Louvre, the management gave away printed maps of France on which Paris was represented by a picture of the store.

Bon Marché may have been described as a 'bewitching palace' by its customers, but it was also a hard-nosed business. It succeeded in the ultimate objective of the consumer age, which was to manufacture new kinds of desire – to get people to buy things they had never imagined they needed. In doing so it set new standards for bourgeois respectability. Browse through the store's mail order catalogue and you would discover that women should have not just one coat but a whole range for different occasions – one for visiting friends, one for travel, a coat for the theatre and still another for attending a ball. A respect-able home should have a variety of forks for every purpose: eating meat, fish, oysters, olives and strawberries. And don't forget special spoons for soup, dessert, sugar, salt and mustard. Your house should have an abundance of bedsheets, patterned curtains, and a separate dining room where you placed a fine set of dishes on a table cloth accompanied by matching linen serviettes. New outfits would be required for seaside holidays and playing tennis. Children should have a little sailor suit at hand for days out. The catalogues and other forms of advertising spread these fashions and tastes amongst white-collar workers and throughout the provinces, with a consequent homogenising effect on French society. Bon Marché – which still exists today, although somewhat less grand – not only reflected bourgeois consumer culture, but helped to create it. Soon it had imitators across the globe eager to create their own empires of desire.[13]

We are direct descendants of all those customers who poured through the doors of Bon Marché in the nineteenth century. Our shopping malls, with their retail outlets and eateries, cinemas and children's play areas, are faithful to the Bon Marché tradi-tion, in which shopping and lifestyle are merged into one. This fusion has utterly transformed the art of living, in three differ-ent ways: by promoting consumer values, by deepening status anxiety, and by robbing us of personal freedom.

We must recognise, first, that our consumerist habits are much less of our own choosing than we like to imagine. 'The culture of consumer capitalism may have been among the most nonconsensual public cultures ever created,' argues the social historian William Leach.[14] He and other historians of shopping have shown how corporate retailers, from Bon Marché to Coca-Cola, have gradually forged this culture over the past hundred and fifty years. One of their main tools for doing so has been advertising. Those early Bon Marché catalogues have since metamorphosed into an incessant barrage of enticing images to make us spend our money. Whether on television, in maga-zines, on billboards or online, we are subject to constant assault. See enough images of a beautiful couple relaxing in a spacious

*The main staircase of Bon Marché, around 1880. The department store was 'part opera, part theatre, part museum'.*

home with stylish Scandinavian furniture, sleek laptops, minimalist light fittings and wearing earthy organic clothes, and we eventually come to believe that this world is valuable and what we should aspire to. We want to become like them. John Berger described this power of consumer advertising a generation ago in *Ways of Seeing*:

Publicity is not merely an assembly of competing images: it is a language in itself which is always being used to make the same general proposal. Within publicity, choices are offered between this cream and that cream, that car and this car, but publicity as a system only makes a single proposal. It proposes to each of us that we transform ourselves, or our lives, by buying something more. This more, it proposes, will make us in some way richer – even though we will be poorer by having spent our money.[15]

We also become spiritually poorer. Consumerism encourages us to define freedom as a choice between brands. It asks us to express who we are through the language of products, while at the same time shaping our ideals of what it is important to own. The good life becomes a matter of satisfying consumer desires to the detriment of alternatives like spending time with our families, enjoying our work or living ethically. Our values become material values. This is a historical legacy that few of us have escaped and none of us can ignore. Whenever we purchase anything beyond our essential needs, we should ask how we have come to acquire this desire. Can we honestly say that it is a free choice, or should we admit that the marketeers at Nike, Gap, L'Oreal or Ford have something to do with it? And if the latter is true, are we satisfied to accept the vision of the good life they have manufactured for us?

The rise of shopping has also produced a second difficulty, that of 'status anxiety', a term popularised by the writer Alain de Botton. Since at least the eighteenth century our sense of self-worth and standing in society has become intimately tied to what we earn and how we spend it. Money has been endowed with an ethical quality, he writes, so 'a prosperous way of life signals worthiness, while ownership of a rusted old car or a threadbare home may prompt suppositions of moral deficiency'.[16] If we fail to display financial success, to wear the right clothes or drive the right car, we feel diminished in the eyes of the world, a lesser person. And that matters to most of us.

In an effort to avoid status anxiety and enjoy the comforts and pleasures of a consumer lifestyle, we embark on a quest to accumulate material possessions and luxury experiences, just as

Aristide Boucicaut would have advised us to do. But psychology research over the past two decades has shown that this is an unlikely path to human fulfilment for all but those at the lowest income levels. The happiness gurus tell us that once national income reaches £12,500 a head, further rises in income do not contribute to higher life satisfaction.[17] In other words, buying more consumer products does not increase our level of personal wellbeing in the long term: after treating ourselves to a sports car it will immediately spike up but then settle down to its earlier level. This is a pattern familiar to drug addicts. Purchasing a new car, or a holiday home in the South of France, or a Dolce & Gabbana suit, just doesn't make that much difference to most people's wellbeing.

Part of the problem is that as we get wealthier, money begins to warp the relationship between our wants and needs. We come to believe we 'need' a winter holiday in the sun or a kitchen extension, and are rarely satisfied with what we've got. That's why an astonishing 40 per cent of Britons with incomes over £50,000 a year – that is, in the top 5 per cent of earners – feel that they cannot afford to buy everything they really need.[18] We then find ourselves working harder and harder to earn the money to satisfy our consumer desires, and ratchet up our levels of personal debt in the process, but in return fail to receive the benefits we had imagined. This may leave us with a discontented yearning for even more luxuries, keeping us on a treadmill that ultimately breeds anxiety and depression. Adam Smith recognised the dangers of consumerism in the eighteenth century. The pleasures of wealth, he said, produce 'a few trifling conveniences to the body' but leave people just as exposed 'to anxiety, to fear, and to sorrow; to diseases, to danger, and to death'.[19] Nike might tell us to just do it, but when it comes to shopping we would be wise to ask, why do it?

Even if you have an unusually steely mind that is immune to the influence of the advertising industry and the dilemmas of status anxiety, the history of shopping has left us with a third problem which has a devastating potential to drain away our personal liberty. It was identified in the 1850s by the naturalist Henry David Thoreau. 'The cost of a thing,' he wrote, 'is the amount of what I will call life which is required to be exchanged for it, immediately or in the long run.'[20] In Thoreau's view, the cost of that new leather jacket you bought was not the price written on the tag – it was the three days of your labouring time needed to purchase it. Buying a sofa might cost twenty days, and a car three hundred. We pay not with our wallets but with the precious days of our lives.

Perhaps you love your job so much that you don't mind working extra hard to meet the financial demands of your shopping wish list. But only a minority can honestly make this claim: most people say they would rather work less if they could. When we buy ourselves the latest iPod, go for a big night out or take on a hefty mortgage, we should instinctively calculate the number of hours or days we will have to work in order to pay the bill. The figures can be alarming. Consumer culture is asking us to exchange days of our lives as the price of membership. But is each of our Faustian shopping bargains really worth it?

The answer is a clear 'no', according to Thoreau. He believed that the path to a fulfilling and adventurous life lay not in shopping till you drop, but in discovering the pleasures of an unmaterialistic lifestyle that offers an abundance of free time. As we shall see, he was a prime mover in efforts to create an alternative to the addictions of consumerism, and helped turn simple living into an art form.

## Simplicity, simplicity, simplicity

If we think we are affluent, we're wrong. That's according to anthropologist Marshall Sahlins, who in the 1970s argued that the truly affluent societies were hunter-gatherer communities. Our desire for consumer products compels us to spend most of our waking hours working to pay for them, leaving us with little free time for family, friends and idle pleasures. But Aborigines in Northern Australia and !Kung indigenous people in Botswana worked only three to five hours a day to support themselves, and, Sahlins points out, 'rather than a continuous travail, the food quest is intermittent, leisure abundant, and there is a greater amount of sleep in the daytime per capita per year than in any other condition of society'.[21]

This may have been an excessively rosy depiction of what in reality was a difficult and precarious existence, where food was often far from abundant and famine never far from the mind. There is nothing enviable about poverty. Nevertheless, Sahlins' point is still pertinent: once we have met our subsistence needs, we might be better off if we lived more simply and on less money. This is especially relevant in an age when working hours are on the increase and many people feel their jobs are robbing time from other parts of their lives. Our current predicament is odd, since the Victorians believed that working hours would progressively diminish as productivity rose, so that the great dilemma for future generations – for us – would be how to occupy our leisure time. As the economist John Maynard Keynes put it in an optimistic essay written in 1930, 'Economic Possibilities for Our Grandchildren', the primary challenge facing mankind in the future would be 'how to use his freedom from pressing economic cares, how to occupy the leisure, which science and compound interest will have won for him, to live wisely, agreeably and well'.

If only he had been right. It is certainly true that from around 1900 until the 1980s working hours did fall in both Europe and North America. But in the past two decades this trend has reversed. In 1997 the US surpassed Japan as the country with the longest working hours in the industrialised world, with an average of forty-seven hours a week.[22] Across Western Europe working hours are going up, particularly in the UK. The typical full-time employee in the EU works forty hours a week, whereas for the UK the figure is forty-four hours, and UK employees are more likely than the Swedes, French or Danes to be working over fifty hours a week.[23] These figures also fail to register the way work follows us home much more than in the past: Keynes had no idea that we might spend our weekends constantly checking our phones for an urgent work message. Although Westerners are now working far fewer hours than in the nineteenth century, and also compared with factory labourers in developing countries, surveys consistently show that many feel they are working too hard and too much. This is in part because they have noticed their own working hours rising over a relatively short time period, but also because of heightened stress levels, as employees are expected to get more and more done within increasingly tight deadlines. One-third of Canadians, for instance, describe themselves as workaholics.[24]

A simpler, less costly lifestyle may be the most effective form of liberation from our culture of overwork, as well as from the dilemmas of status anxiety and our addiction to shopping. But if we want to wean ourselves off consumerism and train ourselves up as experts at simple living, how might we go about it? What inspiration can we draw from the past, so that simplicity is not a matter of scrimping frugality but rather a way of making our lives more beautiful and purposeful?

Simple living has a venerable history in nearly every major civilisation. Socrates believed that money corrupted our minds and morals, and that we should seek lives of material moderation rather than douse ourselves with perfumes or recline in the company of courtesans. When the shoeless sage was asked about his frugal lifestyle, he replied that he loved visiting the market 'to go and see all the things I am happy without'. His pupil, the Cynic philosopher Diogenes – son of a wealthy banker – held similar views, living off alms and making his home in an old wine barrel. Jesus continually warned against the 'deceitfulness of riches', and devout Christians soon decided that the fastest route to Heaven was imitating his simple life. Many followed the example of St Anthony, who in the third century gave away the family estate and headed out into the Egyptian desert where he lived for decades as a hermit, creating a vogue for desert monasticism.

Undoubtedly some have approached simplicity as a quaint affectation: Marie Antoinette constructed a toy village at Versailles where she could temporarily escape lavish court life by dressing in peasant garb and milking perfumed cows next to a picturesque watermill. Such pretence has been more than matched by hard-core simple livers like Mahatma Gandhi, who spent decades in rural communes practising self-sufficiency, making his own clothes and growing vegetables, while simultaneously attempting to overthrow the British Empire. In nineteenth-century Paris, bohemian painters and writers like Henri Murger – author of an autobiographical novel which was the basis for Puccini's opera *La Bohème* – valued artistic freedom over having a sensible and steady job, living off cheap coffee and conversation while their stomachs growled with hunger.[25] For all these individuals simple living was a personal choice driven by a desire to subordinate the material to the ideal – whether that ideal was based on ethics, religion, politics or art. They all believed that embracing something other than money could lead to a more meaningful and fulfilling existence.

The last place one might expect to find a strong tradition of simple living is in the home of material excess and worship of Mammon, the United States. Yet it has been a site of radical experiments in simplicity for over 400 years. The search for alternatives to consumer capitalism, and ideas for adopting a simpler life, lie within this hidden history.

Colonial America was a refuge for religious radicals fleeing persecution in Europe and intent on establishing a holy life in the New World. Best known were the pious Puritans who preached simplicity and wouldn't permit the playing of music, games of chance or other immoral activities in their homes. But the real radicals were the Quakers – officially the Religious Society of Friends – a Protestant sect whose followers began settling in the Delaware Valley in the seventeenth century. As well as being pacifists and social activists, they believed that wealth and material possessions were a distraction from developing a personal relationship with God. The early Quakers were fanatical about what they called 'plainness'. It was easy to spot them: they wore unadorned dark clothes without pockets, buckles, lace or embroidery. Sumptuary guidelines issued in 1695 decreed that 'none Wear long lapp'd Sleeves or Coats gathered at the Sides, or Superfluous Buttons, or Broad Ribbons about their Hats, or long curled Periwigs … and other useless and superfluous Things'.[26] Plainness was also sought in speech. They refused to address

*Plain and simple dress at a Quaker meeting around 1640. Religious guidelines forbade the wearing of fancy clothing with lace, ribbons or buckles. Quakers today follow the spirit of this tradition by avoiding clothes which display corporate designer labels.*

people by their honorific titles, and used the familiar 'thee' and 'thou' instead of the more respectful 'you'. They even objected to the names of the months and days of the week because they referred to Roman or Norse gods such as Mars (March) and Thor (Thursday). So January became 'First Month', February 'Second Month', while Sunday was 'First Day', Monday 'Second Day', and so on.

The worship of simplicity did not last long. As with the Puritans, many Quakers found the temptations of the land of plenty too much, and started up successful businesses and indulged in proscribed luxuries. One of their most eminent members was William Penn – founder of Pennsylvania – who converted to Quakerism at the age of twenty-two. Although declaring, 'I need no wealth but sufficiency', he managed to live like an aristocratic for the next fifty years, until his death in 1718. Penn didn't have just one wig, he had four. He also owned a stately home with formal gardens and thoroughbred horses, which was staffed by five gardeners, twenty slaves and a French vineyard manager. This was hardly a good example for orthodox Quakers, who rejected not only material wealth but also the institution of slavery.

In the 1740s a group of determined Friends led a movement to restore Quakerism to its spiritual and ethical roots in plainness and piety. Its leading figure was a farmer's son named John Woolman. Today largely forgotten, he has been described as 'the noblest exemplar of simple living ever produced in America'.[27] Woolman did not have a brilliant intellect or fine oratory skills. The power of his message came from the fact that he was a humble and humane man who lived by his beliefs. He did far more than wear the traditional undyed clothes and hat of the first Quaker settlers. After setting himself up as a tailor and cloth merchant in 1743 to gain a subsistence living, he was soon faced by a dilemma: his business was too successful – he felt he was making too much money. In a move not likely to be recommended in any business school today, he set himself the task of reducing his profits, for instance by trying to persuade his customers to buy fewer and cheaper items. But that didn't work. So to further diminish his income, he abandoned retailing altogether, and supported his family with a little tailoring and tending an apple orchard.[28]

Woolman was a man of principle. On his travels, whenever receiving hospitality from a slaveholder, he insisted on paying the slaves directly in pieces of silver for providing the comforts he enjoyed during his visit. Slavery, he said, was motivated by 'the love of ease and gain' and no luxuries could exist without others having to suffer to create them.[29] In an early example of ethical shopping and fair trade, Woolman boycotted cotton goods because they were produced by enslaved workers; today he would surely refuse to buy cheap clothes made in Asian sweatshops. After years as a pioneering campaigner against slavery, in 1771 he learned of the poverty being caused by the enclosure of common lands in England, and decided to travel there as a missionary. But upon boarding the ship he was so disturbed by the excessively ornate woodwork in his cabin that he spent the next six weeks sleeping in the steerage with the sailors, sharing 'their exposure, their soaking clothes, their miserable accommodations, their wet garments often trodden underfoot.'[30] After arriving in London, he felt compelled to visit Yorkshire, where he had heard social conditions were harshest. Yet once he discovered the cruelty inflicted on the horses used for the stagecoach trip, Woolman, characteristically, decided to walk – a distance of over 200 miles. Not long after the exhausting journey he contracted smallpox. The disease soon killed him. He was buried in York, wrapped in cheap flannel in a plain ash coffin.

Today John Woolman appears as somewhat eccentric, even foolhardy for his cause. But his story is instructive. It certainly shows that simple living is far from the easiest option in life. If you're not ready to sacrifice a few luxuries and creature comforts like travel in horse-drawn carriages, then simplicity is probably not for you. It also helps to be driven by something larger than self-interest, as Woolman was by his religious ethics. Is there some framework of belief – such as social justice or low-carbon living – that can act as a beacon guiding our actions and keeping us from temptation? Perhaps the greatest lesson emerges from one historian's conclusion that Woolman 'simplified his life in order to enjoy the luxury of doing good'.[31] For Woolman, luxury was not sleeping on a soft mattress but having the time and energy to engage in social work, such as the struggle against slavery. That was his route to personal fulfilment. Simple living is not about abandoning luxury, but discovering it in new places.

Nineteenth-century America witnessed a flowering of utopian experiments in simple living. Many had socialist roots, such as the short-lived community at New Harmony in Indiana, established in 1825 by Robert Owen, a Welsh social reformer and founder of the British cooperative movement.[32] Others were inspired by the Transcendentalist philosophy of the poet and essayist Ralph Waldo Emerson, who preached material simplicity as a path to spiritual truth, self-discovery and union with nature. While the Quakers lived out their ideals in a religious community full of rules and regulations, the Transcendentalists were much more apostles of individualism. The most famous of them, who remains an icon for simple livers across the world today, was a rather prickly character with a liking for bad puns and civil disobedience, Henry David Thoreau.

After completing his studies at Harvard in 1837, Thoreau rejected traditional career paths like business or the Church, working instead as a teacher, carpenter, mason, gardener and surveyor. He despised the growing commercialism in New England, and was incensed when in an attempt to buy a blank notepad for his poetic thoughts, all he could find was a lined ledger for financial bookkeeping. Money was colonising the American mind. Thoreau's response was to become an advocate of 'simplicity, simplicity, simplicity'. His big break came in 1845, when Emerson offered him use of some land at Walden Pond, near the town of Concord, Massachusetts, where he could put his ideals to the test.

For two years Thoreau lived alone in a ten by fifteen foot woodland cabin he built himself for a cost of only $28.12 – less than what he paid for a year's rent at Harvard. It contained little more than a bed, a desk, a few chairs and some favourite books. 'I went to the woods because I wished to live deliberately,' he recorded in *Walden*. 'I wanted to live deep and suck out all the marrow of life, to live so sturdily and Spartan-like as to put to rout all that was not life, to cut a broad swath and shave close, to drive life into a corner, and reduce it to its lowest terms.' As part of his experiment in self-sufficiency, he grew beans, potatoes, peas and sweetcorn, which provided for most of his meals. Selling the surplus earned him enough money to buy staples like rye, Indian meal and salt, from which he made unleavened bread. Occasionally he caught fish for his dinner and once roasted a mischievous woodchuck that had ravaged his bean field.

Despite the long frozen winters and sparse surroundings, Thoreau relished the experience and spent his time writing, reading and observing nature. Each day began with an invigorating and restorative plunge into the pond, often followed by an entranced immersion in the surrounding wildlife:

Sometimes, in a summer morning, having taken my accustomed bath, I sat in my sunny doorway from sunrise till noon, rapt in revery, amidst pines and hickories and sumachs, in undisturbed solitude and stillness, while the birds sang around or flitted noiseless through the house ... I grew in those seasons like corn in the night.

Out of these quiet mornings and attempts at self-sufficiency grew his philosophy of simplicity. 'I am convinced, both by faith and experience, that to maintain oneself on this earth is not a hardship but a pastime, if we will live simply and wisely,' he wrote. 'A man is rich in proportion to the number of things which he can afford to let alone.' While the Quakers preached austerity and abstinence, Thoreau's innovation was to show how simple living could be uplifting and enrapturing in its beauty.

Thoreau's adventure now appears a utopian dream: we can't all just go off and build a hut in the wilderness (especially on a friend's land). But Thoreau never thought that simple living meant abandoning civilisation. In fact, his cabin was only a mile from Concord, and as he openly admits in *Walden*, he went there every few days to hear the local gossip and read the papers. Thoreau was a pragmatist who believed we could learn to turn our backs on the money economy while staying within the company of everyday society. Our real task was to avoid the lures of consumerism and indulge in low-cost pleasures like watching the sunset, talking to interesting people, reading the classics, and thinking.

The most vital lesson from Thoreau concerns work. He should be remembered as one of North America's supreme masters of idling. His sojourn at Walden Pond was less a spiritual quest than an effort to learn to live on as little money as possible so as to minimise his labouring hours and maximise his leisure time. And in this he succeeded. After returning to live in Concord, he worked as a part-time surveyor, which left him ample hours for nature walks, writing and reading. He claimed that in six weeks he could earn enough to live on for an entire year. Today, the inheritors of his legacy are not so much those who live alone in the wilderness but town and city dwellers who have been disciplined enough to cut back their expenses so that they only need to work three or four days a week. Like Thoreau, they have discovered that simplicity is a route to gaining what in the overworked West has become one of the most valuable forms of affluence and wealth: time itself.

The history of simple living in the United States does not end with Thoreau. There were the hippy communes of the 1960s, followed by the rise of an ecologically conscious anti-consumerist movement in the 1970s drawing its inspiration from cult books such as E. F. Schumacher's *Small Is Beautiful* (1973), which argued that our aim should be 'to obtain the maximum of well-being with the minimum of consumption'. Many of its adherents became advocates of 'voluntary simplicity', a philosophy which promotes conscientious rather than conspicuous consumption, and a life that is 'outwardly simple, inwardly rich'.[33] But as we sit here in the twenty-first century, we need to ask what steps we could take in order to lead such an existence. Can we really live deep and suck all the marrow from life without having to constantly take out our wallets?

The most practical starting point is to follow Thoreau and cut back on everyday consumer spending. If he were alive today, I am quite sure he would buy most of his clothes second-hand from charity shops. I can see him burrowing around for kitchen utensils in flea markets, yard sales, and at car boot sales, that peculiarly British gathering where people sell their used household goods – anything from baby clothes to bicycles – at knock-down prices out of their cars. He would grow most of his vegetables on his allotment, support the local farmers' market and rarely eat out in restaurants, preferring to entertain around his kitchen table. His home would have a rustic beauty, containing furniture made with his own hands from reclaimed wood plucked out of nearby skips. What he couldn't make himself would be found on websites like Freecycle, where people give away belongings they no longer want. I imagine he would be living on a canal boat or in a tenant-run housing cooperative rather than in a large home in a fashionable suburb, eager to avoid the burdens of a big mortgage. Thoreau would probably have a solar-powered laptop, and use free Open Source software like OpenOffice, rather than pay Microsoft for the privilege of typing his words. He would get around by bike and public transport, having long since sold the car his parents bought him as a graduation present. His holidays would be a walking trip in a national park accessible by train, rather than a beach vacation in Sri Lanka. He would vow never to work more than twenty-four hours a week. And the main financial question of his life would not be, 'How much money would I like to earn?' but rather, 'What is the minimum I need to live on?'[34]

It is understandable that in a culture geared towards enjoying consumer luxuries, and where social standing is so closely related to displays of wealth, many people are reluctant to embrace a more thrifty way of life. We want our children to wear new, pristine clothes, suspecting that those from a charity store are a bit shabby and smelly. We want our friends or colleagues to admire our tasteful homes, and are pleased when somebody comments on our stylish haircut. For most of us, status anxiety is a shadow obscuring the possibilities for simple living. We can hardly help but want to keep up with the Joneses, whether they are neighbours, workmates, old school pals or some idealised family invented by the advertising industry or TV that lurks in the back of our minds. The bohemian writer Quentin Crisp, who spent most of his life living in a rented bedsit, had a solution: 'Never keep up with the Joneses. Drag them down to your level. It's cheaper.' But the reality is that we probably can't bring them down to our level. So what can we do? Compare ourselves to people other than the Joneses.

One of the most powerful freedoms we possess is to choose who we compare ourselves to for our sense of social worth. To give a personal example, when my partner and I announced we were having twins, some of our better-off friends said, 'Oh, you'll have to move since your house is so small.' But friends in our neighbourhood said, 'Well, it's lucky you live in such a big house!' Whose perspective were we going to adopt? We had a choice of who would be our peer group and we opted to take our inspiration from friends who thrived with their families in homes no larger than our own. Nobody dictates who each of us selects as our peers. We are even at liberty to imagine they include the ghosts of simple livers from the past like Thoreau, Woolman or Gandhi. I doubt they would worry if you served them a meal on plates that didn't match.

Simple living is about more than cutting down your daily expenses or rethinking your points of social comparison, however. It is also about community life. Human flourishing is difficult to achieve alone. One of the damaging results of consumerist ideology is that it has encouraged an extreme culture of possessive individualism where we are primarily interested in our own pleasures and looking after Number One. That is why Monopoly is the most popular board game in the West: the sole aim is to accumulate personal wealth and property.[35] Fifty-five per cent of Americans under thirty think they will end up being rich. 'And if you're going to be rich,' writes Bill McKibben, 'what do you need anyone else for?'[36] This obsession with self-interest has blinded us to the role that community can play in creating the social bonds that do so much for our sense of wellbeing. We should remember what Aristotle told us – that we are social animals, as gregarious as bees. The problem is that a confederacy of forces including suburbanisation, long work hours, television and the consumer drive itself have eroded civic life across the Western world. We barely know our neighbours, shop in faceless hypermarkets and no longer have time for singing in the local choir. Given the failure of consumer materialism to boost our levels of personal wellbeing, it would be a wise move to reclaim community life.

What many people fail to notice is that doing so can be remarkably cheap. In fact, it can save you money, since you no longer need to derive so much existential sustenance from pricey shopping expeditions. Some community activities I'm thinking of are in part designed to help save money, such as joining babysitting circles, car-sharing clubs or time-bartering networks like Local Exchange Trading Schemes. Others just happen to be low cost, like playing music with friends in your living room, meeting people from different cultures down at your allotment, and volunteering at the nearby hospice or as a leader of a Girl Guide troupe. We become surrounded by a web of human relationships that sustain us at least as much as a weekend away in a plush hotel. It is curious that Thoreau did not stress the importance of community for sucking all the marrow from life. Perhaps this was because he did not feel its absence, living near a small town where he knew so many of the inhabitants when he walked down the main street. But if he could observe our isolated, hyper-individualist lives today, I believe he would recommend a healthy dose of community immersion, which offers the prospects of deep living without requiring regular trips to the hole in the wall.

So we can scale down luxury spending, avoid comparison with the Joneses and rediscover our community roots. But there is one final lesson from the history of money for the art of simple living: to expand the free, moneyless spaces in our lives. Imagine drawing a picture of all those things that make your life fulfilling, purposeful and pleasurable. It might include friendships, family relationships, being in love, the best parts of your job, visiting museums, craftwork, political activism, playing sport and music, volunteering, travel, and people watching. There is a good chance that the most valuable of these cost very little or are even free: it does not cost much to put on a puppet show with your kids or walk along a river with your closest friend. The humorist Art Buchwald said it well: 'The best things in life aren't things.' What Thoreau and other simplicity lovers would suggest is that we should aim, year on year, to enlarge these areas of free and simple living on the map of our lives. Let them take up the space once occupied by expensive foreign holidays or boutique items for our wardrobes.

Reducing the role of money in our lives, and shaking off dependency on it, does not mean that we will be deprived of luxuries. The word 'luxury' comes from the Latin for 'abundance'. We have been taught to think of it in material terms – fine wines, fast cars, first-class travel. But we can also have an abundance of intimate relationships, meaningful work, dedication to causes, uncontrollable laughter and quiet time to be with ourselves. There are no shops which sell such luxuries, nor can they be bought with the winnings from a lottery ticket. Yet these are the luxuries which, ultimately, matter the most to us and constitute our hidden wealth.

# Discovering the World

# 7

# Senses

How we love to marvel at the senses. The miracle of touch: premature babies who receive regular massages gain weight 50 per cent faster than those who do not. The wonders of smell: the exquisite scent of violets soon fades because it contains ionone, which short-circuits our sense of smell – but a minute or two later the fragrance will return. Or the intrigue of synaesthesia, a neurological condition which creates connections between the senses: for Rimsky-Korsakov the key of C major was white, while for Duke Ellington, a D evoked dark-blue burlap.[1]

These are the kinds of examples you might find in a book on the science of sense perception, which focuses on the physical and biological aspects of the senses. But our sense experiences are also a product of culture and history. The society we live in teaches us how to use our eyes, ears and other sense organs, shaping our journeys through the doors of perception. Different cultures make sense of the world in their own ways. If you were visiting the Andaman Islands in the Bay of Bengal and met a native Ongee woman, instead of saying, 'How are you?', she would greet you with, 'How is your nose?' If she wished to refer to herself in the middle of the conversation, she would point to her nose. This is because smell is the most important sense for the Ongee, and odour is considered to be the vital force which holds the universe together.[2] In Western culture, by contrast, vision has the place of prominence, which is why so many of our common expressions are based on sight: I see what you mean, that's my perspective, the mind's eye, your worldview, what you see is what you get, great to see you. It is unlikely that a hearty 'Great to smell you!' would go down well with your new work colleague.

The history of the senses reveals a disquieting truth: many of us live in a state of acute sensory deprivation, a hidden form of poverty that pervades the Western world. Unless we happen to be keen-eared musicians or fine-nosed perfumers, there is a good chance we are failing to cultivate the full range of our sensory faculties. Can you really say that all your senses are highly attuned, that you regularly nourish them and give them the attention they deserve? As you eat your breakfast or walk to work, how alert are you to all the sounds, tastes, textures and scents around you?

Failing to nurture our senses not only detracts from our appreciation of the subtleties and beauties of everyday experience, but also strips away layers of meaning from our lives. Yet curing ourselves of sensory deprivation is not, as you might expect, about indulging in luxuries like dining on truffles or locking ourselves in a dark room and listening to a Beethoven symphony at full volume, exhilarating though this may be. It is much more about gaining a deeper understanding of how our various senses have come to shape, filter and even distort our interactions with the world – and also how culture has moulded our sensory experiences.

What can the past tell us about our ways of sensing? First, we need to challenge the ancient myth that we have five senses, liberating ourselves from its strictures and recognising that we possess several additional senses. Then we must discover how vision has become so dominant amongst the traditional senses during the past 500 years, especially how the eye has exerted tyranny over the ear and nose. At that point we will be ready to seek inspiration from two of the most sensually perceptive individuals in history – one a foundling who was locked away alone in a dark dungeon for most of his youth, the other a brilliant writer who was both deaf and blind. They hold the keys to unlocking the latent power of our sensory selves.

## The myth of the five senses

If you share the common belief that there are five senses – sight, hearing, touch, smell and taste – it is time to think again. The five senses are a myth, a historical invention that has been leading us astray for over 2,000 years, leaving us with an excessively narrow conception of what we can sense of the world. How did the five senses become accepted knowledge, who deserves the blame and why does it matter?

In ancient Greece, where the senses first became a subject of sustained discussion, there was no consensus on what they were or how many we had. Plato believed our senses included not only sight, hearing and smell, but also perception of temperature, fear and desire, while taste did not even make it onto his list. In the first century, Philo of Alexandria argued that there were seven senses, one of which was speech, an idea that seems odd to us now, since we think about the senses as passive recipients of data. Yet in the classical era the senses had a more active role and were considered almost as media of communication. The eye, for instance, was thought to send out rays which touched the object it was perceiving, much as words emanate from our mouths.

It is Aristotle who bears responsibility for the doctrine of the five senses. Reflecting the Greeks' obsession with order and symmetry, he claimed there must be a perfect correlation between the elements and the senses. Since there were five elements – earth, air, water, fire and the mysterious quintessence or 'fifth essence' known as ether – there must also be five senses. So he rejected Plato's suggestions of fear and desire, and condensed the various sensations of temperature, wetness and hardness into the single sense of touch. Adding this to sight, hearing, smell and taste gave him the magic number he wanted. The immense intellectual authority of Aristotle meant that this rather arbitrary theory that there were five physical senses became the standard during the Middle Ages, and has remained so culturally powerful that schoolchildren are still taught it today.[3]

Yet during the Middle Ages a new and more expansive conception of the senses also become popular – one which almost no schoolchild will have ever heard about. This was the belief that in addition to the five 'outer senses' identified by Aristotle, there were five 'inner senses'. These inner senses are now forgotten, but for hundreds of years, until the seventeenth century, they were considered scientific fact. Their most famous proponent was Avicenna, an eleventh-century Persian physician and philosopher, who drew on the theories of the ancient Roman anatomist Claudius Galen to argue that an essential part of our sensory apparatus could be found in the ventricles, three fluid-filled cavities in our heads.

The front ventricle was thought to house the vital *sensus communis*, the 'common sense', an organ which acted like a processing plant, organising the information from the outer senses such as sight and taste, which flowed into it via the nerves. The common sense was needed, for example, to distinguish the perception of whiteness from sweetness. Although this was all anatomical nonsense and we might chuckle at the idea of a 'common sense' today, even advanced Renaissance thinkers such as Leonardo da Vinci were firm believers in it. 'The common sense,' he wrote, 'is that which judges of things offered up to it by the other senses.' Just behind the common sense, within the front ventricle, sat a second inner sense called imagination, where images received from outside were stored. The middle ventricle contained an organ usually known as fantasy, which enabled us to visualise things we had never before seen, such as a golden mountain or a unicorn. Alongside it was instinct, a faculty which, according to Avicenna, would prompt us to run away if we saw a wolf, while the rear ventricle contained the inner sense of memory.

When the English scholar Robert Burton discussed the inner senses in his 1621 treatise *The Anatomy of Melancholy*, he was particularly keen to warn his readers about the dangers of fantasy. Although it could stimulate poets and painters, during sleep 'this faculty is free, and many times conceives strange, stupend, absurd shapes.' In melancholic people, he added, this inner sense 'is most powerful and strong, producing many monstrous and prodigious things'.[4]

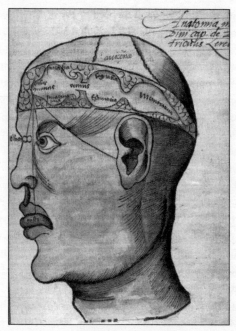

*The three ventricles of the brain and the location of the inner senses, from the*
Margarita philosophica *(1503), an illustrated encyclopaedia widely used as*
*a university textbook in sixteenth-century Germany. It shows how the outer*
*senses of hearing, vision, taste and smell all meet in the common sense – the*
sensus comunis – *in the front ventricle.*

The doctrine of the inner senses did not last beyond the
Enlightenment. It was first undermined by scientific discoveries in the sixteenth century which showed there was no direct
connection whatsoever between the ventricles and any of the
sensory nerves. It became even more unfashionable a century
later, when Descartes' distinction between mind and body suggested that thinking could take place purely in the mind, without
any sensory inputs. This was a conclusion he reached by means
of his famous method of doubt, arguing that an evil demon could
be mischievously creating all his sensory experiences – rendering them illusions – but that the one and only thing he knew for
certain was that he, René Descartes, was thinking. The result,

*cogito ergo sum*, drove a sharp wedge between mental states and our sensory worlds.[5]

We should not, however, be too dismissive of the idea of the inner senses. Current neurological research shows that particular parts of the brain, or neural relationships within it, are responsible for capacities such as memory and imagination, so medieval physicians were perhaps not so mistaken after all. And most of us have experienced those uncanny moments, celebrated by Proust, when an unexpected smell or taste suddenly evokes a long-lost memory, perhaps of a childhood holiday or our grandmother's kitchen. This kind of intimate connection between our outer and inner worlds would hardly have surprised Avicenna. Most importantly, recognising that for centuries people were convinced we had around ten senses is a reminder that our own conception of the five senses might be too constricted, and that there may be more sensory possibilities than we had previously imagined. It's just common sense.

In fact, the current scientific consensus is that we possess up to ten senses, which work closely together to create our perceptual experiences – a 'sense' being defined as a physical mechanism by which information from the outside world enters our central nervous system. In addition to the traditional Aristotelian five, some five further senses have been identified over the past century. Thermoception is a sense physiologically distinct from touch which enables us to detect temperature differences – just as Plato suggested. Now close your eyes and slowly move the tip of one finger to touch your nose. If you happen to miss your nose, then your proprioception is askew. Sometimes also known as kinaesthesia, proprioception is the awareness of your body parts in relation to one another, and the sensation of their movement through space. Ask someone to pinch you, and you will have encountered nociception, your sense of pain. Practise juggling while standing on one leg and you will be cultivating equilibrioception, your sense of balance – the main organ for it, the vestibular labyrinthine system, can be found in our inner ears. Finally, human beings possibly have a weak sense of direction, magnetoreception. In the ethmoid bone just between our eyes and behind our nose is a tiny crystal of magnetite, which is like a compass that orients us within the earth's magnetic field. Animals such as homing pigeons, bats, bees, migratory salmon and dolphins also possess this magnetic mineral. Nobody really knows how it works, but if you are the kind of person who never seems to get lost as you are wandering around a new city, it could be that your sense of magnetoreception is in optimal working order.[6]

Aristotle may have had one of the biggest brains in ancient Greece, but his idea of the five senses was certainly not one of his best. Giving up this myth is a sensory liberation and the beginning of a new adventure in human experience. We might begin, for example, by cultivating our sense of balance. One of the reasons I do yoga – badly – is to improve my balance on the tennis court, as I have a tendency to lose my footing when hitting ground strokes. We could also work on developing our kinaesthetic sense, useful for anybody who spends long hours at a computer. It is common for many people to end up hunched over their keyboard because their shoulders gradually creep forward as they type. But if you become kinaesthetically aware of the position of your shoulders in relation to your upper body and hips, it is possible to notice the creep as it happens, so you can correct your posture. If you seek a more dramatic way to nurture your new senses, you could follow the example of Lawrence of Arabia, who apparently made a habit of testing the limits of his sense of pain by seeing how long he could hold on to a burning match before it turned to ash in his fingertips. But before taking this all too far, we need to explore the regrettable episode of how sight came to dominate the other senses in Western culture.

## The tyranny of the eye

Over the past 500 years the way we perceive the world has undergone a radical transformation. While sight is generally considered our biologically dominant sense – the visual cortex is the largest sensory centre in the brain – it has taken on an exaggerated importance in our lives. We have extended the influence of vision further than nature ever intended, and our other senses, especially hearing and smell, have faded into the background, undergoing what cultural historians refer to as 'sensory decline'.[7] There was a time when there was greater equality between the senses, when people were more aware of what they heard and smelled. But now we are less likely to hear the birdsong as we hurry to work, and gulp down our coffee without paying attention to the wafting aromas – a scent crime the Ongee would never commit. The eye has become a sensory tyrant that distracts us from cultivating the rest of our faculties. According to David Howes, a prominent anthropologist of the senses, we must liberate ourselves from 'the hegemony which sight has for so long exercised over our own culture's social, intellectual, and aesthetic life'.[8]

While some people are born with a particular sensitivity to sound or smell, there is overwhelming evidence that we live in a primarily visual culture. Supermarkets sell us tomatoes which look red and juicy but are often tasteless. Advertising relies more on images – on television, billboards, websites – than on other sensory inputs. We exhibit our wealth and status visually, having an elegant home or driving a stylish car. We typically judge people as attractive by their looks: their facial features, the shape of their body, the clothes they wear. That is why we say 'love at first sight', rather than, say, 'love at first sniff' – even though we are often aware of someone's perfume or body odour. Teenage girls aspire to be supermodels, admired for their appearance rather than their minds. The main way we learn and gain knowledge is not by listening or doing but by reading and looking – the visual world of books, whiteboards and computer screens. No holiday is complete without a set of photos that can be recalled instantly on our phone, originally an audio device that has now been enhanced with visual features. Talk to someone who is blind and you become conscious of how the English language is pervaded by visual idioms – a sight for sore eyes, look before you leap, beauty is in the eye of the beholder. 'Seeing is believing,' we say, not realising that the original expression from the seventeenth century was 'seeing is believing, but feeling's the truth'.[9] Feelings are now out of fashion, and all that matters is what the eye can see. We have come to inhabit a world of surface appearances.

Could we really alter our approach to perception and become more attuned to neglected senses like hearing and smell, which have been eroded by our visual culture? Could we regain the sensory curiosity we once had as children – constantly tasting, sniffing, touching? This is where history can play a role. We need to return to a time before sight came to monopolise our senses in the eighteenth century, when our heightened awareness of sound and scent gave more depth and complexity to everyday life. If we wish to develop a more balanced approach to the senses, we must understand how the eye came to exert its rule over the ear and nose.

When we think of classical civilisations, we may conjure up images of philosophers in togas, bloody battles and exploited slaves. But what did the ancient world smell like? We would undoubtedly be struck by the pervasive use of perfumes. While today we dab on a little perfume or cologne for a night out, a wealthy Athenian man might have applied several different scents: marjoram to his hair, sweet mint to his arms and thyme to his neck. Accompany him to a fashionable dinner party, and you could be adorned with a wreath of roses, then wafted with scent from perfumed doves fluttering above your head. When King Antiochus Epiphanes of Syria held public games in the second century BC, everyone who entered the stadium was anointed with scents such as saffron, cinnamon and spikenard, and upon leaving they received crowns of frankincense and myrrh. The Romans scented not only their food and homes, but also their domestic animals, and Nero's palace was strewn with rose petals. Incense and other fragrances were used extensively in religious rituals and were believed to unite humans with the gods. Scent was not just a matter of individual taste, but a feature of public life.

The appreciation of scent was extended in the Middle Ages by the Crusaders, who brought back exotic spices and perfumes from the East to Europe. The spice box became an essential feature of the medieval kitchen, and food was prepared not simply to stimulate the taste buds but to provide olfactory delights. Hampton Court Palace, home to Henry VIII, contained a spicery, a special room where spices were ground into powder. For centuries, the international spice trade connecting Asia, Africa and Europe was fuelled by the desire not just for commercial profits, but to satisfy our increasingly refined senses.[10]

The widespread use of spices, perfumes and pomanders – scented cases often worn around the neck – which prevailed in Europe until the eighteenth century, helped to create a highly scented culture with a sophisticated approach to smell which now eludes us. When Parisians went for walks, they were just as likely to notice the smells as what they saw along the way, due to what one historian calls 'a collective hypersensitivity to odours of all sorts'.[11] Metaphysical poets such as John Donne were as much infatuated with the scent of their lovers as with their visual beauty: 'As the sweet sweat of roses in a still, / As that which from chafed musk cat's pores doth trill, / As the almighty balm of th' early east, / Such as the sweat drops of my mistress' breast.'

Fragrance was not, however, simply a sensory indulgence. It was also a necessity, a tool to block out the foul odours and pestilential smells that constantly assaulted the nostrils. Consider this description of an eighteenth-century city from Patrick Süskind's novel *Perfume* (1985):

> … there reigned in the cities a stench barely conceivable to us modern men and women. The streets stank of manure, the courtyards of urine, the stairwells stank of mouldering wood and rat droppings, the kitchens of spoiled cabbage and mutton fat; the unaired parlours stank of stale dust, the bedrooms of greasy sheets … People stank of sweat and unwashed clothes; from their mouths came the stench of rotting teeth, from their bellies that of onions, and from their bodies, if they were no longer very young, came the stench of rancid cheese and sour milk and tumorous disease. The

rivers stank, the marketplaces stank, the churches stank, it stank beneath the bridges and in the palaces.

Today, in our deodorised society, we can hardly imagine the fetid stench of the past. But equally we cannot easily imagine the obsession with perfumes and other fine scents. We have lost the acute alertness to smell that our ancestors once possessed. Since the rise of personal hygiene and public health in the nineteenth century, we no longer consider scent to be a matter of great importance – smell has been downgraded in our ranking of the senses. While we should be pleased we no longer have stinking chamber pots under our beds, the scent vacuum that has emerged in the West is a loss for the art of living. As the cultural anthropologist Edward Hall has pointed out, 'The extensive use of deodorants and suppression of odour in public places results in a land of olfactory blandness and sameness that would be difficult to duplicate anywhere else in the world. This blandness makes for undifferentiated spaces and deprives us of richness and variety in our lives.'[12] History calls on us to rediscover our former sensitivity to smell and to become more alive to the scent-scape that surrounds us.

The decline of smell cannot alone explain why sight in particular has become so dominant today, ruling over the other non-visual senses. We must now turn to four further historical developments that altered the balance of the senses towards the eye, the first of which was the gradual shift from aural to visual culture that took place from the fifteenth century.

A major finding of twentieth-century anthropology was the vibrancy of the spoken word in many preliterate societies. Storytelling was often at the centre of community life, and knowledge – whether concerning religion, hunting or childcare – was transmitted verbally. In West Africa, this oral tradition remains embodied in the griot, a kind of walking cultural encyclopaedia who relates local history and folklore in poetry and song, and who may also be an adept satirist as well as a musician. In medieval English and Celtic society, this role belonged to bards, professional poets whose songs and tales were depositories of family and martial history in an era pre-dating the extensive use of writing. Few outside the aristocracy and clergy knew how to read or write. In the Middle Ages people didn't read the Bible, they heard the word of God spoken out loud. They didn't keep address books or diaries, nor did they learn their trade from training manuals. Speech was the pre-eminent medium of human knowledge, and memory the art which supported it.[13]

Then came Johannes Gutenberg. His invention of the movable type printing press in the 1430s was the most momentous event in the history of the senses. According to the cultural critic Marshall McLuhan, it created a 'twist for the kaleidoscope of the entire sensorium', sparking a communications revolution in which 'the eye speeded up and the voice quieted down'.[14] The printing press made the process of acquiring knowledge not only more readily available, but also more private and visual. Information and ideas were increasingly conveyed on the page, and oral traditions slowly began to unravel. The bard went out of business and the book took his place. As the publishing industry and public education expanded in later centuries, and we became buried under a proliferation of books, newspapers and magazines, the typographic culture instigated by Gutenberg gradually took over our lives. Our pre-modern forebears would be shocked at how many hours most of us spend each day reading or writing, and staring at letters, numbers and images on electronic displays. If there is a single factor explaining our increasing bias towards vision, the printing press is it.

A second force distorting the senses in favour of the eye was the Protestant Reformation in the sixteenth and seventeenth centuries. There had always been distrust of the senses within Christian thought. In the Middle Ages, Thomas Aquinas argued that 'man is kept away from a close approach to God' by pleasures of the flesh and the senses.[15] The ideals of chastity and virginity unequivocally denied the sense of touch. The rise of flagellation in the thirteenth century, in which physical pain was self-inflicted on the body in imitation of the suffering of Christ, was a punishment of the senses – even if the devout occasionally whipped themselves into a state approaching sexual ecstasy. But radical Protestant reformers took a more systematic approach to the repression of the senses. They banned the burning of incense in their churches, which was part of a broader assault on scent. In *The Anatomy of Abuses*, published in 1583, the English Puritan Phillip Stubbes warned women that the time would come when 'instead of pomanders, musks, civets, balmes, sweet odours and perfumes, they shall have stench and horrour in the nethermost hel'. Stimulating the taste buds was also subject to disapproval: food should be simple, and lavish feasting treated with suspicion. The eye was usually spared criticism in this puritanical drive towards sensory austerity, since it allowed people to view the grandeur of God's creation.[16]

Vision was given a substantive boost in the eighteenth century. During the Enlightenment, argues the historian of the senses Constance Classen, 'sight became allied with the growing field of science'.[17] The microscope was the visual tool at the centre of emerging fields like biology, the telescope made possible the discoveries of astronomy, and chemical experiments recorded what was observed when gases mixed together. The empirical truths of the universe were seen, rather than heard or detected with other senses. Scientific knowledge was deposited in visual aids such as maps, charts and diagrams. Seeing was transformed into believing, vision into understanding. The Enlightenment was a visual age, in which a shining light helped us to better see the structures of reality. Scientific method naturally lent itself to the use of the eye, and the increasing importance of science in public culture served to deepen the inequality between the senses.

A fourth force, which also emerged in the eighteenth century, was the visual display of wealth and property amongst the European bourgeoisie. Bourgeois culture privileged the eye. The purpose of wearing a fine coat, riding in an elaborate carriage or living in a grand home was not simply to enjoy them for their own sakes, but to enable others to visually admire them. This nexus between the eye, wealth and social status was evident in the development of landscape painting. Consider Gainsborough's well-known work *Mr and Mrs Andrews* (1750), which hangs in London's National Gallery. Its most interesting feature is not

*Thomas Gainsborough,* Mr and Mrs Andrews *(1750). The couple's property in rural Suffolk extends as far as the eye can see, a vision not just of naturalistic beauty but of material prosperity.*

the superb brushwork of the cloud formations, but the fact that the lucky couple clearly wish for all the world to see their vast rural estate stretching into the distance behind them. 'Among the pleasures their portrait gave to Mr and Mrs Andrews,' writes the art critic John Berger, 'was the pleasure of seeing themselves depicted as landowners and this pleasure was enhanced by the ability of oil paint to render their land in all its substantiality.'[18] Can you smell the money? No, but you certainly can see it.

The legacies of the past are not always easy to detect in daily life. Have we really become as addicted to vision as the history of the senses seems to suggest? Anybody who avidly listens to podcasts on their morning commute or who cannot resist the smell of bacon or is taking a course in aromatherapy would probably say their ears and noses are in perfectly good shape, and that they have not succumbed to the tyranny of the eye. Yet have a look at the typical suburban garden.

Gardening is one of the most popular pastimes in many Western countries: Britain has more than 20 million devotees. While some people treat their gardens as mini wildlife sanctuaries or vegetable plots, the majority approach gardening as an exercise in visual aesthetics. What matters more than anything else is how the garden appears to the eye. Does the mixed border have a pleasing combination of colours, heights and shapes? Are there enough plants with 'winter interest', which remain attractive throughout the year? Is the lawn a neat and pristine carpet? Is there space for cheerful window boxes full of bright and vibrant annuals, or for an area of colourful bedding plants? How about a double-flowered camellia in the front bed, and a striking deep purple clematis, 'Polish Spirit', climbing up behind? When I worked as a gardener, it became obvious to me that the primary objective of contemporary garden design is to create a visually pleasing picture.

Most gardeners do not realise, however, that before 1700 visual beauty in gardening was not nearly as important as it is today. Take, for instance, the history of rose cultivation. Until modern times, roses were mainly grown for their scent, not their appearance. In his *Natural History*, written in the first century, Pliny the Elder provides a detailed discussion of which climates produce roses with the finest perfumes, and how to pick a rose to preserve its scent. Roses were featured in medieval and Renaissance gardens especially for their fragrance, explaining why Shakespeare declared, 'a rose by any other name would smell as sweet' – rather than 'would look as lovely'. In one of the most popular gardening books of the seventeenth century, top prize goes to the damask rose for possessing the 'most excellent sweet pleasant scent'. But parallel to the general demise of odour in the West, fragrance faded as a desired attribute of the rose from around the eighteenth century. New cultivars were increasingly bred for their size and colour, with little attention given to scent. In the 1890s a historian of gardening was moved to write, 'a rosery of today would astonish the possessors of gardens in the Middle Ages, and the varied forms and colours would bewilder them, yet in some of our finest-looking roses they would miss, what to them was the essential characteristic of a rose, its sweet scent!'[19] The deodorised roses that fill so many gardens today are a symbol of the stranglehold that the eye has on the rest of our senses.

A similar story can be told about the evolution of garden

design. The earliest gardens were created not just for pleasure and beauty, but to convey symbolic meanings – to stimulate the mind through allegory and metaphor. Enter an ancient Persian 'paradise garden' and you would have to cross water channels, which represented the four rivers of heaven. Once inside you would find a profusion of fruit trees, symbolic of the fruits of the earth created by God. Chinese gardens were also full of allegorical meanings. One hundred years before the birth of Christ, the Han Emperor Wei designed a parkland containing artificial lakes and islands to represent an old myth about the dwelling places of immortal beings. In medieval Europe plants were frequently grown for their symbolism, which was often based on biblical tradition or ancient folklore. A lily alluded to the purity of the Virgin Mary, a violet to humility and patience. Rosemary was a symbol of remembrance, while myrtle and roses represented love. This tradition was later revived, but only briefly, by the Victorian language of flowers.[20]

Just as roses lost their fragrance, so the symbolism was bred out of garden design in favour of visual enjoyment. It began with the rise of formal geometric planting and topiary in the French Renaissance, which reflected a classical enthusiasm for visual order and symmetry. The craze for landscape gardening led by Capability Brown in the eighteenth century gave precedence to creating fine pastoral vistas. The most significant shift, however, was the growing popularity of the English cottage garden in the nineteenth century, which transformed the private garden into a visual canvas to be covered with harmonious colours. The high priestess of this movement was Gertrude Jekyll, who remains one of the most influential garden designers of the last 200 years. 'The purpose of a garden is to give happiness and repose of mind,' she wrote, 'through the representation of the best kind of pictorial beauty of flower and foliage.' The colours at a gardener's disposal should be treated like an 'artist's palette', and design was in essence an exercise in colour composition. Jekyll, who had always wanted to be a painter, treated the garden like an impressionist watercolour, where the principal concern was to convey delicate visual images.[21]

It is true that some contemporary gardeners are becoming more interested in the sensory stimuli of scent and texture, and there are occasional experiments in symbolic design, such as Charles Jencks' 'Garden of Cosmic Speculation' in Scotland, based on the structure of DNA. But gardening today remains largely frozen in the pictorial mode of the nineteenth century. An excessive focus on satisfying the eye has drained away the sensory complexity, multi-layered meanings and self-expression that permeated the gardens of the past, and replaced them with the 'colourful show' celebrated in gardening magazines. 'In our century,' concludes a historian of plant symbolism, 'flowers have been trivialized.'[22]

We now occupy a hyper-visual society. Sight has increasingly become the default filter for our sensory experiences, and our perceptions of sound and scent may be more dulled than at any other moment in Western history. Neither has taste been able to compete with sight, even though we have become more adventurous eaters over the past half-century, experimenting with such things as tabbouleh and Sichuan prawns. The result is not only that most of us fail to develop the sensory sophistication at our biological disposal, but that we are becoming accustomed to the superficial realities of surface impressions. We will enjoy a film for its 3-D special effects even if the story and acting are lousy, or admire a politician who comes across well on television even if their policies lack substance.[23]

Yet there is a way out of our sensory deprivation, a means of replenishing the full spectrum of sensation. We need to step into the shoes of people who have developed such extreme levels of sensory awareness that they have had a more nuanced experience of everyday life. Let's turn to two individuals who can provide us with the inspiration to cultivate our neglected senses, and to expand human consciousness itself.

## The possibilities of darkness

On the afternoon of Monday, 26 May 1828, a shoemaker in the German town of Nuremberg noticed a bewildered youth dressed in peasant clothes wandering helplessly around the streets. He could mutter only a few incoherent words, and was found to be carrying a letter stating that he had been born in 1812 and was the son of a deceased cavalry officer. He was able to write nothing more than his name: Kaspar Hauser.

After spending several weeks detained as a vagrant in the local gaol, he was taken in by Dr Georg Friedrich Daumer, a professor and philosopher, who slowly taught him to speak. Kaspar eventually revealed his incredible story: for as long as he could remember, he had been locked up in a dark cell two metres long and one metre wide. He was given bread and water daily by a man he never saw, slept on a bed of straw, and his sole possession was a carved wooden horse. Who was this strange foundling, only four foot nine and with an unusual talent for drawing, who seemed to have come from nowhere? Could he possibly be the heir to the royal throne of Baden, who had been kidnapped and imprisoned by unscrupulous rivals to prevent his accession? The mysteries surrounding the teenager deepened in 1829, when he was attacked by an unknown assailant. In 1833 he was assaulted once more – he claimed by a stranger – receiving a stab wound in the left breast. Within a few days he was dead. Some thought he was the victim of political intrigue. Others that he had accidentally taken his own life. The riddle of Kaspar Hauser has never been solved.

For all the uncertainties, what we do know is that he had extraordinary sensory abilities. These were meticulously recorded by a respected jurist, Anselm von Feuerbach, who had taken a personal interest in his case. Feuerbach noticed 'the almost preternatural acuteness and intensity of his sensual perceptions', which may have developed through being imprisoned in darkness for so many years and having to make the most out of the few stimuli available to him. Careful experiments and observation revealed that Kaspar had remarkable eyesight and could virtually see in the dark. At twilight, when most people could pick out only a few stars, he could already see hundreds in their various constellations; at sixty paces he could distinguish individual berries in a cluster of elderberries, and tell them apart from adjacent blackcurrants. His hearing was equally highly attuned, and he was easily able to recognise people from the sounds of their footsteps. His sensitivity to smell became famous. He could tell apart apple, pear and plum trees at a great distance simply by the smell of their leaves. But scent was also a cause of considerable distress. 'The most delicate and delightful odours of flowers, for instance the rose, were perceived by him as insupportable stenches, which painfully affected his nerves,' recorded Feuerbach. He could even smell dead bodies under the ground, which would make him break out in a violent sweat. Having lived in the constant temperature of the dungeon, he was hypersensitive to heat and cold: the first time he touched snow, he screamed out in pain.

Most extraordinary of all was Kaspar's perception of magnetic fields. When the north pole of a magnet was pointed at him, he felt drawn towards it, as if a current of air was coming from him. The south pole, he said, blew upon him. When two incredulous professors conducted several experiments designed to deceive him, they found that Kaspar indeed possessed a definite and powerful magnetic sense – one of the 'extra' senses that, as noted earlier, has been identified by contemporary scientists.[24]

What can we learn from the sensory biography of Kaspar Hauser? Certainly that environment can alter our sensory skills, sharpening them to unexpectedly high levels. His sensitivity to smell was similar to that which has been found in many feral children, suggesting, according to Constance Classen, 'that this sense may be by nature of great importance to humans and that it loses its importance only when suppressed by culture'.[25] So if we made a regular effort, we too might be able to smell the leaves of a fruit tree, or learn to distinguish the subtly different scents among varieties of apple. It is also noticeable how quickly Kaspar's superhuman sensitivity faded. Within a few months of escaping the dungeon he was so accustomed to being in natural and artificial light that his night vision began to disappear, and while he could still walk in the dark he could no longer read or discern tiny objects in darkness. His palate adjusted rapidly: initially averse to almost any food besides bread – his staple diet for years – he quickly came to eat most meats. He also complained that his keen hearing deteriorated after immersion in society. Culture and context, it seems, are playing a constant game with the senses, shifting the balance between them, encouraging them sometimes to bloom but at other times to fade. The opportunity before us is to take part in the game, searching for ways to help expand our sensory faculties.

Along with Kaspar Hauser, there is one other sensory icon we should never forget: Helen Keller. Born into a prosperous family in northern Alabama in 1880, Helen had a normal childhood until she was nineteen months old, when she suffered from a terrible illness – probably meningitis – which left her deaf and blind. Over the following years she developed into a headstrong and aggressive child. She would lock unsuspecting family members in their rooms and then hide the key, and throw violent tantrums when she didn't get her own way or was frustrated at her inability to express herself. But when Helen was seven years old, her life changed entirely. Her father sought the advice of Dr Alexander Graham Bell – not only the inventor of the telephone but a renowned expert in deafness – who suggested employing a teacher from the Perkins Institution for the Blind in Boston. A few months later, Anne Mansfield Sullivan arrived to live with the family in Alabama.

Annie's method of teaching Helen to communicate was to 'speak' into her hand, using a series of hand signs that represented the letters of the alphabet, a kind of fingered Morse code. At first Helen was unable to make any connection when the word d-o-l-l was spelled into one hand as she held her doll in the other. But there soon occurred one of the most life-changing moments in sensory history, when Annie thrust her pupil's hand under a spout of water. As Helen recorded in her autobiography:

As the cool stream gushed over one hand she spelled into the other the word *water*, first slowly, then rapidly. I stood still, my whole attention fixed upon the motions of her fingers. Suddenly I felt a misty consciousness as of something forgotten – a thrill of returning thought; and somehow the mystery of language was revealed to me. I knew then that 'w-a-t-e-r' meant the wonderful cool something that was flowing over my hand. The living world awakened in my soul, gave it light, hope, joy, set it free!

Helen had learned that everything had a name, and that the manual alphabet was the key to knowledge. 'As we returned to the house every object which I touched seemed to quiver with life.'[26] Within a few hours she had added thirty more words to her vocabulary. Soon she was reading Braille, and only three months after the water revelation, Helen wrote her first letter. Although shrouded in a dark, soundless world, Helen's intellect flowered. In 1900 she entered Radcliffe College, and four years later was the first deaf-blind person ever to graduate from an institution of higher learning. Following university, Helen established herself as a writer and lecturer, a passionate advocate for the deaf and blind, and a socialist activist. Her fame spread and she met the great and the good of her age – from Mark Twain to President Kennedy – usually with Annie Sullivan by her side, translating into her hand. Her autobiography, *The Story of My Life*, sold millions and was made into the Oscar-winning *The Miracle Worker*, a film produced during her lifetime which she was never able to see.

Helen's life is often remembered as an uplifting tale of personal triumph over extreme physical adversity. But it is just as much an inspiration for how to develop our sensory selves. Like Kaspar Hauser, Helen had extremely sharp sensory abilities. But unlike him, she revelled in the pleasures of her senses, and could express her perceptual experiences with a poetic beauty. Her writings take us into the most sublime and complex sensory world imaginable. Helen possessed what she called 'a seeing hand':

Ideas make the world we live in, and impressions furnish ideas. My world is built of touch-sensations, devoid of physical colour and sound; but without colour and sound it breathes and throbs with life ... The coolness of a water-lily rounding into bloom is different from the coolness of an evening wind in summer, and different again from the coolness of the rain that soaks into the hearts of growing things and gives them life and body. The velvet of the rose is not that of a ripe peach or of a baby's dimpled cheek. The hardness of the rock is to the hardness of wood what a man's deep bass is to a woman's voice when it is low. What I call beauty I find in certain combinations of all these qualities, and is largely derived from the flow of curved and straight lines which is over all things ... Remember that you, dependent on your sight, do not realize how many things are tangible.[27]

Helen listened to classical music through its vibrations and could tell the age and sex of strangers through the resonance of their walk on the floorboards. One day, when wandering through a favourite wood, she felt an unexpected rush of air coming from one side, and knew that nearby trees she loved must have been recently felled. She could recognise all her friends instantly by their smell. She even claimed to comprehend colour through the power of analogy: 'I understand how scarlet can differ from crimson because I know that the smell of an orange is not the smell of a grape-fruit.' Yet she recognised the limits of her knowledge, for she could never sense a room or a sculpture in its entirety, and was always piecing together the small portions of the world her fingers could touch at any one moment.

What is Helen Keller's message for the art of living? 'I have walked with people whose eyes are full of light, but who see nothing in wood, sea, or sky, nothing in city streets, nothing in books. What a witless masquerade is this seeing! ... When they look at things, they put their hands in their pockets. No doubt that is one reason why their knowledge is often so vague, inaccurate, and useless.' Our task, it seems, is to take our hands

*Helen Keller in sensory communion with nature, around 1907.*

out of our pockets, and cultivate all our senses. That is how we might both nourish our minds and, ultimately, deepen our experience of life.[28]

## The knees of Lazarus

The senses can be a challenging dimension of everyday life. Some people feel they are victims of sensory assault – a constant bombardment of images and cacophonous noise compels them to seek calm and silence, to tune out of their senses. Others lead such busy lives that they have no time to appreciate the sensory universe. Yet if we had Helen Keller as a constant companion throughout each day, we would surely recognise that the senses are a gift, and be encouraged to make cultivating them a personal priority. How should we go about tuning in rather than tuning out?

I once asked an unsighted friend to design a sensory tourist trail of Oxford. The starting point, she said, would have to be the chapel of New College in Oxford University, where there is a sculpture of Lazarus by Jacob Epstein. I asked her why. 'Touch him,' she said, 'he has the most beautiful knees in the world.' From here, a trip to the Covered Market to lose oneself amongst the swirling medieval scents of smoked fish, butchers' sawdust, wild mushrooms and cobblers' shoe leather, followed by a blindfolded walk along the towpath of the Thames. Again I was intrigued. 'It's not just about feeling the cool breeze off the river or hearing the flapping wings of the Canada Geese,' she explained. 'There's an edginess walking along the towpath, a sense that you could almost topple in at any moment if you lose your footing. It keeps you on your toes, in a state of complete awareness.' The tour would end at the Ashmolean Museum. 'I once had an art historian show me his favourite portrait painting there,' she told me. 'I asked him to describe it and he started telling me about brushwork and composition and all sorts of rubbish. And I said to him – *but how has the artist made the face look human?* He didn't have an answer to that, because he had never really looked at his favourite painting.' If my friend were the tour guide, visitors would be asked to describe paintings to her, so they learned to see them with fresh eyes.

We might each think of ourselves as sensory travellers, embarking on tours of our local landscape to discover its hidden depths and beauties. Could you create a sensory itinerary for exploring your neighbourhood, or even your own home? Or we might simply decide to focus our awareness on the smell and texture of the food we eat each evening, looking for exactly the right words to describe our culinary experiences. What does the skin of a ripe plum smell like, and what does it feel like in our mouths? We might equally endeavour to hone our non-traditional senses, for instance by doing yoga or the Alexander Technique to develop our kinaesthetic sense of bodily movement and balance. We should also appreciate our senses as a potential source of consolation. I once overcame a broken heart by taking a walking trip along the Welsh coast, each day concentrating on a difference sense – smell, sound, sight. It was not just a distraction from my personal pain, but a more positive immersion in the present, almost a meditative act.

The senses are one of the most precious ways we have to learn about the world, and about ourselves. Most of us have hardly begun to harness their latent power. Turning on our senses is a forgotten freedom we all possess, and can add new dimensions of meaning and experience to our lives. It is time we opened ourselves to all the delights, surprises, curiosities and memories that lie in wait for us.

# 8

# Travel

'To travel is to dispel the mists of fable and clear the mind of prejudice taught from babyhood, and facilitate perfectness of seeing eye to eye.'[1] This was the creed of Thomas Cook, the unlikely inventor of the package holiday and founder of the most successful travel company of the nineteenth century. Today the firm still bearing his name sells the usual array of bargain trips to beach resorts, luxury cruise vacations and weekend getaways to romantic cities. But it all began with a very different mission. In the early 1840s, Cook, a lay Baptist preacher and fanatical member of the temperance movement in the English Midlands, had a brilliant idea. He would organise a train trip for poor working people from Leicester to attend a temperance meeting in the nearby town of Loughborough, where a series of pious ministers would call on them to abstain from the demon drink and take the path to God.

Although this may not be your idea of the perfect holiday break, on 5 July 1841 more than 500 people boarded Cook's specially hired train and made the twenty-two-mile journey to Loughborough, accompanied by a brass band which had squeezed in with them. The holidaymakers, who had each paid one shilling for their trip, listened to rousing speeches espousing the benefits of teetotalism, enjoyed a picnic lunch and finished the day with games of blind man's bluff, group dancing and a cricket match. Cook followed this trailblazing instance of organised mass tourism with package tours to Europe and the Holy Land, keeping prices low so that overseas travel was open to labourers and office clerks, rather than being the monopoly of the bourgeoisie and upper classes. In 1861, 1,000 people, including 200 cotton mill workers from Bradford, travelled to Paris for a return fare of just one pound. Cook believed his tours should offer workers not only leisurely respite from routine jobs, but provide opportunities to broaden the mind through new cultural encounters. Travel, he claimed, could create 'universal brotherhood'.

Despite this vision, Cook died a bitter man in 1892, aged eighty-three. By then his firm was a household name and one of the world's first globally recognised brands. But since the 1870s, when his son John Mason Cook took over, the company had become increasingly commercial in its goals. It now cultivated a wealthy clientele, amongst them European royalty and Indian maharajahs, and promoted only the most profitable routes. Selling their new travellers' cheques became more important than organising spiritual excursions or forging mutual understanding across borders. Thomas was eventually sidelined from company operations by his ambitious son. And with that, the history of travel had lost its greatest missionary.[2]

The story of Thomas Cook & Son is a parable for today, and asks us to consider how we travel and what role we want it to play in our lives. Is it enough to spend our holidays lying in the sun with a cocktail by our side or doing short rambles from a rented country cottage, or should we, like Thomas Cook, view travel as a way of changing who we are? Why do we so readily queue up to catch a glimpse of the *Mona Lisa* or have our photo taken in front of the Taj Mahal? How should we engage with other cultures on our travels, and what kinds of journeying are most likely to transform our approach to the art of living?

The advisors in your local travel agency are unlikely to provide answers to these questions. The most informative advisors, I believe, are the travellers of history. They can inspire us to travel in ways that Thomas Cook would have admired, and which heed the warning of the Roman poet Horace, who wrote, 'they change their climate, not their soul, who rush across the sea'. There are four historical 'persona' we might seek to emulate, each of which represents a different style of travel: the pilgrim, the tourist, the nomad and the explorer. You may identify with one or more of them. They can help lead us on journeys that deepen our souls, not just our suntans.

## Pilgrim

Each year more than half a million people make the pilgrimage to Graceland, the former home of Elvis Presley in Memphis, Tennessee. They pay homage at his grave, then file dutifully past his memorabilia, including a selection of his famous sequinned jumpsuits, and finally leave after buying an Elvis T-shirt. But is 'pilgrimage' the right word to describe a visit to Graceland? The traditional religious pilgrimage that is central to all the world's major faiths, and which draws believers to kiss the worn-down toe of St Peter in Rome, to circle around the Ka'ba or to bathe in the holy Ganges, has two vital ingredients: a meaningful destination, and an arduous and potentially life-changing journey. While some Elvis fans may weep at the sight of his tombstone, few will have struggled to reach Graceland. They are most likely to have flown into Memphis or arrived on a coach tour. This hardly compares with the expedition of St Helena, mother of the Roman emperor Constantine, who in her seventies travelled by land with her entourage via Byzantium and Anatolia, resting overnight at sixty different locations, to make the first Christian pilgrimage to Jerusalem in 327. And it bears even less resemblance to the journeying of Ibn Battuta, the Muslim Marco Polo, who visited Mecca four times during a 75,000-mile odyssey in the fourteenth century that took him from his birthplace in Tangier as far as India and Ceylon, and which lasted almost thirty years.[3]

Pilgrimage remains important today because it suggests a way of travelling that has been lost in our more secular age. The pilgrims of history had little interest in having a leisurely vacation. They were true travellers in the original sense of the word: 'travel' derives from 'travail', meaning to suffer or toil. Their journeys were a challenging rite of passage that gave their lives a sense of purpose and expanded their experiences and imaginations. This was certainly the case for two of the most original of all pilgrims, one a seventeenth-century Japanese poet, the other a peace pilgrim who walked from Delhi to Washington as an act of political protest.

Born in 1644 into a family of Samurai, Matsuo Bashō distinguished himself in his youth as a writer of the seventeen-syllable haiku form. After training in Zen meditation with a Buddhist priest, he became a recluse, writing verse in a hut on the outskirts of Edo, now Tokyo. In the last ten years of his life, however, Bashō set off on several pilgrimages around Japan, carrying little more than his inkstone, brush, paper and overcoat. Explaining the purpose of his journeys, he wrote:

> Following the example of the ancient priest who is said to have travelled thousands of miles caring naught for his provisions and attaining the state of ecstasy under the pure beams of the moon, I left my broken house on the River Sumida in the late August of the first year of Jyokyo (1684) among the wails of the autumn wind.[4]

Bashō belonged to a Japanese tradition of Buddhist pilgrimage in which travelling itself was considered a path of personal progress towards enlightenment – or as today's self-help texts put it, the journey mattered more than the destination.[5] What really motivated him was not simply bowing down in front of Buddhist shrines, but having experiences on his travels that would develop his self-understanding. He sought inner rather than outer journeys. On his most famous trip, recorded in *The Narrow Road to the Deep North*, Bashō sold his home then spent over two years as an itinerant wanderer in the northern provinces of the island of Honshū, sometimes alone, sometimes with a companion. Naturally he visited Buddhist pilgrimage sites such as mountain temples, but the unique feature of his journey was also to make pilgrimages to non-religious places that contained great personal meaning for him. He went to the secluded hermitage of his meditation master Bucchō, visited old friends and family, and paid homage to famous willow and pine trees that had been mentioned in the works of his poetic predecessors.

Bashō's emotional sensitivity was matched by acute sensual awareness. The ageing poet would pause to hear the call of a cicada, or to feel a breeze on his face:

Blessed indeed
Is this South Valley,
Where the gentle wind breathes
The faint aroma of snow.

Bashō realised that the best way to make a spiritual inner journey was on foot, even if it made travelling more physically demanding. Walking in his straw sandals, rather than racing along on horseback, allowed him the time to contemplate the beauties of a cherry tree, to speak to other travellers on the road, to admire an autumn moon and to drink in the natural landscape around him. The regular rhythm of his steps induced a state of meditative calm, permitting his mind 'to gain a certain balance and composure, no longer a victim to pestering anxiety.'[6] He also had an adventurous streak, and seemed to revel in making random deviations in his travels or getting lost and discovering unexpected villages. Bashō was the last person who would have buried his nose in a map, and the first person to turn wandering into an art form.[7]

While the majority of pilgrims are inspired by a god to undertake their journeys, one of the twentieth century's most radical pilgrims was inspired by an atheist philosopher. In 1961 Satish Kumar, a former Jain monk, was sitting in a café in Bangalore when he read that Bertrand Russell had been arrested at an antinuclear demonstration in London. Turning to his friend Prabhakar Menon, he said, 'Here is a man of ninety committing civil disobedience and going to gaol. What are we doing?'

This question prompted an idea: they would make a Pilgrimage for Peace, walking from India to Moscow, Paris, London and Washington, visiting the four nuclear capitals in protest against the bomb. If you think this was a crazy plan, even more extraordinary was that they decided, as a matter of principle, to undertake their journey absolutely penniless, believing that money

*Bashō, decked out in full pilgrim regalia, pauses in his wanderings to share the mid-autumn festival with two farmers.*

would act as an obstacle to genuine human contact. Without money, they would be forced to speak to people, asking for their hospitality, and in doing so would be better able to spread their political message.

Setting out from Gandhi's grave in Delhi in 1962, the pair travelled more than 8,000 miles over a period of two years, almost entirely on foot. Wherever they went, they found supporters of their cause who generously gave them food and shelter. Their host in Kabul presented them with a fur cap in preparation for a trek through the mountains to Herat. In Iran, someone saw them walking in tattered shoes, so bought them replacements. An Armenian mother gave them four packets of tea to deliver to the four world leaders, with the message that if they get mad and think of pressing the nuclear button, they should stop and have a fresh cup of tea to calm down. 'That will give them a chance to remember that the simple people of the world want bread not bombs, want life not death,' she said.

Although Kumar and Menon eventually reached the four nuclear capitals, they were refused audiences with presidents and prime ministers. They evaded the Soviet authorities' attempt to deport them by escaping Moscow and walking for forty-five days through the snow to the Polish border. In Paris they were thrown in a filthy gaol for protesting against nuclear weapons outside the Presidential Palace. Their pilgrimage captured the imaginations of peace activists around the world, and they became media celebrities wherever they went. They had tea and cake with their hero Bertrand Russell in his remote Welsh cottage, and while in the United States met Martin Luther King, who welcomed them into his home.

In some ways their pilgrimage was a failure. 'We met no one on the walk who didn't want peace, but no one seemed to know how to achieve it,' wrote Kumar in his autobiography. Yet he was able to take solace in the spiritual dimension of his travels. 'In wandering I felt a sense of union with the whole sky, the infinite earth and sea ... It was as if by walking I was making love to the earth itself.' And by relying on help from strangers during their moneyless travels, they discovered how much goodness and solidarity there was across the world. 'A common humanity emerged – whether we slept in comfortable beds or on the floor of a barn or under a tree, it was all a gift.'[8]

What would it mean to undertake a pilgrimage today? One

lesson from the travels of Bashō and Satish Kumar is that we should choose a destination that is personally meaningful, involving a journey to the roots or source of something significant – your family history, or perhaps your political beliefs. You might travel to the village in Ireland where your great-grandmother was born, visiting her grave and the streets she would have played in as a child. Having trained as a nurse, you could make a pilgrimage to inspiring sites from the history of your profession, such as the military barracks in Üsküdar, Turkey, where Florence Nightingale treated wounded soldiers in the Crimean War.

A second lesson is that the journey should be a challenge, and ideally involve walking. Jetting in to our pilgrimage destination then taking a taxi to a five-star hotel would not have impressed Bashō. We ought to spend time travelling, giving ourselves enough headspace for contemplation and going at a sufficiently slow pace to appreciate the beauties and sorrows of the landscape, whether it is a mountain range or an inner-city slum. Forget the car: put on some straw sandals and start walking under an open sky. We should also be dealing with situations of adversity, so the journey becomes a quest to learn about ourselves. This does not require leaving home without any money in our pockets, like Satish Kumar, with the prospect of having to beg for our supper each night. All I mean is that it can be an edifying experience to forgo our regular comforts for a while and be forced to push ourselves to reach our goal. I once went with my partner on a pilgrimage from our home in Oxford to visit my parents in Germany. It began with a ride on the Number 5 bus to the train station. Then multiple train trips, first to London, then on the Eurostar to Brussels, and another rail trip across the border to the Mosel valley. From there we took a boat downstream, then walked with our rucksacks for several days along the river and surrounding ridges, wild camping up in the beech forests. It was hard work, the rucksacks weighed us down and our feet hurt. One night our tent was almost stampeded by a frisky wild boar. But it was, as they say, character building. When we finally knocked on my parents' door, in desperate need of a shower, I felt it was somehow appropriate to have made such an effort to reach two of the most important people in my life.

The final lesson, for which we can thank Bashō, is that we should cultivate ourselves as wanderers. Most people want to get to their holiday destination as swiftly as possible, and view travelling to their seaside apartment or ski chalet as a necessary evil they must tolerate before their real vacation begins. But the pilgrimage tradition suggests we should not obsess about our destinations. We can set ourselves an objective but it may not matter if we never arrive, as long as the journey has taught us something about the art of living. Maybe a final destination is even something to avoid. Bashō would advise us not to plan the routes of our travels too carefully, and even to throw away the map or satnav if we are brave enough. Permit yourself to become lost – that is the best way to find yourself, he would surely say. As you walk through a big city on your journey, allow the sun to be your guide, or follow curious smells or unusual sounds, using your senses as a compass. Before reaching your destination, get off the train at a station whose name intrigues you, or where nobody else is disembarking, placing your hopes in serendipity. As a pilgrim you will discover that the journey is not a means to an end, but an end in itself, just as Constantine Cavafy recognised in his poem, 'Ithaka' (1911):

> Keep Ithaka always in your mind.
> Arriving there is what you are destined for.
> But do not hurry the journey at all.
> Better if it lasts for years,
> so you are old by the time you reach the island,
> wealthy with all you have gained on the way,
> not expecting Ithaka to make you rich.

## Tourist

When I was fourteen, my parents took me out of school in Sydney for three months to go camping around Europe. We visited over a dozen countries and saw all the sights, especially in Italy. I climbed the Leaning Tower of Pisa, filed past great Renaissance works of art in the Uffizi Gallery in Florence, went on a gondola ride in Venice, and in Rome wandered through St Peter's Basilica and gazed up at the Sistine Chapel ceiling. Along the way I sent postcards of these places to friends and family, bought souvenir replicas of what I had seen, admired all the best views and was the subject of hundreds of photographs in front of statues and cathedrals.

Why?

Why did we visit so many galleries when both my father and I had little interest in art, and immediately felt sleepy in a roomful of Old Master paintings or Roman statues? Why reverentially enter so many churches when we were all non-believers? Why take an expensive gondola ride lasting only half an hour, knowing full well that it was a tourist rip-off? Why photograph me eating an ice cream outside Dante's house, when I had little idea who he was?

The reason, of course, is that this is what it is to be a tourist and 'do' a city. Visiting famous artworks, architectural monuments and sublime views has come to constitute the standard itinerary for millions of travellers. But how can we explain why, upon arriving in Paris for the first time, we immediately rush off to the Louvre, up the Eiffel Tower, then over to Versailles? Unravelling this historical mystery can introduce us to more original ways of being a tourist and discovering different cultures.

European tourism emerged in the seventeenth century when aristocrats, especially from England, began travelling around the continent on what became known as the 'Grand Tour'. Accompanied by a retinue of servants, tutors and guides, wealthy young men – and sometimes women – embarked on a cultural voyage lasting several years that generally took them through France, Holland, Germany, Switzerland and eventually to the ultimate destination of Italy, where they could find not only the finest Renaissance masterpieces, but also the ancient Roman sculptures and other antiquities that their classical educations had taught them to revere. As Samuel Johnson observed in 1776, a 'man who has not been to Italy, is always conscious of an inferiority, from his not having seen what it is expected a man should see'.[9] These privileged tourists had little contact with local people outside the social elite, and viewed travel as a journey into the artistic past rather than an encounter with the human present.[10]

Tourism experienced a huge expansion in the nineteenth century when the growing middle classes found themselves with enough income and leisure time to travel, and could take advantage of the new railway networks to do so. But where should they go? The most definitive answer was provided by a German publisher, Karl Baedeker. From 1839 he began producing a series of best-selling and iconic travel guides that soon dominated the international market. For nearly a century Baedeker set the itinerary for the bourgeois traveller in Europe, North America and much of Africa and Asia, and few would leave home without the latest edition, with its trusty red cover, for their destination of choice. Just as Baedeker was himself a collector of autographs, his travellers became collectors of countries, ticking them off an imaginary list, gradually accumulating the world's geography with his help, as many people still do today with their bookshelf displays of Rough Guides and Lonely Planets.

Baedeker's main principle was that the handbooks should enable people to travel completely independently, so they were not reliant on hired guides or servants like the Grand Tour aristocrats, and could be free of the herd-like travel arrangements of group operators such as Thomas Cook. Open the pages of a Baedeker and you would find remarkably detailed information on transport, hotels, eating, tipping and shopping, as well as dozens of fold-out maps. But the bulk of each guide contained the all-important recommendations for what to see and how to see it. This is the realm in which Baedeker helped forge an enduring ideology of tourism, of which we are the unsuspecting inheritors.

His guidebooks largely imitated and popularised the itinerary and tastes of the Grand Tour for the new bourgeoisie. The emphasis was on the very artworks and architecture that had been deemed an appropriate cultural education by the European upper classes.[11] Galleries, museums, churches and palaces dominated the pages, so that travel became equated with seeing 'high art', although he also gave some space to alpine excursions or visits to bazaars. The guide to Central Italy noted that 'both in viewing the monuments of architecture and in inspecting the works of plastic art, the traveller is advised to surrender himself to the influence of the greatest and best examples'.[12] How would you know which were the greatest and best? This could be discovered by using Baedeker's celebrated star rating system, an innovation stolen from his rival, the British travel publisher John Murray.[13] Two stars were given to an unmissable attraction, and either one star or none to others.

Baedeker prided himself on the accuracy and detail of his books, which bordered on the obsessive. Typical is the description of the two-starred cathedral in Siena, which runs to three pages of tiny typeface. He informs us that the cathedral is 97.5 yards long, 27 yards wide, and that the transept is 56 yards in length. Why it is important to know this is not clear. He then reveals that the marble pulpit is held up by nine granite columns, though anybody wishing to count them could no doubt do so for themselves.[14] Baedeker lists ninety-four works of art in the cathedral that deserve our attention – mainly frescoes and statues – far too many for anyone to take in. I find only one of them genuinely intriguing: 'a silver casket, by Francesco di Antonio (1466), contains an arm of St. John the Baptist'.

Apart from the star ratings, Baedeker guides became known for their numbered itinerary routes, which told travellers exactly what to visit, in what order, and how long they should take. You could see everything of interest in Siena within two days, according to the 1909 handbook. On the first morning you should visit Via Cavour, then the Piazza del Campo and the Palazzo Pubblico, followed by the parish church of San Giovanni, and finally the cathedral museum. The afternoon was reserved for the cathedral itself, its famous library, and then a fourteenth-century Gothic palace.[15] Baedeker's tourists were understandably exhausted after rushing from site to site, eyes fixed on the street map, and busily filling their heads with statistics about church architecture.

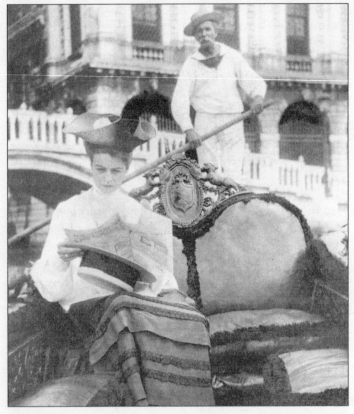

*Eleanor Roosevelt taking a gondola ride during her honeymoon in Venice in 1905. As a teenager she had travelled Europe guided by a Baedeker, which recommended that all new arrivals in Venice should immediately make a two-starred 'Voyage of Discovery' by gondola to see the sixty architectural gems along the Grand Canal.[16]*

It is unsurprising that the Baedeker became an object of playful ridicule. In the 1985 film adaptation of E. M. Forster's novel *A Room With a View* (1908), the heroine Lucy Honeychurch has the following exchange with the minister of the Anglican church in Florence:

*The Reverend Mr Eager*: So, Miss Honeychurch, you're
     travelling. As a student of art?
*Lucy*: No, I'm afraid not.
*Mr Eager*: As a student of human nature, like myself?
*Lucy*: I'm here as a tourist.
*Mr Eager*: Indeed? We residents sometimes pity you poor
     tourists not a little. Handed about like parcels from
     Venice to Florence to Rome, unconscious of anything
     outside Baedeker, anxious to get done and go on
     elsewhere. I abhor Baedeker. I'd fling every copy in the
     Arno.

Reverend Eager would probably hold these opinions today.
Tourist guidebooks have made little progress since the demise
of the Baedeker in the 1930s, when the firm became tinged with
Nazi associations, even publishing a handbook to occupied
Poland in 1943, complete with justifications for the German
invasion.[17] Most contemporary travel guides still send us to
visit the same galleries, churches and views, even if they have
added some information on idyllic beaches, trendy nightclubs
and budget accommodation options. If you've ever backpacked
around Europe, you may have noticed that you keep spotting
the same people at museums and hostels in different cities
along your route – because everyone has similar guidebooks.
It is absurd that, in the twenty-first century, we are still largely
following the tourist trails favoured by the aristocrats of the
Grand Tour. Although Karl Baedeker hoped to foster independent travel, his legacy has been to prevent tourists from thinking
for themselves, and following their own curiosity and instincts.
Perhaps guidebooks should only be our occasional travelling
companions, best used in an emergency.

More significantly, Baedeker and his imitators have taught
us to believe that a church facade is of greater interest than other
facets of a city, such as vegetable markets, street fairs, cafés, graf-
fiti, community centres or children's playgrounds. We have been
similarly taught to celebrate the geometric proportions of this
facade rather than to think about the workers who spent their

lives building it. The tourist guides assume that travel is about visiting historical buildings and other man-made objects rather than discovering the living people who create the contemporary human landscape.[18]

I believe that the real monuments worth visiting are people. That is where the fascination of travel truly lies. Following his early journeys in Sudan in the 1930s, the British explorer Wilfred Thesiger wrote that 'ever since my time in Northern Dafur, it has been people, not places, nor hunting, not even exploration, that have mattered most to me'. I think he's right. If you think about your own holidays, often the most memorable ones are those when you befriended the barman in a small village, or when a rickshaw driver took you to his home to meet his family. Such experiences give us insights into unknown worlds. We must reinvent tourism and move beyond the high-culture legacy of Baedeker and the Grand Tour. Our aim should be to become observers of – and even participants in – other people's daily ways of living. Directing our antennae towards the social practices of different countries and cultures can not only illuminate new possibilities for how we conduct our lives, but reveal how strange our own ways might be.

When I first travelled around Spain, for instance, I noticed something unusual about the bars: parents brought along their children, who would often stay up until late in the evening. In England you would rarely find kids in a pub on a Saturday night, and they were frequently banned from entry. Then there was the culture of drinking. Glasses of wine or beer were quite small in Spain, and people ate snacks with their drinks, whereas the English would sit themselves down with a huge pint glass of beer, drinking on an empty stomach, with the inevitable inebriating result. Once I began living in Spain, I became addicted to their shopping habits, which involved buying food each morning from several small, independent stores, enabling me to meet people from my neighbourhood and offering a sense of community that I had never before enjoyed. Some of these approaches to living have stayed with me since I left Spain – I still shop locally each day and drink from small Spanish glasses at home. They have offered me a very different form of inspiration than walking the hallowed hallways of the Prado Museum.

Visiting other countries is, however, becoming an old-fashioned way to travel. In the era of climate change, taking a high-carbon aeroplane flight for a long weekend is increasingly viewed as a social embarrassment and ethically unsavoury. At the same time, growing immigration has meant there are probably more foreign cultures alive in your own country than at any moment in the past. These shifts suggest a more creative way to be a tourist, which is to explore the world of strangers on your doorstep, in the place where you already live. I live in a city of more than 100,000 people, but have only had genuine conversations with a minute proportion of them. When I went to my Muslim neighbour's wedding feast, my partner and I were the only white faces amongst several hundred British Asians whom we had never met. After nearly a decade in Oxford, I am still at the earliest stages of exploration.

We should see ourselves as backyard anthropologists, delving into the unknown minds we walk past every day – or meet at a neighbour's wedding – discovering the wisdom inside other people's heads and creating bridges of mutual understanding. You might strike up a conversation with the woman working at the bike shop and find out she is a Baha'i. You could volunteer at a local refugee support centre and meet your first Congolese doctor, or become a host to foreign language students, so the world comes to you. Perhaps you might embark each Saturday morning on a visit to a different 'greasy spoon' café, and encounter a universe of second-generation Italians and Cypriots. You will not need a Baedeker on these journeys, nor have any need to queue up at the airport or spend a fortune on hotels.

As a society, we should be thinking about ways to nurture these possibilities. Just imagine if hotels contained state-sponsored crèches open to both foreign visitors and local people, allowing not only the children to play with each other but their parents to meet and talk. Or if public parks held regular conversation picnics where a tourist could sit with a local pensioner to discuss their different perspectives on life. A town in Denmark has originated the idea of the 'human library' where you can 'borrow' bistro chefs, asylum seekers, former drug addicts and other volunteers for an hour of conversation. The human library movement has now spread to more than twenty countries. This is the kind of innovation required to take tourism into an adventurous future.

## Nomad

'Our nature lies in movement; complete calm is death,' wrote the seventeenth-century French thinker Blaise Pascal. This quote, which I first encountered in *The Songlines* (1987), Bruce Chatwin's homage to nomadism, obsessed me throughout my twenties. It offered the romantic notion that human beings were in essence nomads who could only feel a sense of wholeness if continually on the move like Bedouin tribesmen crossing the desert by camel from oasis to oasis. Chatwin described how we had been permanent travellers for millions of years, hunters and gatherers who followed the migratory pathways of bison or moved camp with the seasons, and had only become sedentary 10,000 years ago with the rise of agriculture.[19] According to him, we were by nature restless beings, and the desire to be 'settled' and have a fixed home filled with personal possessions was a historical novelty that would ultimately fail to satisfy our inner yearning to wander.

I subsequently spent much of my twenties and early thirties travelling – visiting and living in different countries, renting rooms, sharing flats, staying in hostels – doing my very best not to put down any roots. I went from England back to Australia, then on to Spain and the United States, via repeated long stays in Guatemala. My life was one of suitcases and boxes, address changes and passport stamps. This apparently nomadic lifestyle not only satisfied my innate feeling of restlessness, but gave me freedom from the trappings of modern civilisation. I was not burdened with having a mortgage that tied me down to a regular job or a particular city. I tended to live quite simply, without accumulating the domestic detritus – sofas, beds, televisions, tables, clothes – that a consumer society thought necessary for sedentary living. I agreed with the fourteenth-century Islamic philosopher Ibn Khaldun, who wrote that nomads 'are more removed from all the evil habits that have infected the hearts of settlers'.[20] If I wanted to learn Spanish I could move to Spain. If I fell in love, I could follow my lover anywhere in the world. I allowed myself to mythologise nomadism, conveniently forgetting that for most nomadic peoples travel was a matter of economic necessity rather than a lifestyle choice, that they usually followed established routes rather than meandering from here to there, and that they did so together with family and tribe rather than alone, which is how I had always pictured my nomadic self.

Over time, I felt that creeping desire for permanence that comes to so many people as they grow older. By my thirties, I was getting tired of being a self-styled nomad. I dreamed of having a room of my own, where I could unpack my boxes of books, paint the walls the colours I wanted, and have the time I needed to become part of a community. A decade later, now with a home and family, I know that my former sense of restlessness has not completely left me. My feet are occasionally itchy, and part of me secretly envies the Hindu tradition in which men aged over fifty, once they have fulfilled their family duties, leave for ever to become wandering ascetics, or *sannyasi*.

How can we travel like nomads today, in the modern world? One approach is to have a non-sedentary life, as I did during my 'global nomad' period. This is the path pursued by many of those who have no permanent home, ranging from hobos and itinerant migrant workers to UN staff employed in humanitarian relief and teachers of English as a foreign language who move country from year to year. I imagine, however, that a genuine nomad – say a Bakhtiari herder from Iran or a Nukak hunter-gatherer from the Colombian Amazon – would hardly see their own lifestyles reflected in such examples. Most nomads don't take flights abroad, inhabit cities, receive *per diems* or keep their books in storage.

A more plausible way to explore nomadic experience is a form of travel that people tend to either love or hate: camping.

Nomadic peoples were the world's first campers, staying in temporary and easily constructed shelters like lean-tos, tipis or yurts, spending most of their lives outdoors in nature as part of a small community, and relying on fire to warm themselves and cook. Camping not only captures the essential spirit of nomadism, but is something we can easily replicate. It requires little more than pitching a tent with friends and family in a lush rural valley or on a cliff top overlooking the sea, and immersing ourselves in a simpler way of living.

Camping for pleasure is not, however, a direct descendant of nomadic culture. It emerged in the nineteenth century in response to a variety of social forces. First, the Romantic movement encouraged communing with the beauties of nature, while also glorifying the life of the outlaw or lone outsider who rebelled against organised society. According to the historians of camping, Colin Ward and Dennis Hardy, works like Friedrich Schiller's *The Robbers* (1781) and George Borrow's nineteenth-century gypsy tales 'idealised the brigand or gypsy camp whose carefree occupants lived a simple, heroic life under the stars, contemptuous of settled town dwellers in their smug, dull comfort'.[21] A second influence was the age of empire. European powers in Africa and Asia were busy trekking into the dark hinterlands, pitching their bell tents and erecting barrack huts as they attempted to extend their control over indigenous lands. Camping was necessary for colonial expansion, and became a way of life not only for the troops, but for the pith-helmeted explorers and missionaries who either led the way or followed in their wake. A final factor was the rise of emigration. Hundreds of thousands fled Europe in the nineteenth century to create new lives in Australasia, the United States, Canada and South Africa, working as trappers, lumberjacks and ranchers, or lured by the glint of gold rushes. A specialist industry grew up to supply their needs – tents, camp beds, stoves, kettles, camp matches and coffee. Their tales of rough adventure were soon popularised in the press back home. Camping was becoming part of the cultural imagination.

By the early twentieth century, camping for pleasure was

ready to launch itself as a form of mass recreation. Its leaders were the organised youth movements of the period, such as the Boys' Brigade and the Church Lads' Brigade, which began taking mostly working-class boys on camping expeditions. The best known of them all, however, was the Scout movement. In the summer of 1907, Robert Baden-Powell, a lieutenant-general in the British Army, led the first experimental scout camp, at which twenty boys slept for around a week under canvas on an island off the Dorset coast. After Baden-Powell published *Scouting for Boys* the following year, such was the enthusiasm for this new pastime that groups of youths from across Britain began setting up their own troops, before any central organisation had been established. By the 1930s, more than a million British children were members of either the Boy Scouts or Girl Guides, and nearly all of them had been on a camping trip. Alternative, less militaristic groups were also emerging, such as the Woodcraft Folk, with its emphasis on international peace, friendship and social cooperation. It was partly the prospect of camping that made these youth movements so attractive to generations of young people.[22] The only reason I joined the Church of England Boys Society in suburban Sydney in the 1980s was because it offered bush camping trips; religion was the last thing on my mind.

Camping today exists in many forms, not all of which resemble the nomadic experience. Modern caravans are so well-appointed with television sets and other luxuries that they can be little different from people's own homes. The accompanying caravan parks often provide entertainment complexes complete with mini-golf, swimming pools and cinema screens, which could hardly be more different from a Bedouin encampment. You might have better luck visiting a New Age eco-camp, where you can stay in a solar-powered yurt or tipi, although the daily activity list is more likely to include meditation sessions than a nomadic pursuit such as herding goats. There is also the option of becoming what Australians call a 'grey nomad', which refers to retirees who spend most of the year camping in motor homes or recreational vehicles (RVs), moving from site to site around the country and throughout the year, having exchanged sedentary retirement for itinerant freedom.[23]

If your aim, however, is to touch something of our long history as nomadic travellers, it would probably be best to return to basics. That means putting a tent on your back and hiking with friends or other members of your tribe to some wild and isolated place for a week of camping. You will not need your iPod or hairdryer, just the kind of essential provisions that those first youth campers took with them a hundred years ago: some food, matches, a knife and wet-weather gear. The beauties and freedoms of camping are in its simplicity. And it is simplicity that ultimately defines the nomadic alternative. As twilight approaches, all you need do is light a fire and, sitting under the stars, stare into the flickering, mesmerising flames, like all the nomadic peoples before you.

## Explorer

What kind of traveller do you implicitly model yourself on? If not a pilgrim, a tourist or a nomad, you might see yourself as an explorer. School textbooks typically depict explorers in a heroic light: Christopher Columbus, Ferdinand Magellan and Francis Drake were, they say, adventurers and discoverers who risked their lives to fill in the blank spaces on our maps, expanding the world's geographic imagination. Yet for all the romantic associations, there is a darker side to reveal, which is that the history of exploration is inseparable from the history of racism. From the Spanish conquistadors of the Americas to the colonial expeditions in nineteenth-century Africa, explorers have been united by a widespread belief that the cultures they encountered were inferior to their own. Charles Darwin provides an example. When he arrived in Tierra del Fuego in 1834 on board the survey ship HMS *Beagle*, the 27-year-old naturalist declared the local inhabitants to be 'savages of the lowest grade'. Taking note of their 'filthy and greasy' skin and 'hideous faces bedaubed with white paint', he wrote in his journal:

Viewing such men, one can hardly make oneself believe that they are fellow-creatures, and inhabitants of the same world. It is a common subject of conjecture what pleasure in life some of the lower animals can enjoy: how much more reasonably the same question may be asked with respect to these barbarians![24]

That is why Mary Kingsley is such an unusual figure. Born in London in 1862, Kingsley received no formal education, yet by raiding her father's library managed to teach herself chemistry, mechanics and ethnography. She also immersed herself in the memoirs of explorers, and in 1893, filled with enthusiasm for foreign travel, embarked on her first trip to West Africa. She was a rare woman in a man's world, travelling alone most of the time, climbing the mountain peak of Great Cameroon and canoeing down the rapids of the Ogooué River. She is remembered by ichthyologists for discovering three species of small fish, which are duly named after her, and for being one of the most intrepid early female explorers, happy to stare a leopard in the eye.[25] 'Being human, she must have been afraid of something,' Rudyard Kipling wrote of her, 'but one never found out what it was.'[26] What made her truly remarkable, however, was her attitude to the so-called 'African races'.

A notorious letter Kingsley wrote to the *Spectator* newspaper in 1895 began with the accepted Victorian belief that 'the African races are inferior to the English, French, German, and Latin races'. But following this assertion, she broke the taboos of her age by arguing that the natives were far from being immoral savages. 'I have lived among and attempted to understand the Africans,' she explained, and in mental and moral affairs the African 'has both a sense of justice and honour', while 'in rhetoric he excels, and for good temper and patience compares favourably with any set of human beings'. Africans were no more cruel than any other race, she believed, and although their funeral rites might appear strange, they were little different from those of the ancient Greeks. Kingsley was ahead of her time in realising there was no such thing as the 'negro', noting that 'there is as much difference in the manners of life between say, an Ingalwa and a Bubi of Fernando Po, as there is between a Londoner and a Laplander'. While the gentlemen readers of the *Spectator* considered her views a shameless defence of barbarians and cannibals, she caused further uproar by comparing Africans favourably to Protestant missionaries, suggesting that the natives' good qualities 'are very easily eliminated by a course of Christian teaching'.[27]

The example of Mary Kingsley suggests we should rethink the meaning of being an explorer. The greatest explorers have not been those who pushed back the geographic frontiers on colonial maps, but rather those who have travelled beyond the frontiers of their own prejudices and assumptions – whether they are based on race, class, gender or religion. A successful expedition is one which challenges and alters our worldview, liberating us from the narrowness of deeply ingrained beliefs that we have often unconsciously inherited from culture, education and family. Mary Kingsley's experiences of travel did just this, exploding the racial prejudices about Africans that were the stuff of the Victorian drawing room. When an explorer returns from their travels, they will ideally have been invigorated not just by mountain air or desert landscapes, but by fresh perspectives on the world, and may find themselves inspired to take up a political cause, question their own privileges or abandon some cherished belief about God or human nature. We should return to the wisdom of Thomas Cook, who believed that the ultimate purpose of travel was to clear our minds of prejudice.

We must rewrite the history of travel, filling it with a new pantheon of worldview explorers. Forget Columbus or Pizarro, whose expeditions to the Americas paved the way for centuries of exploitation, such as the enslavement of indigenous people by the Spanish to work deep in the Potosí silver mines in the Andes, where hundreds of thousands of them died and were crippled during the colonial period.[28] Mary Kingsley is someone to admire. Apart from her, there are two other travellers whose journeying provides models for the future of exploration.

One of them is the farmer, journalist and politician William

Cobbett. Like George Orwell a century later, Cobbett ventured into his own country, setting out on travels through provincial England in an attempt to understand how the rise of industrial society was affecting the rural population. Travelling in the 1820s on horseback, usually with one of his sons or a manservant, he visited small towns and villages, trotted through agricultural lands, chatted with labourers trudging the roads, and all along the way kept a mental note of what he saw and heard for articles in the radical journal he edited, the *Political Register*, and for the travel book he published in 1830, *Rural Rides*.

Cobbett was appalled by the starvation wages and poverty of the agricultural workers he encountered. In *Rural Rides* he intertwined lyrical descriptions of the countryside with a devastating depiction of the havoc being wrought upon people's lives by the agricultural revolution and nineteenth-century capitalism. Noticing the rich abundance of food produced in the Wiltshire Avon valley, he exclaimed:

> What injustice, what a hellish system it must be, to make those who raise it skin and bone and nakedness, while the food and drink and wool are almost all carried away to be heaped on the fundholders, pensioners, soldiers, deadweight, and the other swarms of tax-eaters! If such an operation do not need putting an end to, then the devil himself must be a saint.[29]

Cobbett made sure to stop to talk to people and stay in local inns. He also practised self-discipline by fasting during his travels, and gave away what he saved on meals to the poor labourers he met.[30] His most admirable trait, though, was an ability to change his mind. Cobbett was a stubborn and prejudiced man who had a long list of hates including Anglican parsons, bankers, Scots and Quakers. But to his credit, he was willing to revise his opinions based on the experiences of his travels. Although expressing disdain for people from the North of England, once he travelled there he shifted his view and came to appreciate not only their farming techniques, but also their independence of mind. Similarly, in 1816 he had publicly criticised the Luddites for their hostility to machinery. But after seeing with his own eyes how machines had destroyed the jobs of women who had worked carding and spinning wool to make broadcloth, he admitted that 'mechanic inventions' have 'been productive of great calamity in this country'.[31] Travel, for Cobbett, was an antidote to the narrowness of his own worldview.

William Cobbett's journeys suggest that one way to be an explorer, and stretch the boundaries of our own worldview, is to embark on travels which are 'social projects'. Just as Cobbett chose to explore rural poverty, we can make a choice to travel in a way that is likely to give us radically new experiences that may challenge our customary ways of thinking and living. This is precisely what many (though not all) gap-year students are doing when they opt to spend six months working with street kids in Bogotá or volunteering in an orphanage in Romania. I once went for a summer to Guatemala and volunteered as a human rights monitor in a village of Mayan war refugees. This led to another trip, where I spent a week with balaclava-wearing Zapatista rebels and international activists in the Mexican jungle, discussing strategies to combat neoliberalism. These experiences fundamentally altered my attitudes towards politics, money, friendship and the kind of work I should be doing. As William Cobbett realised, this type of travel can easily take place much closer to home. You could volunteer in a shelter for people with mental illnesses, or for an organisation replanting lost hedgerows. Each year we might spend a week of our holidays engaged in similar project-oriented travel. Even that single week could have a major impact on our lives.

One of the towns Cobbett passed through was Stroud, in the Cotswold Hills of Gloucestershire. Almost a hundred years later, this was the birthplace of the poet and writer Laurie Lee, whose way of being an explorer differed from the 'social project' approach. Like Cobbett, he wished to expand his worldview, but the journey he undertook as a young man was less directed, more open to chance and possibilities. I think of Lee as an 'existential explorer', someone who consciously sought to escape from the confines of their limited experiences of life and the limits of social convention, yet without any clear idea of how to broaden their horizons, beyond feeling the need to encounter the freedoms of the open road. So on a summer morning in 1934, aged just nineteen, he abandoned the sleepy country village that was his home and, as he put it, 'left to discover the world'. Like the wandering pilgrim Bashō, he took few possessions – a tent, a fiddle, some biscuits and cheese – and set out on foot. He was now free, but he also felt 'affronted by freedom', sensing the burdens of his new liberty and responsibility for making his own way in life. Why did he leave the place of his childhood, his mother and siblings, his steady job as an office clerk in Stroud?

> I was propelled, of course, by the traditional forces that had sent many generations along this road – by the small tight valley closing in around one, stifling the breath with its mossy mouth, the cottage walls narrowing like the arms of an iron maiden, the local girls whispering, 'Marry, and settle down.'

Lee walked a hundred miles to London, worked there for some months as a labourer, then continued his journey to the coast and jumped on a boat to Spain. Over the course of the next year he walked across the country by foot, earning a living busking with his violin, sleeping outdoors or in flea-ridden guest houses. Reading his memoir of these formative travels, *As I Walked Out One Midsummer Morning* (1969), you become aware of his eyes and mind gradually opening through his meetings with peasants and gypsies, writers and soldiers. As he wandered through the Spanish landscape, Lee noticed the growing political tensions, and when he finally reached the southern coast, he was trapped by the outbreak of the civil war. Rescued by the British navy along with other travellers and expatriates, he eventually returned home.

Yet he could not stay there. He had left the Cotswolds far behind him. 'I'd been away two years, but was little the wiser for it,' he wrote. 'I was twenty-two, woolly-minded, and still naïve in everything, but I began to realize I'd come home too soon.' Lee was drawn back to Spain. This time, however, it was not as a busker, but as a soldier. His travels had, unknowingly, given him a political education, and he felt compelled to join the republican struggle against the fascists. 'I hadn't consciously chosen it as a Cause but had stumbled on it by accident, simply by happening to be there.'[32] So he set out from England once more, this time to the French Pyrenees. From there, with the help of some anarchist villagers, he made a dramatic and dangerous journey over the mountains and down into Spain, where he joined the International Brigades and entered the stream of the rest of his life.

Unlike William Cobbett, Laurie Lee could never have predicted his pathway when he first left home. But he knew he had to leave, even if he was not sure where to go. The power of existential exploration is this strange mixture of certainty and uncertainty. You feel compelled to turn your back on the past, but through not knowing your exact destination, you remain open enough to embrace the offerings of different ways of living and thinking that you may happen to encounter, which lie waiting in places beyond your imagination.

Travel today is often approached as a form of escape. We long for 'getaway' holidays that offer temporary relief from the strains of our jobs or pressures of family life. We want to relax and switch off for a while, without having to be stuck in commuter traffic or to cook meals for our kids every day. So we dream of lying on a secluded beach or treating ourselves to a few nights in a top hotel. Vacations like this are often just what we think we need to rejuvenate before throwing ourselves back into our normal lives. They are a form of survival mechanism.

At first glance, the approaches to travel I have discussed – as a pilgrim, tourist, nomad and explorer – might seem like too much effort if you are in search of escape and looking to put up your feet and take it easy. Can you really be bothered to set out on some wandering pilgrimage or a conversational journey into your local community? We might remember, though, that embarking on an experimental journey can be viewed as 'time on' – an integral part of our lives – rather than 'time off'. We may well return in an altered state, having discovered worlds which appear on no maps, and in no guidebooks.

# 9

# Nature

NAKED HE PLUNGES INTO MAINE WOODS TO LIVE ALONE TWO MONTHS. In August 1913 the *Boston Post* ran this headline for a report about a part-time illustrator and former hunting guide, Joseph Knowles, who had stripped off in front of a crowd of journalists and marched into the Maine wilderness for a sensational 'man versus nature' experiment. Intending to live off the land just 'as Adam lived', Knowles took no equipment with him – no knife, food, clothes or map. His aim, he said, was 'to prove that man, though handicapped with the habits of civilization, is the physical equal of his early ancestors'.

Over the course of his adventure, Knowles became a celebrity. Every few days he wrote a journal on birch bark using charcoal, leaving his dispatch in a secret spot for a *Post* journalist to collect and convey to the world. The eager public read how the 44-year-old had fashioned shoes from rushes, made fire by rubbing sticks together like a caveman, and had dined on berries, trout and even venison – having strangled a deer with his bare hands. On 24 August they were astounded to discover that he had lured a bear into a pit and clubbed it to death, making a coat from its skin. When a healthy Knowles emerged back into civilisation, draped in bearskin, tens of thousands greeted his motorcade as it passed through Boston. Knowles spoke of the virtues of a simple, primitive life, and declared that he had been on a spiritual journey. 'My God is in the wilderness,' he said, 'the great open book of nature is my religion. My church is the church of the forest.' Knowles went on to write a bestseller, *Alone*

*Joseph Knowles, moments before his departure into the Maine woods in 1913.*

*in the Wilderness* (1914), and toured the vaudeville circuit with his dramatic story. Accusations that his venture was a fraud neither dampened his popularity nor prevented the Maine authorities from fining him $205 for killing a bear out of season.[1]

Joseph Knowles' instant fame reflected a new public fascination with the wilderness that had not existed in the United States a century earlier: when Henry David Thoreau had published his first book of nature travels in 1849, it sold only a few hundred copies. But it also showed how divorced Americans had become from nature. Most people were now living in the big cities or small towns, not out in the woods or on the prairies like the early pioneers. Knowles stood out because he was an exception to the rule, and was treated as much a freak as he was a hero. Who was this incredible Tarzan who could wrestle a bear to the ground?

The response to Knowles reflects the complex human relationship to the natural world. Today, most of us are not much different from those Boston newspaper readers a hundred years ago. We have a yearning for nature, and dream of escaping the city to ramble in the countryside or hike up a mountain. Yet we are also desperately alienated from nature. It is something we watch voyeuristically on television in wildlife documentaries and outdoor survival programmes, or cultivate in our tame suburban gardens. Few people make a habit of sleeping out under the stars or alone in forests.

So how should we relate to nature, and what role should it play in our lives? And why treat nature as an 'it' – are we not, after all, part of the natural world? Our approaches to nature have changed radically over the centuries, with equally radical implications for the ways we choose to live. These changes have occurred in three realms: nature as an object of beauty, as a source of mental wellbeing and as an economic resource.

## How woods and mountains became beautiful

Forests have always had a role in human society. They have been a source of building timber and firewood, of wild game and foods like mushrooms, and have been sites of spiritual veneration, especially in pagan traditions. They have not, however, always been considered places of beauty. During the Middle Ages, especially in parts of Northern Europe, they developed a reputation for being places of darkness and fear, the home of evil spirits, trolls and wild beasts. In Germany you might have been attacked by werewolves or a semi-human Wild Man, a kind of ogre covered with coarse hair who ate children and ravished maidens. Anglo-Saxon folk tales, such as the eighth-century *Beowulf*, frequently set the action in menacing forests, a legacy inherited by the stories of Tolkein, in which friendly hobbits are petrified at the thought of having to pass through the haunted Fangorn Forest or the shadowy Mirkwood. Out of this medieval vision comes our word 'savage', derived from *silva*, meaning a wood, much as 'panic' comes from the ancient Greeks' dread of running into Pan, the half-man, half-goat lord of the woods.[2]

This wary, negative attitude towards wild landscapes, particularly dense forests and mountains, began to permeate culture and language. A poetical dictionary from the seventeenth century suggested that appropriate words to describe a forest were

*A Germanic Wild Man wielding an uprooted tree trunk by Hans Holbein the Younger (1528). After the Middle Ages these men became progressively less hairy and aggressive. Many German towns still celebrate a medieval festival each January in which the inhabitants dress up as Wild Men and dance around, swinging tree trunks.*[3]

'gloomy,' 'dreadful' and 'uncouth,' and when William Bradford stepped off the *Mayflower* in 1620 onto the wooded shore of Plymouth Harbour, he described the scene as a 'hideous and desolate wilderness'. In the late seventeenth century Celia Fiennes, a pioneering woman traveller, thought the Lake District to be 'desert and barren' and its mountains 'very terrible', a stark contrast to our vision of it today as one of the most beautiful places in Britain. More generally, in many parts of Europe mountains were derided as 'deformities', 'warts', 'boils' and 'monstrous excrescences', probably because they were so difficult to cultivate. Where such ideas prevailed, few people would have thought to stop to admire a mountain view, and no self-respecting artist of the Renaissance would have painted a craggy, snow-capped peak.

By the eighteenth century, however, mountains and other natural landscapes had become objects of the highest aesthetic admiration. This shift was thanks to the Romantic movement, which revolutionised the Western perception of nature. According to the art historian Kenneth Clark, its defining moment was in 1739, when the English poet Thomas Gray, while visiting the French Alps, declared to a friend, 'Not a precipice, not a torrent, not a cliff, but is pregnant with religion and poetry.' Mountains were no longer an unproductive nuisance or the home of Wild Men and bandits, but the ideal place to find the soul of man and commune with the divine. It wasn't long before Goethe was swimming naked with his friends in mountain lakes, and pallid poets were scrambling up escarpments. By middle age, Wordsworth was believed to have walked 180,000 miles, much of it in his beloved Lake District, and in the late nineteenth century the English led the way in a new European craze of mountain climbing. Woods and trees were increasingly believed to be worthy of devotion. In 1872 a group of German students from Göttingen University spent the night under the moon in an ancient oak grove, swearing Druidical oaths of friendship and fraternity, their hands linked by garlands of oak leaves. The Victorians published books venerating ancient trees, and in 1879 Gerard Manley Hopkins wrote of his sorrow at the felling of a row of poplars outside Oxford, 'O if we but knew what we do / When we delve or hew – / Hack and rack the growing green!' Overturning centuries of fear and revulsion, the Romantics had transformed nature into a source of the sublime.[4]

The medieval Church had done its best to stamp out the pagan worship of trees, rivers and other features of the natural world. True Christians had little time for ancient folk festivals such as May Day – rooted in the Celtic celebration of Beltane and the Germanic Walpurgis Night – when revellers lit bonfires and wrapped themselves in leaves to become Green Men. That was for Druids and backward peasants, not for the Children of God. Romanticism was a threat to the established Church because it took religion back to nature. Coleridge had his poetic character Christabel pray beneath a huge old oak, and while climbing a Lakeland pass during a violent thunderstorm the poet exclaimed, 'God is everywhere.' If you could, like Coleridge, see God everywhere in nature, what need was there for preachers and crucifixes and Sunday Services? The philosophy of Transcendentalism, which emerged in North America in the nineteenth century, was influenced by these Romantic ideas. 'Nature is a symbol of the spirit,' declared Ralph Waldo Emerson in 1836, encapsulating the Transcendentalist ideal that nature is the proper source of religion. Immersion in nature, believed Henry David Thoreau, could elevate mankind from the coarseness of material life to a higher spiritual plane.[5]

This startling change in Western attitudes towards nature drew on the collective memory of pagan traditions, but romanticism was also a response to economic and social upheavals. The veneration of nature was a product of its degradation and growing scarcity. Mass agriculture was laying waste to wild places, and the clearing of old-growth forests was considered necessary for the advance of civilisation. Millions of acres of ancient woodland were lost in England between 1500 and 1700. By the eighteenth century the country was covered with places named 'forest', 'grove' or 'park' which had been turned over to crops and pasture. This process was exacerbated by the most scandalous example of privatisation in British history, the 'enclosure' of common lands by the upper classes, which escalated from the Tudor period onwards. Between 1760 and 1837, using dubious Acts of Parliament, the elite stole some 7 million acres of land – much of it woodland – which had previously been publicly owned, and converted it to profitable agricultural use.[6] The stately homes that so many people admire and visit today were often built with money made from destroying woods that had stood for centuries.

Romanticism was equally a response to urbanisation and industrialisation. In the eighteenth century, the philosopher Jean-Jacques Rousseau popularised the notion that modern society was a corrupting force, creating inequality and fuelling obsessions with wealth, status and moral vice. In the state of nature, he believed, we were essentially good. Although he never used the term himself, Rousseau was associated with the idea of the 'noble savage', who became a primitive icon of the Romantic movement. As the industrial revolution progressed, city dwellers were struggling against poverty, suffocated by coal smoke and succumbing to cholera epidemics. In 1810 William Blake wrote of the 'dark satanic mills' that were destroying England's 'green and pleasant land' and turning workers into machines. Rural life was increasingly imagined as an idyllic alternative to urban squalor – just as it still is now.[7]

The Romantics' contribution to the art of living was to show how nature could help us discover our souls. Most of us can appreciate the kind of beauty and spiritual depths that they began to sense in the eighteenth century. If you have ever stood in a secluded woodland grove, silenced by the beauty of dappled sunlight passing through the whispering leaves, you have entered the Romantic mode. If you have climbed a mountain, and stared with awe and wonder at the immensity of creation, then you have viewed the world through Romantic eyes. In my early twenties, I began following in the footsteps of my Romantic literary heroes. I scaled peaks in the Lake District with Coleridge's notebooks in my hand, treading the same pathways. I walked through German forests with Goethe looking over my shoulder. I swam in luminous Italian grottoes where Byron had frolicked in the 1820s. I listened to the ice crack on a Massachusetts lake, inspired by Thoreau. These experiences took place without any thought of God: nature, I realised, was impressive enough in its own right. The beauty I found in these

*In paintings like* The Mountains at Lauteraar *(1776), Caspar Wolf depicted the terrifying beauty of the Swiss Alps. Hikers scramble up the rocks to admire the view. Before the rise of romanticism in the eighteenth century, few travellers would have recognised this as a beautiful landscape deserving of their attentions.[8]*

places, and that indescribable sense of communion with nature that I often felt, would have been understood by the Romantics, even if they may have made fun of my self-conscious attempts to imitate them.

The problem with romanticism is that it can be a little too pristine. Reading the great poets of the era, it often appears that it was all about gazing at sublime views and appreciating the changing light, rather than really delving into the wilderness and getting yourself grubby and mud-splattered. In the past two decades, the Romantic vision has been updated through a new cult of the wild. We can read books which entice us to root about in the bracken and climb up trees during storms, rather than follow the example of Wordsworth and serenely contemplate a gently swaying daffodil. In *Wild* (2006), an account of a seven-year journey into the heart of our wild natures, Jay Griffiths tells us that we are all 'homesick for wildness'. The human spirit, she says, 'has a primal allegiance to wildness, to really live, to snatch the fruit and suck it, to spill the juice. We may think we are domesticated but we are not. Feral in pheromone and intuition, feral in our sweat and fear ... this is the first command: to live in fealty to the feral angel.'[9] Her advice is to get dirt under our fingernails and have ice cracking on our lips, to wander in lonely places and experience the fear of the night. It is not so much beauty that we should seek in nature, but savagery.

We can indeed escape the confines of our plastic, halogen, digital lives by stepping out the door into nature, searching for beauty and meaning like the Romantics, or perhaps a more savage variety of the wild, if we can find it. But we might also draw lessons from our pagan ancestors. We could join those who have been reviving the ancient spring festival of May Day, which is celebrated right across Europe, dressing ourselves in green garlands and dancing around the maypole. Similarly, we might decide to observe the summer and winter solstices, perhaps treating them as times when we don't work, and choosing instead to walk across the hills or plunge into cool rivers as the sun rises. It is not necessary to be a Druid to embrace the pagan spirit, or to prostrate yourself before an oak or Stonehenge. We can each create our own rituals to get in tune with the natural rhythms that existed long before the beat of our iPods.

## Biophilia and the ecological self

Although human beings have searched for beauty in nature, an alternative has been to test themselves against it. This more confronting relationship with the natural world may be familiar to those who pursue extreme outdoor sports. Since the Victorian era, mountaineers and rock climbers have been pitting their physical prowess and mental stamina against vertical cliffs and walls of ice. Why do they do it? When the British mountaineer George Mallory was asked in the 1920s why he wanted to climb Everest, his famous – and possibly apocryphal – reply was, 'Because it's there.' But that doesn't explain very much. Some extreme athletes seek the adrenaline that comes with taking risks, or thrive on achieving goals they have spent months training for, or hope to enter a state of 'flow' where the past and future melt away and they become completely absorbed in a timeless present. There are those who love the solitude of being in a wild, lonely place, while others desire the kudos that comes with their heroic ventures, just as Joseph Knowles did.

Understanding the mentality of people who challenge themselves in the harshest natural environments provides an insight into the role that nature can play in nourishing our minds and bodies, and even into the boundaries of our sense of self. A revealing case concerns Christopher Johnson McCandless, who in the early 1990s abandoned civilisation for the remote Alaskan wilderness. Although from the recent past, he is representative of a long tradition of American adventurers and frontiersmen, stretching back to Daniel Boone in the eighteenth century, who were lured by romantic dreams and personal challenge to survive alone in the rawness of nature.

Chris McCandless grew up in the wealthy suburbs of Virginia, where his father was a successful space scientist who had designed radar systems for NASA. Chris always had an adventurous spirit: at the age of two he had got up in the middle of the night and toddled down the street into a neighbour's home to raid the sweet drawer. He was an intense and earnest teenager but also had a gregarious side and loved to bang out honky-tonk tunes on the family piano. Although not keen to attend college, he succumbed to parental pressure and went to Emory University, where he was an A-grade student. But immediately after graduating in 1990, Chris vanished. He gave his $25,000 savings to charity, drove out into the Nevada desert where he abandoned his car, then burned the money left in his wallet. At last he was free. Over the next two years he became a professional hobo. He jumped trains, camped out in the wilds of South Dakota and almost killed himself kayaking down the Colorado River. He changed his name to Alexander Supertramp and told nobody who knew him of his whereabouts.

In April 1992, Chris was finally ready for what he called his 'great Alaskan adventure'. He hitchhiked north and walked into the wilderness carrying little more than a bag of rice, a hunting rifle and a sleeping bag, intent on spending a few months living off the land in total isolation. By chance he discovered an abandoned bus, which he made his temporary home. Over the following weeks he learned to shoot game and cut hunting trails with his machete, and kept up a simple diary. 'No longer to be poisoned by civilization he flees,' Chris wrote in the third person, 'and walks alone upon the land to become lost in the wild.' Revelling in his freedom, he declared, 'I am reborn. This is my dawn. Real life has just begun.' Another joyous entry read simply, 'CLIMB MOUNTAIN!' On a piece of wood he carved 'Jack London is King', paying homage to his childhood hero who a century earlier had romantically portrayed outdoor life in Alaska and the Yukon in classics like *The Call of the Wild*.

By late June the hunting had become difficult, food was running low and he was rapidly losing weight. It was time to leave. He packed his rucksack and walked back the way he had come. But the shallow river Chris had crossed on his trek into the ranges was now swollen into a raging torrent and was too dangerous to cross. Without any map to guide him out – unknown to him there was a safe crossing point a few miles downstream – he felt he had no choice but to return to the bus. There he remained, increasingly scared and lonely. His rice was gone and he was forced to scavenge for berries. Then, on 30 July, came a fateful entry in his diary: 'Extremely weak. Fault of pot. seed. Much trouble just to stand up. Starving. Great jeopardy.' He had, it seems, misidentified a plant in his botanical guide and accidentally been eating poisonous wild potato seeds. In large quantities they cause emaciation and eventual death from starvation.

Chris died not long after his hundredth day on the bus. Three weeks later, his body was found by hunters, zipped up in his sleeping bag.

In the book *Into the Wild* (1996) – also made into a film – Chris's biographer Jon Krakauer attempts to understand what had driven him to such an extreme escape from society and embrace of the wilderness. Part of the answer emerges in a letter Chris wrote to an elderly man he had met, just before leaving for Alaska:

So many people live with unhappy circumstances and yet will not take the initiative to change their situation because they are conditioned to a life of security, conformity, and conservatism, all of which may appear to give one peace of mind, but in reality nothing is more damaging to the adventurous spirit within a man than a secure future.

Chris thought that the greatest mistake we could make in life was to swap our individual freedom for the deceptive comforts of stability and financial security. Real life could never be found by having a nice house and garden in the suburbs. Like Rousseau, he believed society and its obsession with money corrupted our inner goodness. While on the bus he meticulously read and annotated his favourite authors such as Thoreau and Tolstoy, revealing his admiration for their rejection of industrial society and their belief in an ascetic lifestyle close to nature. In the nineteenth century, according to the cultural historian Roderick Nash, journeying into the American wilderness appealed to the Romantic individual who was 'bored or disgusted with man and his works'. Chris was such a Romantic, admittedly of the more edgy, feral variety.

Yet beneath the Romantic vision lay a deeper, psychological explanation of his actions. Chris was running away from his dysfunctional family. He hated his controlling father and was haunted by memories of violence in the family home. In his late teens he was devastated when he discovered that his morally upright father had had an affair. Only the wild could offer him the mental solace he needed. The British psychiatrist and rock climber John Menlove Edwards regarded climbing as a 'psycho-neurotic tendency', in which the climber finds refuge from the inner torment that frames his existence. Chris was tormented and his escape into the wild should be read, ultimately, as a self-imposed nature cure – which happened to go horribly wrong.[10]

The story of Chris McCandless provides a vital clue for understanding the topography of the human mind. It suggests that nature is intimately related to our mental wellbeing. Since the 1980s this phenomenon has had a name: biophilia. Coined by the Harvard evolutionary biologist Edward Wilson, it refers to our 'innate tendency to focus on life and lifelike processes'. We are drawn to nature 'like moths to a torchlight'.[11] Biophilia explains why, like Chris McCandless, we often find ourselves inexplicably attracted to wild places as a cure for our ills. If we feel anxious or stressed, we know that a quiet walk in a leafy wood or along the coast path in sight of the sea will help restore mental calm. Even an hour weeding in the garden, smelling the dank soil, hearing a little birdsong and noticing the first shoots of spring, can be restorative.

Wilson and other biophilia experts argue that the reason why a touch of the wild can be so healing has roots in the depths of human psychohistory. For millions of years our primordial brains evolved on the semi-wooded grasslands of the African savannah. We feel most psychologically at ease when inhabiting similar landscapes, or when by the water's edge, which for so long was a sign of abundant food. Conversely, we can have a negative biophobic response to inhospitable landscapes, such as dense forests or parched deserts, which our ancient inner brains register as places to avoid. An environment devoid of nature altogether – such as our tarmacked megacities – can be seriously bad for our health. Why do we cheer up our offices with a few pot plants? Biophilia.[12]

Although the word is new, biophilia has always been with us. Samuel Hammond, an American lawyer who began camping in the Adirondack Mountains in the 1840s, wrote: 'I have generally gone into the woods weakened in body and depressed in mind. I have always come out of them with renewed health and strength, a perfect digestion, and a buoyant and cheerful spirit.'[13] That buoyancy was a biophilic response: nature healing both body and mind. No doubt those Romantic poets mesmerised by mountain streams were not only seeing beauty and religion in nature, but were also having an unconscious biophilic reaction to the landscape, such as when Wordsworth spoke of the 'soothing influences of nature'.[14] It may be that the antipathy towards wild woods in the Middle Ages was in part a biophobic reaction to a dangerous environment, but equally the cultural myths about the dark and menacing forests might have been too powerful for our instinctive biophilia to overcome.

The scientific evidence for biophilia has grown rapidly in recent decades. A study showed that patients in a Pennsylvania hospital who had their gall bladder removed and who had a view of greenery outside their windows recovered more quickly and required fewer painkillers than those whose rooms looked out on a brick wall. Horticultural therapy projects demonstrate the positive effects for people with mental illnesses of digging an allotment or tending a garden, while dozens of studies of recreation experiences in the wilderness reveal that stress mitigation is one of the most noticeable benefits. Neuropsychologists have more success with their patients when treating them in lush conservatories than in sparse clinical rooms. Children as young as five have significant reductions in the symptoms of attention-deficit disorder when they engage with nature, which has prompted the author and journalist Richard Louv to believe that they may actually be suffering from 'nature-deficit disorder'. Unlike children a few decades ago, modern kids spend most of the day staring at computers and television, and have little time or inclination for climbing trees or exploring the bush. As one San Diego fifth-grader put it, 'I like to play indoors better 'cause that's where all the electrical outlets are.' The result can be depression and other mental health problems. Today's children are being starved of the contact with nature they require to meet their innate biophilic needs.[15]

The historically unprecedented extent of urbanisation in the West is a major part of the problem. We are suffering from a nature deficit more than any previous generation. We may not realise it until we spend more time outdoors, away from the high-speed and stressful city lives that have become our worst addiction. Most of us are in need of a curative dose of nature as a regular part of our lives – and thankfully the medicine is unlikely to be as extreme as hiking out into the Alaskan wilderness. As we walk through a local wood or sit watching a river flow by, our anxieties are likely to fade, and we will know that biophilia is doing its gentle, restoring work.

Biophilia also prompts us to radically rethink who we are. For a century, psychoanalysis has assumed that our physical body, our outer skin, provides the boundary of the self. Obvious, right? The mind lies within it, and therapy is the process of intro- spectively exploring our inner being. But biophilia suggests that our minds are, at least in part, located outside our corporeal selves. This view of the self is central to the developing field of 'ecopsychology', founded by the historian and environmental thinker Theodore Roszak. The idea is that if our mental well- being is intimately linked with nature through phenomena such as biophilia, then our psychological self is not separate from nature but part of it. When we look in the mirror, we are only seeing a portion of who we are; the rest is reflected in the scenery in the background. 'The psyche,' says Roszak, 'remains sympa- thetically bonded to the Earth that mothered us into existence.'[16] We possess an 'ecological unconscious' that lies at the core of our being. When we step into the wild, we respect and nurture it. When we destroy nature and live apart from it, we are effectively destroying ourselves. Biophilia reveals the intricate relationship between each of us and the biosphere, and tells us that we are part of Gaia herself.

The notion of a sense of self that extends into the natural world may have little precedent in recent Western history, but it sounds familiar to many indigenous cultures, which see an inte- gral unity between human beings and the earth. 'Is not the sky a father, and the earth a mother, and are not all living things with feet and roots their children?' said the Sioux holy man Black Elk. Or as an indigenous Australian elder explains, 'We are a spirit- ual people who believe we come from the land; in a sense we are the land, and the land owns us.'[17] In the Popul Vuh, the Mayan book of the dawn of life, human beings are described as being made from maize. Such cultures carry the wisdom of biophilia deep within them.

Biophilia has the potential to dramatically transform our thinking about personal identity, and more generally reminds us that the art of living wisely and well may require us to embrace a closer relationship with the natural world. 'I am at two with nature,' quipped Woody Allen. Ironic for a man named Woody, but he was probably more at one with it than he realised.

## How to live after the end of nature

There are moments in history when the art of living undergoes fundamental change. Our understanding of our place in the world is transformed, the parameters of choice are altered and we are compelled to radically reassess what we value in life. The last time this took place was during the industrial revolution, which caused major upheavals in our approaches to work, time, family life and love. Today we are immersed in another of these moments, which stems from the environmental destruction caused by biodiversity loss, climate change and the depletion of non-renewable resources. Species extinction has accelerated exponentially over the past hundred years: many kinds of fish, birds, ferns and beetles are rapidly disappearing on every continent, threatening the collapse of fragile ecosystems.[18] The inhabitants of rich nations bear the main responsibility for abusing the planet, with just 14 per cent of the world's population – from countries like the USA, Japan and Western Europe – having produced 60 per cent of the world's carbon emissions since 1850.[19] This new ecological context has implications not only for how society is organised, but for our conception of the good life, since the unbridled enjoyment of carbon-intensive consumerism – currently the dominant approach to 'quality of life' in the West – no longer seems desirable or even possible. Understanding how we arrived at this turning point, and discovering ways forward, requires a journey into the history of our relationship with nature – not nature as a source of beauty, spirituality or mental wellbeing, but as an economic resource.

Humans have always used the earth to sustain their lives. Yet it was not until the sixteenth century that European culture firmly adopted its most reckless ideology since the Dark Ages: that the world had been created for man's sake, and that nature was there to be plundered for his benefit. It was an ideology based on classical conceptions of human uniqueness, which was reinforced by Christian thought, early capitalism and the development of nation states.

The idea of nature as man's resource had its roots in the belief that human beings were distinct from, and superior to, other creatures that inhabited the earth. Classical sources provided a veneer of justification. Aristotle had said that humans were alone in possessing rationality – and in being unable to wiggle their ears. By the Renaissance, others had suggested that they were the only creatures to have speech, make tools or display a spiritual conscience. But the primary distinguishing quality was usually thought to be reason. In 1610 the English poet and soldier Gervase Markham claimed that horses had no brains at all: he had personally cut open several skulls of dead horses and found nothing inside. The difference between man and beast was most sharply drawn by René Descartes, who in the 1630s argued that animals were mere machines or automata, like clocks, while humans had minds and souls. This soon became the standard view. Surely there could be nothing wrong with using soulless machines to plough your fields, or skewering a few for your evening meal. Medieval Britons rarely ate meat, but by 1726, Londoners were annually killing 600,000 sheep and 200,000 cattle.[20]

Environmental historians also place much of the blame for the pillaging of resources on the established Christian Church. Between the sixteenth and eighteenth centuries, propelled by the development of Europe's money economy, preachers offered resolutely anthropocentric interpretations of the Bible to justify exploiting nature. They pointed out that in Genesis, God gave Adam 'dominion' over the earth: 'Every moving thing that liveth shall be meat for you,' God tells man. In other words, the whole of physical creation – fish, birds, cows, forests – existed to serve man's purposes. This God-given right to ravage nature was reinforced by Christianity's destruction of paganism, in which every tree, river and animal had its guardian spirit. The result, writes Lynn White, was that 'Christianity made it possible to exploit nature in a mood of indifference to the feelings of natural objects'. This was a recipe for ecological disaster.

Although some religious scholars argue that 'dominion' really meant 'stewardship' rather than 'domination', and point out that St Francis preached to birds and wolves, accepted Christian doctrine firmly supported, and even encouraged, an abusive attitude towards the environment.[21]

Religion would have wreaked far less havoc had it not been for the influence of European capitalism, whose rise after the Middle Ages sounded a death knell for the natural world. Capitalism required energy to fuel the drive for profits and growth, and the great technological revolution was the use of coal to power industrial development. It was used to produce bricks, tiles and sheet glass; it was the basis of iron manufacturing; it heated bakers' ovens and family homes. Annual coal production in the Newcastle Basin – Europe's epicentre of coal mining – increased from 30,000 tonnes in 1563 to around 2 million tonnes by 1800.[22] Coal was the secret ingredient of the growing culture of consumption. But it could not happen without the mines creating scars across the landscape and carbon being pumped into the atmosphere. The ideology that the earth existed for the economic wellbeing of the expanding population was so entrenched that most people did not question their actions or consider the consequences. The concept of wilderness conservation did not yet exist. Every standard economics text, from Adam Smith's eighteenth-century classic *The Wealth of Nations* onwards, treated natural resources like coal exclusively as a 'factor of production' – a tool for economic growth.[23] Capitalism required denying any intrinsic value to planetary resources and wild places.

The impact of religion and capitalism was exacerbated by emerging nation states, which viewed their own territory – and their colonies – as a ready resource to expand their power. In Britain, trees were felled on an almost unimaginable scale to build ships for the Royal Navy, decimating the ancient royal forests. At the end of the eighteenth century, a seventy-four-gun ship required 2,000 mature oaks of two tons each. And that was just for the keel. 'To cut down trees,' writes the historian Keith Thomas, 'was to strike a blow for progress.'[24]

It would be wrong, however, to assume that this ideology of

resource exploitation was uniquely associated with Christianity and European economic and political development. A similar pillaging of the wilds took place, for instance, in Japan between the sixteenth and eighteenth centuries. Pre-industrial Japan was as dependent on wood as we are today on oil, and in feeding the population's hunger for timber the old-growth forests on the three main islands were largely destroyed. Trees were needed for everything from building castles, palaces and shrines for the elite – all constructed almost entirely from wood – to providing peasants with firewood and charcoal. By the late 1700s, the country was left with bald mountainsides where there had once been dense woodland, and an increasingly fragile economy due to a crisis of timber scarcity. According to environmental historian Conrad Totman, Japan seemed to be a society 'bent on accomplishing its own destruction'. Japanese poets may have been writing haikus about cherry blossoms, but almost everybody else, especially the ruling Shoguns, was busy chopping the trees down.[25]

The damage began to be mitigated in the eighteenth and nineteenth centuries by reforestation policies in Japan, England and other European countries. Trees even became a profitable crop, and English aristocrats planted them in the tens of thousands on their estates. Yet this managed forestry could hardly make up for the ecological harm wrought over hundreds of years, and nobody could replace the coal and other fossil fuels such as oil and natural gas which were being extracted from the ground. A sign of hope was the gradual development of a conservation ethic in the nineteenth century, partly inspired by the Romantic movement and the emergence of the study of natural history, which fostered curiosity about botany, zoology and geology. The United States created the first national reserves protecting the wilderness – Yosemite in 1864, Yellowstone in 1872 and the Grand Canyon in 1908. Leaders of the US conservation movement such as the Transcendentalist John Muir, founder of the Sierra Club in 1892, became public icons. But none of this was enough to halt economic growth, consumerism and a rising global population from laying waste to the natural world in the twentieth century.

Citizens of the world's rich countries are the inheritors of a 500-year legacy of treating nature as a resource – as a commodity to own, and to devour or squander at will. If everyone on the planet consumed natural resources at the rate of the average European, we would need more than two planet Earths to sustain us. Consuming at the US rate, we would need nearly five.[26] Yet even when faced with such statistics it can be difficult to comprehend our personal impact on the environment, unless we happen to live next door to an open-pit coal mine or an Amazon logging region. My own eyes only began to open when I visited Britain's Eden Project and saw a sculpture called the WEEE man – whose acronym stands for 'waste from electrical and electronic equipment'. It is a huge robotic figure, standing seven metres high and weighing 3.3 tonnes, constructed entirely from electrical products, with its teeth made of computer mouses, its brain from old monitors and its body full of fridges, microwave ovens, washing machines and mobile phones. This menacing creature represents the average amount of electrical equipment each of us will use and throw away during our lifetimes. The WEEE man is the ecological doppelgänger of the typical Westerner. Gazing up at it, I could see that I had been constructing a personal WEEE man all my life, churning through my share of laptops, stereos and other electrical detritus.

We now know the result of our plundering of natural resources and addiction to fossil fuels: man-made climate change. How can we absorb the meaning of this reality? On one level we should aim to educate ourselves about it, for instance by reading books and expert reports on the causes and consequences of global warming, which offer far more depth than the brief news stories on which we base many of our opinions. But we should also look through the lens of cultural history. We have entered a new era, which the environmental writer Bill McKibben calls 'the end of nature'. For most of human history we have imagined nature as an independent force that is larger than ourselves. We have endured its violent storms and long dark winters, marvelled at its beautiful sunsets and felt its cool breezes on our brows. Even when we've inflicted damage – polluting rivers or

223

blowing the tops off mountains – we've never really thought that nature has been broken beyond repair. Until now. Climate change has altered the very fabric of the planet. We have become the weather makers. As McKibben explains,

> We are no longer able to think of ourselves as a species tossed about by larger forces – now we *are* those larger forces. Hurricanes and thunderstorms and tornadoes become not acts of God but acts of man.

This is what the end of nature means. It is the death of an idea – of nature as a separate, wild realm. We have turned nature into something artificial. Next time you exclaim, 'How lovely to see the snowdrops out already!' you must remember that their early appearance has, to some extent, been reconfigured by human beings, whose actions are altering the seasons. 'A child born now will never know a natural summer, a natural autumn, winter or spring,' says McKibben. 'Summer is going extinct, replaced by something else that will be called "summer".'[27] Although we might believe there are still a few pristine places in nature largely untouched by man, like the Alaskan wilderness visited by Chris McCandless, we are mistaken. Climate change is everywhere, touches everything. After 12,000 years in the remarkably stable geological age known as the Holocene, we have moved ourselves into what climate scientists are now calling the Anthropocene, a label signalling our massive impact on the earth's ecosystems.

What does the end of nature mean for the art of living? On the most obvious level it is about putting ourselves on a carbon detox diet. We now understand what this involves: fewer plane flights; bikes, trains and buses instead of cars; switching to green electricity or solar heating; insulating our homes. That is, breaking the ingrained habit of high-carbon consumerism. Some people thrive on the community created by establishing car-sharing clubs and relish the simple joys of having a shower heated by the solar vacuum tubes on their rooftop. Others are reluctant to give up their gas-guzzling four-wheel drives and become experts at denying the significance of global warming. What is clear is that we cannot just rely on governments to take action to limit runaway climate change – we must also rely on ourselves.

On a more fundamental level, however, it is about recognising an astonishing cultural transformation: within only two decades, climate change has shifted the ethical boundaries of what constitutes the good life. Especially in the West, we inhabit an increasingly ecologically sensitive milieu in which carbon-intensive pleasures and lifestyle options are far less enviable or socially acceptable than they used to be. An example is global travel, which until recently was a standard component of what most people considered 'quality of life'. In the 1990s I could think of nothing I wanted to do more than fly all over the world to exotic and adventurous destinations. So I accumulated passport stamps from Indonesia, Mexico, Spain, Sydney, Hong Kong. But as I gradually understood the implications of climate change and learned that flight emissions were by far my largest personal contribution to it, such a lifestyle choice no longer seemed morally defensible, since people in developing countries and future generations everywhere – including my own children – would suffer as a result of my actions. And as public discussion of low-carbon living became commonplace in the new millennium, I also felt increasingly embarrassed admitting to friends that I was catching a budget flight abroad for a holiday. As a result, I have been trying – with mixed success – to wean myself off flying.

This has not simply been a personal choice, but reflects a wider contextual change in the ethical parameters of the art of living. Despite the best efforts of the airline companies, international air travel has lost its moral innocence. Such changes have happened before. Today few people would approve of owning a slave who cooked and cleaned for them, even though this was, in the past, a widespread lifestyle aspiration: enslaving another human being for our pleasures is no longer morally acceptable. The end of nature is challenging us to shift our minds into a new paradigm of the good life which is based not on a high-carbon consumerist ethos, but on a sustainable relationship with our fragile world. As with the transition from the slave economy, the transition from the carbon economy requires us to redefine freedom and discover fulfilment in new areas of our lives, like swapping our usual holiday on a Greek island – which requires a plane flight – for camping in a wild place near our home. As the climate change campaigner and writer George Marshall argues, we need to think about a low-carbon lifestyle not as a hair-shirt option which deprives us of consumer comforts, but as a lighter, smarter way of living in the twenty-first century.[28]

Nature may have ended. But we still need to have a relationship with what stands in its place. Our journey through history has revealed an array of possibilities, from finding beauty and spiritual meaning, to indulging our wild and feral selves; from satisfying our biophilia and ecological unconscious, to living carbon-light so we can limit a warming world. We can be thankful there is an internal harmony to all these approaches. They can be pursued without contradiction, and lead one to the other. Sitting in the shade of an ancient oak can be an aesthetic experience, offer biophilic sustenance and make us realise the value of preserving wild places rather than chopping them down to build new roads for our oil-dependent economies. This is a remarkable confluence of virtues.

The tragedy of our society is that the map we most commonly consult is a road atlas.[29] We need new maps, which take us off the highways and into the unmarked spaces where we can explore the meanings of an untamed landscape. 'In Wildness is the preservation of the World,' wrote Thoreau. Yes, of the world. But also of ourselves.

# Breaking Conventions

# 10

# Belief

On 11 June 1963, a procession of 350 Buddhist monks walked slowly through the streets of Saigon, led by an Austin Westminster sedan. They carried banners denouncing persecution of Buddhists by the South Vietnamese regime of President Ngo Dinh Diem – a member of the country's Roman Catholic minority – and demanding religious equality. When the marchers arrived at the busy intersection of Phan Dinh Phung Boulevard and Le Van Duyet Street, three monks emerged from the car. One placed a cushion on the ground; another was carrying a five-gallon gasoline container. The third, a 65-year-old Buddhist priest named Thich Quang Duc, calmly sat down on the cushion in the traditional lotus position. After being doused in petrol by his colleague, he recited a chant in honour of the Buddha, holding a string of wooden prayer beads.

He then paused for a moment, struck a match and dropped it onto his robe.

Amongst the crowd of onlookers was David Halberstam, a journalist from *The New York Times*:

> Flames were coming from a human being; his body was slowly withering and shrivelling up, his head blackening and charring. In the air was the smell of burning human flesh; human beings burn surprisingly quickly. Behind me I could hear the sobbing of the Vietnamese who were now gathering. I was too shocked to cry, too confused to take notes or ask questions, too bewildered to even think … As he burned he

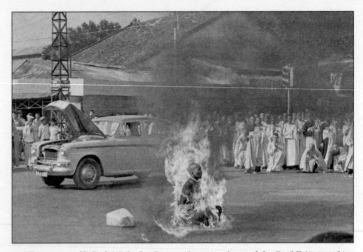

*The power of belief: Malcolm Browne's 1963 photo of the Buddhist monk Thich Quang Duc.*

never moved a muscle, never uttered a sound, his outward composure in sharp contrast to the wailing people around him.[1]

The death of Thich Quang Duc was seared onto the minds of millions by Malcolm Browne's photograph, 'The Burning Monk – Self-Immolation', which appeared on front pages around the world. His singular personal sacrifice discredited the government both nationally and internationally, and contributed to the eventual collapse of the Diem regime.

When Thich Quang Duc set himself alight, he was not only committing an act of political dissent, but sending a message to humanity about the importance of belief. Our beliefs are an integral part of who we are. Few people will give up their lives for them, but most of us have values and principles which we aspire to live by and which help define our identities. We might believe that abortion is morally wrong, or that it is unethical to eat meat, or that there should be no tax on inherited wealth, or that all children should attend state-funded schools. Such beliefs are frequently expressions of religious teachings or political credos.

Our beliefs are a lens through which we see both the world and ourselves. They guide the choices we make but are also a standard against which we can judge our actions. Are we being true to our values and ideals, or is there an uncomfortable gap between what we profess to believe and how we behave in reality? Our beliefs are the mirror in which we can see our integrity or hypocrisy. Beliefs also matter because we so rarely question them. 'Common sense,' declared Einstein, 'is the collection of prejudices acquired by age eighteen.' We may all have beliefs, but we seldom lay them out in a row on the table and subject them to systematic scrutiny. If we were each asked to take out a piece of paper and write down a list of our fundamental beliefs, could we easily do so – and could we justify them? Socrates warned against living an unexamined life. Like a jeweller who holds a diamond up to the light to discern its authenticity, its consistency and flaws, the beauty it contains, so too we should examine our beliefs.

We can turn to history for an illuminating perspective on the beliefs we hold. First, we must reveal the subtle means by which our families, education systems and governments shape our values, often without our realising it. Second, we need to explore what it takes to change our beliefs, for which we can gain inspiration from a seventeenth-century Italian stargazer and a Russian aristocrat who made his own boots. Finally, we can excavate the forgotten lessons from the past for closing the gap between our purported beliefs and our everyday actions. The value of history, we will discover, lies not so much in suggesting what the content of our beliefs should be, but in encouraging us to be more discerning and informed believers, so we can pursue the art of living with an inner integrity.

## The inheritance of belief

A favourite thought experiment amongst philosophers is to imagine that we are not a flesh-and-blood person but nothing more than a brain in a vat. Mad scientists have wired us into a supercomputer which is feeding our neurons with ideas, memories and images, so we inhabit a completely virtual world. We might think we are eating an ice cream, but the experience is really being simulated by a software program. This is a popular theme in science fiction films. Could we be trapped in the prison of our own minds, our whole lives an artificial creation?

It is unlikely that we are brains in vats. But most of us recognise, on some level, that our minds are not fully our own. We know that our brains have been injected since childhood with advertising messages, values from our parents, political propaganda and religious doctrines that are not entirely of our own choosing. When we buy a hamburger from a fast-food chain or brush our teeth with a branded toothpaste, we are at least dimly aware that we may be doing so not just as a matter of personal preference, but because the company is incessantly telling us about the virtues of its products.

None of us like the idea that the choices we make or the beliefs we hold have been manufactured for us. We value thinking for ourselves and making up our own minds. But if we delve into the origins of our cherished beliefs, we are likely to encounter a disturbing truth: that they have been shaped by forces outside ourselves, and often without our knowledge. This is certainly the case when it comes to beliefs connected with religion, nationalism and monarchy.

Where do our religious beliefs come from? Although theologians expend enormous energy debating the various arguments for the existence of a supernatural God, such as 'intelligent design', few people are actually moved to believe in God by intellectual arguments. The primary explanation for religious belief – no matter your religion, class background, age or sex – is that it is inherited from your family and the society you have grown up in. The most comprehensive survey of the academic literature concludes:

> To the question, 'Why do people believe in God?', the best answer remains: 'Because they have been taught to believe in God.' ... The vast majority of believers have been born

into whatever tradition they now follow … Most individuals learn their religion in childhood, as a specific identity, within a specific community.[2]

Religious belief, then, is largely an accident of birth, geography and history. If you were born into a typical family in contemporary Tehran, you would almost certainly be a Muslim and believe in the truths of the Qur'an, just as if you had been born in rural Italy in the nineteenth century, you would have been a Catholic. Acquiring your religion appears to be akin to learning your mother tongue.

This conclusion seems disempowering – most people feel their religious convictions are their own – but it is difficult to escape the evidence. Our parents pass down not only their genes but their religion by taking us to church, mosque or temple, and getting us to say our prayers, to observe rituals in the home and perhaps to attend special religious classes.[3] A major study of religion in the United States since the Second World War, carried out at the University of Chicago, showed that 90 per cent of Protestants, 82 per cent of Catholics and 87 per cent of Jews follow the same religion as the one they were brought up in. If your parents worshipped regularly, there is only a one in ten chance you will have abandoned their religion. Around a third of people leave their religion at some point – often during a period of doubt in their youth – but the majority return to it or convert to a related denomination. In other words, if you grow up believing there is a God, you are unlikely ever to relinquish this fundamental belief and become an atheist or agnostic. Your inherited religious worldview will not easily permit any choices outside a smorgasbord of sects which all take the existence of God for granted.[4] Overall, parents are much more successful at transferring their religious beliefs to their children than they are at passing on their political views, sporting interests or dietary habits.[5]

Parents do not, of course, have a monopoly on determining religious belief. Almost as important as family is the community you live in. If you grew up in a highly religious society, like Ireland or Poland, even if you came from a non-religious household, there is a good chance you will have adopted the prevalent religion, absorbing it from school, friends and the media.[6] This religious culture can also have strong psychological effects, especially in relation to mystical experiences. Visions of the Holy Virgin do not appear to orthodox Muslims or Taoists – only to Catholics or those surrounded by Catholic ideas.[7]

A consequence of inheriting a particular religion from either family or culture is that we also tend to inherit an unquestioning belief in its foundation stories and traditions, whose truths we take on trust. A classic instance concerns Christmas. Most Christians believe that this festival marks a concrete historical event – the birth of Jesus on 25 December. Yet standard scholarly sources put this into doubt. Early Christians in the first two or three centuries did not even celebrate Christmas: the death and resurrection of Jesus was considered far more important than his birthday. In fact, there was no consensus on his actual date of birth, since none of the Gospels were specific about it. Suggestions up to the fourth century included 25 March, 20 May and 18 November. So when did Christmas begin, and why 25 December?

We need to transport ourselves to fourth-century Rome, and the rule of the emperor Constantine (306–37). Romans were accustomed to letting their hair down in December to celebrate three pagan midwinter festivals. First was their favourite party, Saturnalia, usually from 17 to 23 December. This was a time of general feasting, debauchery and bonfires that had been taking place since at least 200 years before the birth of Jesus. Then there was the Kalends celebration on New Year's Eve, full of processions and heavy drinking. According to the fourth-century writer Libanius, houses were 'decorated with lights and greenery' and 'a stream of presents pours itself out on all sides'. Sound familiar? Finally, Romans performed rituals to mark the birth of the Sun God, Sol Invictus, which took place on their date for the winter solstice ... 25 December. The evidence suggests that following Constantine's conversion to Christianity, he – or one of his immediate successors – permitted Christians to celebrate the birth of Jesus as long as its timing coincided with the existing festivities, possibly to appease the largely pagan population or to boost its potential popularity. As historian of religion Bruce Forbes puts it, 'the birthday of the sun god was changed into the birthday of God the Son'.[8]

So when Church leaders say we should return to the 'true spirit of Christmas' – a favourite theme of papal addresses – this may be a more complicated task than we think. The larger lesson of Christmas is that we need to approach the foundation stories of all ancient religions with care, for any truths they contain will almost certainly be mixed with layers of folk mythology. Beyond this, we ought to recognise that religion is overwhelmingly a product of social learning, an inheritance from past generations. We should ask ourselves how we feel about the fact that, for most of us, our religious beliefs as adults could have been predicted successfully by others at the time of our birth.

Alongside religion, nationalism is one of our most potent sources of belief. When I meet fellow Australians, I am almost always struck by the strength of their national pride. They seem offended that I don't support Australia's national sports teams, and generally believe that Australia has the world's best beaches, weather, coffee, food and overall 'lifestyle'. Why would you possibly want to live anywhere else, especially if – like me – you possess an Australian passport?

While allegiance to one's own nation is widespread amongst people from almost every country, it can be difficult to pin down exactly what beliefs are entailed by nationalism. One form of belief is the idea that our nation is superior to others in particular ways, such as cultural achievements, natural beauty or sporting prowess. Australians might believe they have the best food in the world – but so do the French, Italians, Spanish, Peruvians and Chinese. George Bernard Shaw recognised the absurdity of it all when he noted that 'patriotism is your conviction that this country is superior to all other countries because you were born in it'.

A second kind of nationalist belief is that one has a duty to protect the nation when it is under threat. Nationalism can encourage people to sacrifice their own lives on behalf of their fellow citizens, and also rouse them to kill their enemies.[9] It may have been a vital force in the struggles of oppressed peoples against colonialism, but it was also a major cause of the wars of the twentieth century, from the First World War to the conflicts in the former Yugoslavia in the 1990s. This destructive potential of nationalism was obvious to the British poet Wilfred Owen. While witnessing the horrors of trench warfare in 1917, he wrote with unmasked irony, 'dulce et decorum est pro patria mori' – 'it is a sweet and seemly thing to die for one's country'. He was killed in battle seven days before the armistice.

The fascinating thing about nationalism is that it is such a recent phenomenon. Most nation states in Europe and the Americas have only emerged during the past 300 years. Prior to the mid-nineteenth century, you could not have supported an Italian or German sports team, for these countries did not yet exist: they were agglomerations of principalities or parts of empires. Nation states did not appear spontaneously, simply through popular enthusiasm. Forging them required enormous effort on the part of political leaders, who had to convince citizens to give their loyalty not to local communities, ethnic groups or empires, but to the nation itself. How did they perform this miraculous feat of creating national identities, with the result that patriotic beliefs are so deeply held today?

One of the powerful tools at the disposal of nation builders was the use of the education system, where there was a captive audience. Schools were at the front line of creating the imagined community of the nation state, argues the historian Benedict Anderson, playing a key role in 'a systematic, even Machiavellian, instilling of nationalist ideology'.[10] With the emergence of public education in the nineteenth century, children were taught to speak, read and write their national language, to sing the national anthem, and to learn the proud history of their country. So a child born in Provence in the 1880s – when a new system of national education was introduced – would have had their school classes in French rather than the local dialect of Provençal, learned the words of the Marseillaise, and studied great moments of republican history like the storming of the Bastille in July 1789. In other words, they were taught how to be French.

Education still plays this role today, nowhere more so than in the United States, which has been more successful than most nations at instilling patriotism into the minds of its young citizens. Amongst the most effective means of doing so has been the daily ritual of the Pledge of Allegiance. Each morning, across the vast majority of states, millions of children are legally obliged to stand before the Stars and Stripes and recite, 'I pledge allegiance to the flag of the United States of America, and to the republic for which it stands, one nation under God, indivisible, with liberty and justice for all.'

What are the origins of this unusual practice of making a pledge to the national flag, which exists in almost no other countries? Many know that the phrase 'under God' was only added in 1954 in response to anxieties about the influence of godless Soviet Communism. Few realise that the pledge was not created by state or federal governments, but was invented in 1892 by a Christian Socialist, Francis Bellamy, who first published it in a children's magazine. Bellamy unashamedly viewed the pledge as a propaganda device, admitting that the youngest children would be unable to understand it, but through constant repetition it could foster national pride and loyalty to the republic, becoming a means of 'thinking those thoughts for them'.[11]

The pledge gradually spread in popularity, especially after it was adopted by patriotic organisations like the Daughters of the American Revolution at a National Flag Convention in 1923. In the interwar period, America's politicians believed the pledge could help unite a country not only threatened by trade union radicalism and racial divides, but facing the task of integrating millions of immigrants, who would potentially lack loyalty to their new home. It could also help mobilise the nation at a time of war. In 1942, just months after the Japanese bombing of Pearl Harbor, the US Congress officially designated it the national pledge. Throughout the 1960s and 1970s it was the subject of legal wrangling when both pupils and teachers refused to recite

*American schoolchildren of Japanese descent pledging allegiance to the US flag in San Francisco's Little Tokyo district in 1942, photographed by Dorothea Lange. A month later nationalist wartime fervour deemed them public enemies: all people of Japanese ancestry from the city were forcibly placed in internment camps.[12]*

the pledge in protest against the Vietnam War and the treatment of minorities.[13]

The Pledge of Allegiance now stands as an integral element of what has been described as a culture of 'flag worship', which effectively operates as a civil religion in the United States.[14] The flag is an object of almost sacred veneration and repeated attempts have been made to legally ban burning or otherwise desecrating it. Today foreign visitors often remark on the ubiquitous public presence of the flag – such as outside people's homes – and how odd it is that in an apparently free society most children are compelled to swear an oath of allegiance. They are simply noticing the way governments endeavour to embed nationalist beliefs and loyalties amongst their citizens. The problem is that we are particularly good at noticing when this is happening to other people rather than to ourselves.

Belief in the institution of monarchy may not be as globally prevalent as either religion or nationalism, yet it is illustrative of the way we absorb our cultural inheritances. Britain, one of the most monarchy-obsessed countries in the West, provides a good example. Around 80 per cent of British citizens approve of the monarchy: they support the idea that the head of state should be a member of the royal family. It is extraordinary that in the modern democratic age so many people hold an effectively anti-democratic belief in the legitimacy of hereditary rule. One of the main reasons people give for preserving the monarchy is that it is a 'great British tradition' and a time-honoured symbol of national unity.[15] At royal weddings and anniversaries, tens of thousands flock to see the gilded carriage glide by, the ermine cloaks and plumed hats, the gunfire salutes and stately processions. Television commentators reinforce the idea that these are ancient customs stretching back into the mists of time, with remarks like, 'all the pageantry and grandeur of a thousand-year-old tradition', 'a pageantry that has gone on for hundreds of years' and 'all the precision that comes from centuries of precedent'.[16]

This is largely, to put it mildly, nonsense. Most of these royal ceremonies and rituals are creations of the late nineteenth and early twentieth centuries, when the monarchy itself was under threat. They are what historians call 'invented traditions' – conscious efforts on the part of those in power to subtly influence our beliefs by providing a compelling but illusory sense of continuity with the past.[17] The story of how the British monarchy revived itself through the innovative use of invented traditions is one of the great episodes in the history of public relations.

For the first three-quarters of the nineteenth century, the monarchy was an object of public derision and something of a national joke. George IV was ridiculed for his extravagance and womanising, and his marriage to Queen Caroline was an unprecedented public scandal. When he died in 1830, *The Times* bequeathed him a damning editorial: 'There never was an individual less regretted by his fellow creatures than this deceased king. What eye has wept for him? What heart has heaved one throb of unmercenary sorrow?' Can you imagine a national newspaper casting such a verdict on a royal figure today? Moreover, despite what many people might think, Victoria's early reign distinctly lacked regal grandeur. Her coronation in 1838 was an unrehearsed fiasco: the clergy lost their place in the order of service, the coronation ring didn't fit and they didn't bother singing the national anthem. From the very beginning she was criticised in the press for her political meddling and was constantly lampooned by cartoonists. When she effectively retired from public life in the 1860s, the pressures on the monarchy began mounting. With the extension of the franchise and rise of worker organisations, class consciousness was beginning to rival national allegiance. Between 1871 and 1874, eighty-four republican clubs were founded, and Prime Minister Gladstone worried about the 'stability of the throne'.[18]

It was in this atmosphere of crisis that a concerted effort was made to shore up the monarchy, and the nation it represented. The solution? To resurrect belief in the institution of monarchy by inventing traditions. From the 1870s, writes the historian Eric Hobsbawm, 'the revival of royal ritualism was seen as a necessary counterweight to the dangers of popular democracy'.[19] A new era of pomp and circumstance began in 1877 when Victoria was crowned Empress of India – an invented title bestowed by Prime Minister Disraeli – associating her with the glories of the British Empire. For Victoria's Golden Jubilee celebration in 1887, colonial premiers were invited for the first time, and their troops paraded in a masterpiece of ceremonial choreography, while the clergy were fetchingly dressed up in a new wardrobe of embroidered vestments and coloured stoles. Following the festivities, the Archbishop of Canterbury noted with relief that for 'days afterwards, everyone feels that the socialist movement has had a check'. The event was considered such a success that it was repeated ten years later with even more splendour, for the Diamond Jubilee.

In 1901 Edward VII ensured that his coronation would be remembered for its romantic majesty by having a new, fabulously ornate carriage drive him back from the Abbey. He also transformed the state opening of Parliament into a full-dress ceremony, parading through the streets of London and personally reading the speech from the throne. Edward was an innovator even when dead, creating the tradition of British monarchs publicly lying-in-state: a quarter of a million people filed past his coffin in 1910. Other changes followed, for instance in 1917, when the royal family sought to obscure its Germanic heritage by altering its name from the House of Saxe-Coburg and Gotha to the House of Windsor, and introduced the practice of having royal weddings in public rather than behind closed doors.[20]

It was through such invented traditions that the Crown reasserted itself as a patriotic symbol and ensured the allegiance of the labouring classes. The achievements of this political programme are evident today in the overwhelming support for the monarchy, and the fact that there is virtually no serious public debate about a republican alternative. So next time you see people waving their Union Jacks at a fairy-tale royal wedding or some lavish royal parade through London, just remember that you are witnessing the results of a brilliant PR campaign designed to mould the beliefs of whole nation.

I do not want to give the impression that we are empty vessels, ready to have our minds filled by whatever our families, schools or governments choose for us. But we must be vigilant about the beliefs we absorb on issues such as religion, nationalism and the monarchy. So it must be with all our beliefs, from politics to ethics, ecology to equality. We should be constantly probing the sources, biases and veracity of our beliefs. We could also benefit from learning one of the most vital aspects of the art of believing, and that is how to change our minds.

## When the facts change, I change my mind

During the Great Depression, the economist John Maynard Keynes shifted his views and recommendations on monetary policy. When criticised for his inconsistency, he came back with the reply, 'When the facts change, I change my mind. What do you do, sir?' Keynes's reasoning was compelling, and raises a question. How often do we change our beliefs? There may be nothing more difficult than doing so, especially because so many of them – like those stemming from nationalism and religion – are cultural inheritances embedded during our impressionable youths. Moreover, our beliefs can be so ingrained in our psyches that they become an unconscious element of our worldviews. Few white people, for instance, acknowledge that they have prejudices against black people, yet the evidence defies this: white job interviewers regularly discriminate – consciously or not – against black applicants in a host of employment fields.[21]

We need to understand what it might take to change our beliefs. Will we have to be presented with new facts, like Mr Keynes, or perhaps fresh experiences or novel arguments? If we do not know what could alter our beliefs, or are convinced that nothing could make us change them, then there is a danger that we are trapped by dogma. Inspiration for developing a capacity to change our minds comes from two pioneering figures of the past who discarded their old beliefs and took on new ones: Galileo Galilei and Leo Tolstoy.

In the late 1590s, when in his mid-thirties, Galileo still believed in the old geocentric system in which the earth was assumed to be a fixed point at the centre of the universe, with the sun and everything else revolving around it in a symphony of perfect circles. This doctrine, proposed by Ptolemy in the second century, was a cornerstone of Catholic and Protestant belief, having been duly confirmed by Holy Scripture: Joshua had commanded the sun – not the earth – to stand still in the heavens, and King Solomon had said that the sun 'returns to its place'.[22] Galileo, a red-headed mathematics professor at the University of Padua, who also made a living as a maker of surveying instruments, began to have doubts after reading Copernicus's De Revolutionibus, which in 1543 had proposed that the earth actually revolved around the sun. But Copernicus had offered only a hypothesis, rather than scientific evidence, and in any case the idea of heliocentrism defied common sense: if the earth was spinning about, why didn't we all fly off it, and why was it that an object dropped from a tower fell down in a straight line?

The event that changed Galileo's mind – possibly the most explosive moment in the history of belief – took place in January 1610. The previous year he had improved on a recent Flemish invention by making a telescope so powerful that it enabled a ship on the horizon to be seen two hours before it was visible with the naked eye. But now he did something even more astonishing: he pointed his telescope at the sky.

Galileo was so excited by what he saw that in March 1610 he published a twenty-four-page pamphlet, *The Starry Messenger* (*Sidereus Nuncius*), which presented a totally new picture of the universe. He discovered that there were at least ten times as many stars as anybody had ever previously thought. He found that the moon 'does not possess a smooth and polished surface, but one rough and uneven, and, just like the face of the earth, is everywhere full of vast protuberances, deep chasms and sinuosities'. The Galaxy, he now realised, was 'nothing else but a mass of innumerable stars planted together in clusters'. And most astonishing of all, he had spotted four new planets orbiting around a bright star, which turned out to be satellites of Jupiter. This last discovery was his moment of conversion, because he deduced that if these moons could be circling Jupiter while Jupiter itself was circling the sun – already a long-established observation – then the earth, with its own orbiting moon, could be doing exactly the same thing. The whole system of Ptolemy had come tumbling down.

But had it? Even if Galileo was able to convince himself that the Scriptures were mistaken about the truths of nature, he was unable to convince the Church of Rome. For the next twenty years Galileo waged a constant publicity campaign to have the heliocentric vision of the universe accepted, naively thinking that scientific fact would be enough to shift religious belief. In 1616 and again in 1624 he presented himself to the Pope, but was unable to persuade either the papacy or the powerful Jesuit fathers that the earth moved. Unknown to Galileo, the Church's secret police, the Holy Office of the Inquisition, had been gathering evidence for over a decade to bring a case of heresy against him. In 1633, following the publication of yet another heliocentric treatise, the ailing seventy-year-old was summoned to Rome for the trial of the century.

Galileo didn't have a chance against the Inquisition. Of the ten judges, one was the Pope's brother and another his nephew. After twice being threatened with torture, he issued a humiliating recantation, abandoning 'the false opinion that the sun is the centre of the world and immovable, and that the earth is not the centre of the world, and moves'. As punishment, Galileo was put under permanent house arrest and forbidden to leave the confines of his home near Florence. He died there, totally blind, eight years later. The Catholic Church, in its own blindness, did not officially accept Galileo's view of the universe until 1822.[23]

What does Galileo's story mean for the art of living today? Unlike Galileo, most of us never even raise the telescope. We do not turn our gaze towards that which might challenge our long-held beliefs or lifestyle choices. Those who believe in the monarchy seldom want to look carefully at the invented royal ceremonies and rituals, which might undermine the idea that it is a 'great British tradition'. We would rather remain in denial about the way we have been fed nationalistic propaganda all our lives, which serves to prevent us from seeing the common bonds amongst all human beings, and places a boundary on our moral universes. We want to close our eyes to the origins of our religious beliefs in ideas that we have largely inherited from our parents or the community we have grown up in.

But if we want to have a Galilean revolution in our own lives, we need to decide where to point the telescope. What might we dare look at? What information or arguments could we seek? And are we ready for the sacrifices that may be involved, such as feeling ostracised from friends and family? Galileo had extraordinary courage and curiosity to gaze into the starry heavens, for it had the potential to overturn his deep beliefs about the universe, and to challenge the authority of the Church. We too might discover that same courage and curiosity, and look with fresh eyes at our beliefs in realms such as politics, religion, money and love.

Leo Tolstoy was the most famous novelist of the nineteenth century. Yet readers of *Anna Karenina* (1876) or *War and Peace* (1866) are usually unaware that he was also one of its most radical social and political thinkers – as revolutionary, in his way, as Galileo. During a long life from 1828 to 1910, he gradually rejected the received beliefs of his aristocratic background and embraced a startlingly unconventional worldview based on pacifism, anarchism and Christian asceticism. How and why did he do so?

Tolstoy was born into the Russian nobility. His family had an estate and owned hundreds of serfs. The early life of the young count was raucous and debauched, and he gambled away a fortune through a reckless addiction to cards. As he acknowledged in *A Confession* (1885):

> I killed men in war and challenged men to duels in order to kill them. I lost at cards, consumed the labour of the peasants, sentenced them to punishments, lived loosely, and deceived people. Lying, robbery, adultery of all kinds, drunkenness, violence, murder – there was no crime I did not commit, and in spite of that people praised my conduct and my contemporaries considered and consider me to be a comparatively moral man. So I lived for ten years.

His beliefs, and way of life, began to change in the 1850s when he was an army officer. Tolstoy fought in the bloody siege of Sebastopol during the Crimean War, a horrific experience which was the basis of his later pacifism. A decisive event took place in 1857, when he witnessed a public execution by guillotine in Paris. He never forgot the severed head thumping into the box below. It convinced him of the belief that the state and its laws were not only brutal, but served to protect the interests of the rich and powerful. He wrote to a friend, 'The truth is that the State is a conspiracy designed not only to exploit, but above all to corrupt its citizens … Henceforth, I shall never serve any government anywhere.'[24] Tolstoy was on his way to becoming an anarchist. His criticisms of the Tsarist regime in Russia became so vociferous that only his literary fame saved him from imprisonment; others who espoused similar views were not so lucky, such as the anarchist Prince Peter Kropotkin, who was locked up for three years as a subversive before managing to escape.

Tolstoy's travels in Europe brought him into contact with radical thinkers of his day such as Pierre-Joseph Proudhon and Alexander Herzen, and spurred his belief in economic equality and his interest in the educational writings of Rousseau. He founded an experimental school for peasant children based on libertarian principles, and taught there himself. Following the emancipation of the serfs in 1861, and influenced by a growing movement across Russia which extolled the virtues of the peasantry, Tolstoy not only adopted traditional peasant dress, but worked alongside the labourers on his estate, ploughing the fields and repairing their homes with his own hands. For a blue-blooded count, such actions were nothing short of remarkable. Although no doubt tinged with paternalism, Tolstoy enjoyed the company of peasants and consciously began to shun the literary and aristocratic elite in the cities.

His dedication to the peasantry was nowhere more evident than in his famine relief work. After the crop failure of 1873, Tolstoy temporarily stopped writing *Anna Karenina* to organise aid for the starving, remarking to a relative, 'I cannot tear myself away from living creatures to bother about imaginary ones.' He did it again after the famine in 1891, and with other members of his family spent the next two years raising money from around the world and working in soup kitchens.[25] Can you imagine a best-selling author today putting their latest book aside to do humanitarian relief work for two years?

One of Tolstoy's greatest gifts – and also a source of torment – was his addiction to the question of the meaning of life. He never ceased asking himself why and how he should live, and what was the point of all his money and fame. In the late 1870s, unable

Tolstoy Ploughing (c. 1889) by Ilya Repin. *Tolstoy regularly put down his pen to work in the fields. He kept a scythe and saw leaning up against the wall next to his writing desk. A basket of cobbler's tools lay on the floor.*[26]

to find any answers, he had a mental breakdown and was on the verge of suicide. But after immersing himself in the German philosopher Schopenhauer, Buddhist texts and the Bible, he adopted a revolutionary brand of Christianity which rejected all organised religion, including the Orthodox Church he had grown up in, and turned towards a life of spiritual and material austerity. He gave up drinking and smoking, and became a vegetarian. He also inspired the creation of utopian communities for simple, self-sufficient living, where property was held in common. These 'Tolstoyan' communities spread around the world, and led Gandhi to found an ashram in 1910 named the Tolstoy Farm.[27]

Tolstoy's new life was not, however, without its struggles and contradictions. Apart from the fact that he preached universal love yet was constantly fighting with his wife, the apostle of equality was never able to fully abandon his wealth and privileged lifestyle, and lived till old age in a grand house with servants. When he mooted the idea of giving away his estate to the peasants, his wife and children were furious, and he eventually backed down. But in the early 1890s he managed, against their wishes, to relinquish copyright to a huge portion of his literary works, in effect sacrificing a fortune.[28] In his last years, when writers and journalists came to pay homage to the bearded sage, they were always surprised to find the world's most famous author chopping wood with some workers or making his own boots. Given the privileged position in which Tolstoy started life, his personal transformation, if not complete, still deserves our admiration.

Whereas Galileo changed his beliefs through scientific discovery, Tolstoy altered his through experience and conversation, as well as through ideas gathered from his adventurous reading. He realised that the best way to change his worldview, and challenge his assumptions and ideals, was through surrounding himself with people whose views and lifestyles were different from his own. That's why he ceased socialising in Moscow and spent so much time with labourers on the land. In *Resurrection* (1899), Tolstoy pointed out that most people, whether they are wealthy businessmen, powerful politicians or common thieves, consider their beliefs and way of life to be both admirable and ethical. 'In order to keep up their view of life,' he wrote, 'these people instinctively keep to the circle of those people who share their views of life and their own place in it'.[29] Cosseted within our peer group or social milieu, we may think it is perfectly normal and justifiable to own two homes, or to oppose same-sex marriage, or to bomb countries in the Middle East. We cannot see that such views may be perverse, unjust or untrue because we are inside a circle of our own making, which constantly reinforces our worldview. If we want to question our beliefs, we need to follow the example of Tolstoy, spending time with people whose values and everyday experiences contrast with our own. Our task must be to journey beyond the perimeters of the circle.

## Please mind the gap

What is the value of a belief if we do not put it into practice? We get frustrated by politicians who speak of peace but then go to war, or who claim solidarity with the poor but then live luxuriously on the back of company directorships. 'What hypocrites!' we cry out. Yet we are often less aware of, or less concerned by, our own inconsistencies. It is seldom easy to close the gap between our beliefs and actions. Tolstoy couldn't do it. Reconciling our beliefs with our behaviour offers the prospect of a sense of integrity and wholeness, but it usually involves paying some kind of price. Historically, human beings have made five kinds of sacrifice in the endeavour to be true to their beliefs: the sacrifice of life, power, liberty, wealth and relationships.

The most extreme cases are people who have given up their lives for their beliefs, like the Vietnamese monk Thich Quang Duc. I often cycle over the spot in central Oxford where Thomas Cranmer, a former Archbishop of Canterbury, and two bishops, Hugh Latimer and Nicholas Ridley, were burned at the stake for their Protestant beliefs in the 1550s. Apart from religious martyrs, we might think of Socrates, who preferred death by poisoning to renouncing his philosophical views. There are also those who risked their lives in collective struggles for their political ideals, such as the Republican workers and international sympathisers – amongst them George Orwell and Laurie Lee – who in the 1930s took up arms against the fascists in Spain. While in Guatemala in the 1990s, I felt in awe of human rights activists, peasant leaders and trade unionists I met who regularly faced death threats in their campaigns to bring the military to justice for its violence during the civil war, or to get better wages on the coffee and sugar plantations. Many of them were assassinated by extrajudicial death squads.

A second group comprises those who have abandoned power and fame in the name of a belief, such as the Indian spiritual thinker Jiddu Krishnamurti. In 1909, aged fourteen, he was 'discovered' by the mystical Theosophy movement, who declared him to be the 'World Teacher' they had prophesied. He was designated leader of their Order of the Bright Star, a religious organisation with 60,000 followers around the globe. In 1929 he shocked them all by not only resigning his leadership but dissolving the whole order. Krishnamurti had – like Tolstoy

– come to the belief that discovering spiritual truth had to be an individual journey, and all religious institutions were essentially authoritarian and dogmatic, while the believers increasingly used them as a crutch:

> I maintain that Truth is a pathless land … A belief is purely an individual matter, and you cannot and must not organize it. If you do, it becomes dead, crystallized; it becomes a creed, a sect, a religion, to be imposed on others.[30]

You need genuine integrity and humility to give up being messiah of your own religion.

A more common sacrifice than either life or power has been to put personal liberty at risk for a belief. The history of social movements is a record of individuals who have been willing to break the law and face imprisonment for their values and principles. Think of the Suffragettes fighting for the vote in the early twentieth century, or the thousands arrested during the US civil rights movement, having committed acts of civil disobedience. Pick up the annual report of Amnesty International or Human Rights Watch and you will see how common it is for people to jeopardise their freedom for their beliefs, whether it is an Iranian journalist intent on speaking her mind, or a German environmental activist scaling a nuclear power station. Their actions should make us ask ourselves this question: is there any belief for which I would be willing to face a night in prison?

'Be the change you want to see in the world,' said Mahatma Gandhi. That could be the credo of all those who wish to close the gap between their beliefs and actions. Gandhi's speciality was giving up wealth and material comfort for his beliefs. As a young barrister practising in South Africa, he felt increasingly awkward about having servants, so began emptying the chamber pots himself and learned how to wash and starch his own legal collars. He later founded ashrams where the aim was 'to live the life of the poorest people' in conditions of absolute equality. Like other members, he tended the goats, hand-spun cloth and cleaned the latrines – a job traditionally done by the

Untouchable or Dalit caste.[31] Gandhi practised what he preached and died with almost no personal possessions apart from his writings. In a modern world bent on material gain and high consumption, sacrificing wealth is a confronting prospect. Are we willing to put our savings in an ethical investment fund, even if it yields lower returns than a standard fund? Are we prepared to join those who pledge to give 10 per cent of their income to charity, if it prevents us from having an annual holiday in the sun? Would we turn down a high-paying job for a firm whose values are at odds with our own?

A final form of sacrifice involves personal relationships. At the end of his autobiography, *Long Walk to Freedom* (1994), Nelson Mandela wrote:

> I have never regretted my commitment to the struggle, and I was always prepared to face the hardships that affected me personally. But my family paid a terrible price, perhaps too dear a price, for my commitment ... In attempting to serve my people, I found that I was prevented from fulfilling my obligations as a son, a brother, a father and a husband.[32]

The cost of his political actions was not just twenty-seven years in prison, but the painful realisation that he had hurt his loved ones. In the struggle to enact our own beliefs we may not face the same risks as Mandela, yet the potential to damage our relationships could still be there. How will our mother feel if we reject her religious beliefs and take a different path? If we don't believe in private schools, are we willing to sacrifice our children's educational prospects for our own principles? Putting beliefs into practice is never easy when we have multiple obligations.

History is telling us that sacrifice is part of the meaning of belief. How much we are willing to give up is a measure of our commitment. If we cannot contemplate a price, then our belief and dedication to a cause may be weaker than we think. But sacrifices can yield valuable gifts in return. We might each take time to consider what we could, on balance, forgo to enact our beliefs, so we can enjoy the rare gift of personal integrity.

## What transcendence can do for you

One of the most common mantras found in self-help books is 'believe in yourself'. Although self-confidence has a role in the art of living, it is just as important to believe in your ideals. The moral philosopher Peter Singer argues that we are most likely to find personal fulfilment in life by committing ourselves to a 'transcendent cause' – some value or project that is 'larger than the self', for instance human rights, animal liberation or environmental justice. Living by our beliefs, says Singer, will sustain us more than commitment to self-centred desires such as wealth or social status, no matter how pleasurable they may seem.[33]

Yet we must treat our beliefs with care, for it is hardly virtuous to be a blind ideologue or unthinking do-gooder, even for a worthy cause. That is why we should take our fundamental beliefs, lay them out in front of us and examine them one by one. Our approaches to the art of living ought to be informed by a healthy scepticism that can challenge the influence which family, peer pressure, governments and other social forces have on our values and ideals.

Once our beliefs have survived this scrutiny they are ready to be transformed into reality. There may, however, appear to be overwhelming obstacles to doing so. In the face of powerful economic interests, political intransigence and global complexity, it might seem hardly worth fighting for a transcendent social or ethical cause as Singer suggests. As a result, we often retreat into disillusionment, apathy or paralysis. But the story of our beliefs does not have to end there. We can always start with ourselves, and strive to be the change we want to see in the world. That may be a first step, which we take with the courage of Galileo or Gandhi, to creating the alternative futures that inspire us.

# 11

# Creativity

I walk into the headquarters of the aid agency Oxfam. Usually there are weighty reports on gender rights and global inequality stacked on the coffee tables and a video wall shows interviews with drought-stricken villagers in sub-Saharan Africa or flooded rice farmers in Bangladesh. But today the foyer is filled with art: paintings, pottery, sculpture, weaving, jewellery, upholstery and short films. These are not the fruits of a new development project in the shanty towns of Rio but a display of work by staff. It has been made by policy analysts, clerical assistants, fundraisers, security guards, emergency relief workers and accountants. The charity is clearly pulsating with artists who spend their evenings and weekends standing in front of easels or chiselling away in the garden shed. A staff jazz group plays in the corner. The song echoing around the atrium is 'All of Me'. It could hardly be more appropriate, since the employees wish to show that who they are is not just their 'worker selves' but also their 'creative selves', a hidden part of their lives which they normally do not bring to the office each day.

The art show is a reminder of how much creativity matters to people. The word 'creativity' comes from the Latin *creare*, to make or produce, and human beings have always expressed and nurtured themselves through making and inventing things. Some people save their creativity for their leisure time, like the American poet Wallace Stevens who worked as an insurance company executive by day and wrote his poetry long into the night. Others look for it in their jobs, using their imaginations to devise a new marketing strategy or give birth to a path-breaking report. Psychologists are now in general agreement that creativity is good for you and that we all have creative selves just waiting to burst out of us. The business world has picked up the zeitgeist, with companies sending their staff on courses to release their creative potential and turn everyone into a blue-sky thinker.

Creativity may be popular, but what exactly is it, and why does it matter? What are the best ways of cultivating creativity for the art of living? I believe that creativity, as commonly understood, is a dangerous ideal. It is too closely associated with the ideas of originality and innate talent, legacies of Renaissance attitudes that continue to haunt our minds and that are responsible for a famine of creative self-confidence. The more recent view that creativity can be taught has been unable to compensate for this history. Instead, we need to broaden the meaning of creativity so we can pursue it in a variety of ways: through treating ourselves to a daily dose of self-expression, by rediscovering our lost craft skills, and as a philosophy of living that frees us from the strictures of social convention.

## How Michelangelo destroyed the creative spirit

I've always thought of myself as someone lacking in artistic talent. The one subject at high school I disliked was art. I considered it boring and pointless for the simple reason that I found it so painfully difficult, whether drawing, painting or sculpting. Unlike other subjects such as maths or history where I usually did well, my attempts to sketch a bowl of fruit or a human face were derisory. There was little connection between the model before me or the vision in my mind's eye, and what my hand then produced on the sheet of paper. My art teachers didn't help: they repeatedly criticised me, pointing out how my perspective was 'wrong' or my figures 'out of proportion' (if only I had retorted that much of Picasso's art displayed the same mistakes). By the time I was fourteen, I had admitted defeat and condemned myself as being uncreative. This experience was compounded by my musical ineptitude. At primary school I was one of only three people in my year who failed a test singing 'Twinkle Twinkle, Little Star'; while everyone else went off to sing each week, we were ushered into a small room to play with Lego. Humiliation. I also spent seven years half-heartedly learning violin, piano and clarinet, but by the end was still struggling with the basics. Although my father was a fine musician, having won a scholarship to study piano in his youth, I had clearly failed to inherit any of his ability, so finally gave up. As I left my teenage years behind me, I felt a complete absence of artistic self-confidence. I told both myself and others that I couldn't draw to save my life and was totally tone deaf. I saw no point in trying to cultivate my artistic self. The gift of creativity had eluded me.

Those who share my lack of self-confidence should not blame themselves. Instead, they should blame Michelangelo Buonarroti. Or more accurately, the cult of the creative genius that grew up around him. The Renaissance may have produced some of the most remarkable art and literature in European history, but it is also responsible for fostering an elite and disempowering attitude towards creativity from which we are still attempting to recover today.

This attitude had its origins in the two great inventions of the Renaissance. The first was the idea of individuality. According to the Swiss historian Jacob Burckhardt, in medieval Europe 'man was conscious of himself only as a member of a race, people, party, family, or corporation – only through some general category'. This changed towards the end of the thirteenth century, when Italy 'began to swarm with individuality'.[1] Amongst the well-off citizens of Venice, Florence and other cultural centres, it became not only socially acceptable but positively admirable to express your uniqueness. This was reflected in new forms of individualism such as putting a personalised seal on your letters, writing an intimate diary, and distinguishing yourself through your tastes in fashion, art and literature. Individualism may have gone too far in the twenty-first century, having become a form of self-centred narcissism, but in the Renaissance it was a more positive development, helping people shake off the fetters of feudalism and religious dogma that had been crushing self-expression and free thinking for hundreds of years.

The second major invention of the Renaissance, which built upon the new admiration for individuality, was the idea of the creative genius.[2] During the Middle Ages the notion of 'creation' was associated exclusively with God's biblical act of creating the earth *ex-nihilo*, 'from nothing'. No human being could hope to replicate this divine feat. They might become skilled artisans or copyists of nature, but never creators. Renaissance thinkers put an end to God's monopoly on originality and the power of creation.[3] In the fifteenth century, the Florentine humanist Giannozzo Manetti boldly declared 'the genius of man', believing that the human mind had extraordinary capabilities of invention and imagination. And there was one figure whose brilliance was said to outshine all others, who elevated human creativity to a level of sublime perfection not even reached by Dante or Leonardo da Vinci. That person was Michelangelo – sculptor, painter, architect, poet.

Born in 1475, Michelangelo was the first artist to become a legend in his own time. Despite being descended from a noble family, he had humble beginnings and was brought up amongst quarrymen in the hills above Florence, where from the age of six he learned to cut and chisel stone blocks. At fourteen he was apprenticed to a painter's studio, but soon left to follow his deepest passion, carving stone. In his twenties he astounded Europe with masterpieces such as the *Pietà* and the giant statue of *David*, each of which he brought to life out of hunks of Carrara marble. A succession of power-hungry popes began clamouring for his services, leading to a commission to paint the ceiling of the Sistine Chapel in his early thirties. The cantankerous Michelangelo initially refused, claiming he had no interest or talent as a painter, but after four lonely and intensive years up on the scaffolds, he had created the greatest fresco the world has ever known. Towards the end of his life he turned to architecture, designing the dome of St Peter's in Rome, for which he refused any payment, regarding it as a service to the glory of God. Throughout a career that spanned over half a century,

*The face of the Virgin Mary, a detail from Michelangelo's* Pietà, *completed in 1499 when he was just twenty-four. 'It is a miracle,' declared his contemporary Georgio Vasari. 'It is absolutely astonishing that the hand of an artist could have properly executed something so sublime.'*[5]

Michelangelo continued to astound with his artistic invention. He attracted a cult-like following, and several idolising biographies had already appeared before his death, aged almost ninety, in 1564.[4]

Although we may gasp in wonder at his achievements, the hero worship of Michelangelo has damaged the pursuit of the art of living for the last 500 years. Michelangelo's creative talents were seen to be a gift from God. His friend and admirer Georgio Vasari described him as the 'Divine Michelangelo', who in all the major arts had 'a perfect mastery that God has granted no other person, in the ancient or modern world, in all the years that the sun has been spinning round the world'.[6] Vasari – and Michelangelo himself – helped generate the myth that he was a lone genius by concealing the extent to which he relied on help from others; and yet the historical archives of Michelangelo's major commissions are full of bills put in for his use of assistants, at least a dozen of whom worked on the ceiling of the Sistine Chapel.[7] This depiction of Michelangelo's talents helped generate the Renaissance belief that creative genius was not of your own making but could only be bestowed by the Almighty Himself.

The legacy of this idea, which has been a powerful current in Western thought for centuries, is that creativity is not just about originality, but is a product of innate talent rather than a learned ability: either you have the gift or you don't. What is more, the gift of creativity is only granted to a chosen few, so unless you happen to be born into the lucky minority, there is not much hope of excelling in an artistic career. Creativity thus emerged as a thoroughly undemocratic concept, to be enjoyed only by an exclusive elite rather than being open to everyday people.

Since the time of Michelangelo, this is how we have usually thought about creative individuals, whether in the arts or other fields. We are amazed, for instance, by the musical genius of Mozart. At six he was composing minuets, by nine he had written his first symphony and at the age of twelve had completed an opera. No wonder his father described him as the 'miracle which God let be born in Salzburg'.[8] Mozart's own letters bolster the idea that creativity is not a matter of learning or practice, but is a mysterious and inexplicable process that comes from within:

When I am, as it were, completely myself, entirely alone, and of good cheer – say, travelling in a carriage, or walking after a good meal, or during the night when I cannot sleep; it is on such occasions that my ideas flow best and most abundantly. *Whence* and *how* they come, I know not; nor can I force them.[9]

During the Enlightenment in the eighteenth century, the idea of creativity gradually became associated with the sciences, and we now often think of the history of scientific discovery in terms of 'eureka moments', when virtuoso thinkers had blinding insights into the hidden structures of the natural world. Consider Isaac Newton, whose revelation about gravity flashed into his mind when seeing an apple drop from a tree, or the nineteenth-century French mathematician Henri Poincaré, whose breakthrough ideas suddenly emerged from his unconscious while stepping onto a bus or walking on a cliff top.[10] More recently, the British mathematician Andrew Wiles completed his proof of Fermat's Last Theorem after what he described as an 'incredible revelation' that inexplicably came to him one Monday morning in September 1994.[11] Although the idea that science advances through such eureka insights is increasingly under challenge, scientific discovery is still commonly portrayed as an unexpected moment of creative genius.

When I sat at my schoolroom art table in the early 1980s producing yet another unrecognisable still life, the overwhelming sense of creative incompetence I felt was more than self-generated angst. It was also a cultural response, reflecting the fact that I had absorbed a narrow conception of creativity handed down from the Renaissance, generation to generation. Without realising it, I had the ghost of Michelangelo looking over my shoulder, whispering into my ear that artistic ability is essentially a matter of natural talent, and I'm sorry to say, young man, but you just haven't got it. How many of us, I wonder, have sensed the presence of the Divine Michelangelo subtly eroding our creative self-confidence?

During my schooldays nobody told me there was an important shift taking place in the history of creativity that could have offered me the confidence I lacked. This was the emergence of a new movement which viewed creativity as a 'technique' that could be learned, just like you could learn to touch-type or ride a horse. It was a potentially liberating and democratising idea implying that each of us has a creative potential waiting to be realised, and that originality and invention are not primarily innate gifts from God, or the result of a favourable genetic inheritance. Rather, creativity stems from a grounding of appropriate technique and hard work, a view supported by recent research showing that 80 per cent of creativity is acquired through education or training. This has been reinforced by studies suggesting that to become an expert, whether a creative one like a concert violinist or novelist, or in an area such as sport, you need to put in around 10,000 hours of practice – the equivalent of three hours a day, every day, for ten years.[12] So Thomas Edison was not far off when he asserted that 'genius is one per cent inspiration and ninety-nine per cent perspiration', a view which would have had little popularity during the Renaissance.

The technique-based approach to creativity began in 1967 when Edward de Bono coined the term 'lateral thinking'. His emphasis was on using inventive strategies like counterfactual hypotheses and challenging conventional assumptions to solve everyday problems and train your mind. De Bono's classic lateral thinking exercise was the nine-dot puzzle, the task being to join the dots together using only four straight lines without taking your pen off the paper.

It looks easy but most people struggle, assuming that the lines must not extend outside the boundaries of the outer dots. The solution is to break that assumption, which is believed to be the origin of the phrase 'thinking out of the box'.[13]

Clever, but the problem with de Bono's work, and the industry of thinking textbooks it spawned, was that it reduced creativity to mastering a set of analytical skills that would enable you to solve puzzles and find answers. This might have been appropriate for tackling difficult engineering problems or working out why your shop was selling fewer neckties even after lowering the price, but it was unlikely to help you as a creative artist in search of beauty and self-expression.

That is why a second creativity technique became popular in the 1980s, which was to cultivate the right side of your brain. The assumption was that Western society is far too reliant on the logical and rational left brain, and that we need to nurture our more artistic, holistic and intuitive right half if we really wish to discover our creative selves. It was a powerful idea, although the left/right split is considered too simplistic by today's neuroscientists. A typical right-brain exercise asked you to sketch a tree by focusing on drawing the 'negative' spaces between the branches rather than the branches themselves, in order to circumvent the conventional idea of what a branch is supposed to look like. Another activity called 'Morning Pages', developed by Julia Cameron, suggested you write three pages of stream-of-consciousness each morning by hand, which would rid your mind of rational overload and free it up for creative endeavours.[14]

The tragedy of this growing movement in creativity was that by the 1990s it had been largely appropriated by the commercial world. Books and courses were increasingly designed for the business sector, and aimed at helping organisations thrive, rather than the individuals within them. Best-selling creativity gurus became highly paid consultants to multinationals, applying their ideas about mind maps and thinking hats to foster 'business innovation'. Workers were now expected to 'think out of the box' when devising sales strategies or streamlining management processes. While creativity was once an activity assigned to God, artists or scientists, the self-styled 'creative industries' such as public relations and advertising saw themselves as major sources of invention and imagination in society. Advertising firms even began calling their own executives 'creatives'.[15] Photographers were being further lured into doing fashion shoots for glossy magazines, and musicians wrote catchy jingles to help sell cars, running shoes and junk food. By the early twenty-first century, creativity was being directed towards marketing. Its spirit and democratic potential had been drained away.

History has sent us conflicting messages about creativity. The Renaissance legacy tells us that being creative is the preserve of those with innate talent, and requires the pursuit of originality in rarefied fields like the fine arts and sciences. This approach remains too intimidating for most of us. The creativity-technique movement views creativity as a business strategy, and as a skill not much different from learning to drive, while at the same time suggesting that if we want to raise ourselves to the level of experts in creative fields, we need to do thousands of hours of practice. None of these approaches make it obvious how creativity can become a nourishing aspect of everyday life. If we want to reclaim creativity for the art of living, we must rethink its meaning and purpose, tearing it off the gallery walls and bringing it from the corporate blue skies back down to earth. The following three strategies for doing so will not gain you a commission to paint the ceiling of a Vatican chapel or help you sell a new generation of mobile phone. All I can promise is that they will make you feel more creatively alive. The first requires little more than an empty stomach.

## Self-expression: I cook, therefore I am

One of the secrets of traditional Buddhist practice is to bring a sense of mindful awareness to routine tasks like washing up or riding a bicycle, rather than confining it to an hour of sitting cross-legged in a meditation class on a Tuesday night. And so it should be with creativity. We need to identify the moments in each day when we can nurture our creative selves, and not restrict it to a treat only to be enjoyed at a weekly pottery course. You may have already found ways of doing this, perhaps by playing the piano after dinner each evening, or tending your garden with a loving hand and an artistic eye. But one of the most obvious places for a regular dose of creation is cooking. The majority of us spend between thirty minutes and an hour preparing food each day, whether it is simply scrambled eggs on toast or a more elaborate dish like seafood risotto.[16] There lies our opportunity.

Cooking has been considered a creative art since classical times. A few decades before the birth of Jesus, the historian Livy wrote that by the second century BC the Romans were beginning to take food seriously: 'The cook whom the ancients regarded and treated as the lowest menial was rising in value, and what had been a servile office came to be looked upon as a fine art.'[17] The Romans are well-known for their obsession with luxury dining and indulgence in gluttonous feasts. But a well-laid table also needed creative chefs to fill it, so it is not surprising that the Romans invented the cook book. Open the pages of the fourth-century compilation called *Apicius* – named after a famous lover of fine food – and you will find a multitude of tantalising recipes, including roasted flamingo with honey and dates, sea urchins with mint, and a tasty version of asparagus quiche using lovage and fresh coriander.[18]

But it would be wrong to think that creative cooking is all about concocting new and delectable dishes to astound your dinner guests. That would be falling into the trap laid by the Renaissance, which is the belief that creativity should be equated with brilliant originality. No, I think that cooking permits what is really important about creative endeavours, which is to grant us a space for self-expression.

I learned this in the early 1990s while living for a year in Madrid. One afternoon my three Spanish flatmates conceded to teach me the sacred art of making *tortilla española*, the famed Spanish omelette. Virtually a national dish, it traditionally involves slowly frying raw potato and onion in plenty of oil, pouring this into a bowl of beaten eggs, then returning the mixture to the pan. After a tricky manoeuvre flipping the omelette over, you should end up with a beautifully browned and springy discus about an inch thick. After a few failed attempts, I eventually managed to cook a tortilla that met with my flatmates' gastronomic approval. But then I began to play around. I found the omelette a little bland, so tried adding clams, aubergine and even apple, avocado and figs. My patriotic flatmates were completely horrified. I had desecrated the holy tortilla, sullied it with foreign bodies. I shocked them further by parboiling the potatoes to use less oil. They repeatedly urged me to return to the purity of the original recipe. Yet I was too busy enjoying myself – respecting the basic law of using potato, onion and egg, yet adding a personal touch of flavour and inspiration.

*A 1709 Dutch edition of the ancient Roman cookbook* Apicius, *here subtitled* The Art of Cooking. *In the London edition published four years earlier, the printing costs were covered by some of the most creative luminaries of the age, including Isaac Newton and Christopher Wren.[19] Were they secret weekend chefs who could rustle up a mean roasted flamingo?*

Making a tortilla had become nothing less than an act of creative self-expression. It allowed me to try out some of my own ideas and put part of myself into the cooking process. I had a love of clams, so why not toss some into the pan? Even when I later discovered that this was a common practice on the eastern coast of Spain, I was not concerned, since it was not my intention to revolutionise Iberian cooking. I was able to develop my own culinary aesthetic – my sense of what tastes, smells and looks good on a plate. To me there was something beautiful about criss-crossing strips of roasted red and green pepper over the top of the tortilla as if it were a Mondrian canvas.

There was also scope for improvisation, a crucial element of many creative pursuits. In the same way that a jazz trumpeter improvises around the chords of the main tune, I could do the equivalent in the kitchen, which was to open the fridge door to see what happened to be inside that day, and adding it to the tortilla mixture in an unplanned but respectful elaboration of the core recipe. What was the worst thing that could happen if I stirred some leftover popcorn into the tortilla? When life is full of busy schedules and long lists of things that ought to get done, cooking provides a vital outlet for the freedoms of improvisation. 'Life is a lot like jazz,' said George Gershwin, 'it's best when you improvise.'

Cooking a tortilla embodied a final aspect of self-expression for me, which was that the meal I prepared could become a gift to be shared with friends, family and visiting strangers as a nourishing act of generosity. Genuine art, writes Lewis Hyde, is a gift whose value is unrelated to its price, and is an offering which creates a 'feeling-bond' between artist and viewer.[20] When a neighbour dropped around with a fish pie just after my children were born and I had no time to cook, it had all the qualities of an artistic gift. To satisfy the hunger of another is to satisfy their most basic human need, but it is also a sublime form of gift-giving.

One of the great joys of cooking today is that there has been half a century of pioneering writer-chefs such as Irma Rombauer, Julia Child, Auguste Escoffier, Elizabeth David and Fuchsia Dunlop, who have removed the mystique around gastronomy and made it possible for almost anyone to learn how to be a competent cook, without the need for a diploma from the Cordon Bleu school. With a little experience and the courage to deviate from the recipes on the page, cooking dinner after a long day at work can be transformed into an energising act of creation that surpasses the pleasures of collapsing in front of the television and ordering takeaway. Even a frozen pizza can be graced with some inventive extra topping, perhaps arranged in a mesmerising spiral or to resemble a Jackson Pollock drip painting. By putting part of ourselves into the food we make, we give new meaning to the phrase 'you are what you eat'. At the same time, we may come to understand just why the French gourmet Jean-Anthelme Brillat-Savarin declared in 1825, 'The discovery of a new dish does more for the happiness of mankind than the discovery of a star.'[21]

So I say treat yourself to a daily dose of self-expression, whether through cooking, learning to play the guitar or some other potentially creative pursuit. Let it become a habit as regular as walking your dog or brushing your teeth. Avenge the legacy of Michelangelo and rescue creativity from the exclusivity of high art and the cult of the creative genius.

## Homo faber: making things is good for you

In 1914 the German psychologist Wolfgang Köhler conducted an experiment in the Canary Islands with a chimpanzee named Sultan. He placed a banana outside Sultan's cage, just beyond arm's reach, and inside he put a bush covered with small branches. Sultan was then let into the cage. The chimp looked around and spotted the tantalising yet distant banana. Then, noticing the bush, he immediately seized a slender branch, broke it off with a sharp jerk, ran back to the bars and thrust the branch through, using it to drag the banana towards him, at which point he devoured his prize. In another experiment, Sultan managed – after many unsuccessful efforts – to fit two hollow sticks into one another and use them to rake another banana into his cage. This new discovery 'pleased him so immensely', reported Köhler, that Sultan kept repeating the trick and forgot to eat the banana.[22]

Sultan's ability to make tools, and his evident pleasure in doing so, is a deep evolutionary clue to resolving our dilemmas about how to live. Making and using tools is a fundamental element of who and what we are, even more so than for our close relative the chimpanzee. *Homo erectus*, the ancestors of *Homo sapiens*, were employing stone tools 2.5 million years ago. It is with our hands as much as our minds that we have changed the world, through building, spinning, hoeing, hammering and hunting. For thousands of years we have moulded pots, woven cloth, ground corn, raised walls, joined mortise and tenon. As much as being *Homo sapiens*, man the thinker, we are *Homo faber*, man the maker. When children erect a tower of tottering blocks or run to the craft table to cut plasticine stars, they are *Homo faber*. When you experience the satisfactions of knitting a scarf or tiling the bathroom, you are *Homo faber*. To be human is to be a maker of things. To deny this part of ourselves is – almost literally – like losing a limb.[23]

Bringing more *Homo faber* into your life is a second, fundamental way of expanding your creative being. Historically, the main way we have done this is through craft, which typically involves developing a practical skill like carpentry or weaving, and making objects such as spoons or shirts that are useful on a daily basis, unlike a painting that hangs in the hallway. The challenge is that craft culture has been in decline since the eighteenth century and most of us have lost the skills that our ancestors once possessed.[24] Have you made any of the clothes you are wearing, or the chair you are sitting on? Almost certainly not.

No one would have lamented this more than the nineteenth-century writer, socialist reformer and craftsman William Morris. Having trained himself as a weaver, fabric designer and printer, Morris led a revival of traditional handicrafts as a response to the industrial revolution, which was destroying the artisan economy and condemning human beings to tedious toil in factory jobs. Morris's ideas, encapsulated in the Arts and Crafts movement that he founded and which thrived between 1880 and 1910, have helped define the meaning and purpose of craft in the West for the last century.

The chief benefit of being a craftworker, Morris believed, is 'giving us pleasure in our work'. This is largely because it uses 'the whole of a man', requiring a combination of brain work and manual work, rather than numbing us with specialised and repetitive tasks. Instead of sitting in front of a computer screen all day, craft allows us to merge mind and body. Another benefit is the feeling of pride we experience by learning a skill and producing everyday objects which are not only highly functional but also aesthetically pleasing. 'Have nothing in your home that you do not know to be useful and believe to be beautiful,' he advised. A true craftworker takes a healthy pride in their work, doing the task well for its own sake, even if the financial reward does not match their time and effort, and even if their name does not adorn what they make. Craft should additionally be valued because it is an act of political defiance, a rejection of what Morris called 'the commercial system'.[25] It replaces the wage slavery of the capitalist economy with self-sufficiency and self-reliance, offering the prospect of greater individual freedom and wellbeing. When Mahatma Gandhi founded the *khadi* movement in the 1920s, which revived the hand-spinning of cloth to replace imported British textiles as a protest against British colonial rule, he was following in Morris's footsteps, using craft as a political tool.

William Morris is an undisputed champion of *Homo faber*, one of history's greatest thinkers on the idea that making things is good for us. But if craft is so good for us, why don't we do it more? The story begins in pre-industrial Europe, when making was at the centre of everyday life. Wander the streets of late medieval Paris, London or Mainz, and you would have seen the workshops of shoemakers, goldsmiths, ironmongers and coopers. Apprentices in their teens were busily learning the skills of their craft, dreaming of the day when they would produce their 'masterpiece' – perhaps a fine inlaid cabinet – which would gain them the exalted title of Master and allow them to open their own establishment. Of course, some were treated brutally by their employers, and if apprenticed in a tannery they would have to suffer years of pounding dog dung into animal skins. But at least they would probably become members of a craft guild, a kind of trade union which acted as a mutual aid association protecting the members by providing health and old-age insurance, controlling employment in the trade and ensuring standards of workmanship.[26] And the culture of making extended beyond the workplace. If you owned a horse, you may have bought its shoes from a blacksmith, but you would probably have built the stable yourself. If you needed a water well, you would have dug it with the help of your brothers. If your family required a new kitchen table, or clothes for the children, they would have been made at home. Forget calling in the plumber or ordering online – the Middle Ages was the original era of do-it-yourself, when men and women spent their whole lives with calloused hands.

Over the past 300 years, however, *Homo faber* has been in a gradual, deathly decline. We have lost touch with the medieval culture of making, and our soft-skinned hands are now good for little more than tapping a keyboard and sending a text. It started with the machine age of the eighteenth and nineteenth centuries, which ushered in an epoch of creative obliteration.[27] This was when the art of making began to disappear. Its first villain was Jacques de Vaucanson, who was originally famous as the inventor of an ingenious mechanical shitting duck, which Voltaire declared to be 'the glory of France'. Louis XV decided he should make something more useful, and put him in charge of French silk manufacturing, which inspired Vaucanson to design a loom that wove silk threads far more quickly than human hands. In the 1740s and 1750s his machines became so widely used in Lyons that weavers assaulted him whenever he appeared on the streets.[28] As factories and mills rose up across the increasingly smoke-filled European landscape, then spread to North America, the skilled craftworker became largely redundant, only surviving in cultural pockets such as the New England Shaker communities, a radical Protestant sect that retained a tradition of fine woodworking into the twentieth century.

The demise of *Homo faber* accelerated in the consumer age of the nineteenth and twentieth centuries, when we lost the art of mending. We became increasingly dependent on buying manufactured household goods and gradually developed an addiction to shopping that was incompatible with maintaining the old craft skills. Chair making, for instance, was radically transformed in 1859 when the German-Austrian cabinetmaker Michael Thonet created his renowned 'Chair No. 14'. Made using a unique steaming process and mass production techniques, over 50 million of these were sold between 1860 and 1930. By the early twentieth century, if you needed a dining chair, you went out and bought a No. 14 or some similar factory model, without even thinking of making it yourself. Then, when it had a wobbly leg, rather than fixing it, you would purchase a whole new chair. I only have to walk down my street and peek into the skips to see the results of this wasteful, throwaway culture – they are full of abandoned chairs, bookshelves and other domestic items. Most of the chairs are easily repairable but the majority of people don't know how. I am as much a culprit as anybody else: I have a hole in one of the socks I'm wearing, and because I have no darning skills, my socks will probably soon end up in the bin. William Morris – and no doubt his wife too – would have been able to stitch up the hole beautifully.

The final stage in the decline of *Homo faber* is the computer age, which began in the late twentieth century and in which we are still immersed. This is the era when we lost not the art of making or mending, but the art of practical understanding. Technology has become so complex that we no longer know how anything works. Fifty years ago you could probably figure out how your typewriter operated and fix it at a push, but most of us don't have a clue how our computers function. What really goes on inside the whirring box where the hard drive lives? Today's cars have so many computerised components that even trained mechanics have trouble repairing them. We have also become deskilled by modern technology, so that architects design with specialised software that renders them unable to draw, and bakers make bread by pushing a button rather than kneading dough. The result is almost total alienation from the material objects around us, eroding the possibilities for a culture of craft. Craft no longer seems a feasible option.[29]

William Morris, and his contemporary John Ruskin, dreamed of returning to a mythical golden age of the medieval craft-worker.[30] But if we want craft to become a renewed source of creativity in our lives, we have to move beyond such nostalgic visions. The contemporary economy provides little scope for making a living as a potter, glass-blower or hand-loom weaver. Some years ago I trained with one of Britain's last remaining master chair-makers, who taught me the ancient craft of making a 'greenwood' chair, completely by hand using fresh timber and a pole lathe, without any nails, glue or power tools. The experi-ence was just as Morris described it: the merging of mind and body, the creation of a rustic object that was both beautiful and functional, the pride of learning and completing, the sense of self-sufficiency and connection with nature. But when I returned home and began making the chairs in my workshop, it soon became clear that this was no way to support myself financially. Each chair took a minimum of thirty hours from start to finish, and, given the market price, even if I could sell them immediately I could scarcely pay the rent.

I realised then that it would be more realistic, and possibly just as fulfilling, to introduce a 'craft mentality' into the work I was already doing rather than pursue the Arcadian dream of earning my livelihood as a chair bodger.[31] I could try to write my articles and books keeping in mind the ideal of doing a task well for its own sake, making an effort to refine and sculpt the prose even if it might be possible to get away with more turgid expression of my thoughts. Equally, when I gave public talks I could ensure that the visuals were both useful and beautiful, showing slides which conveyed the point with maximum clarity while also having an uncluttered minimalist aesthetic. While it may be easier to introduce a craft approach into some jobs than others, we can all strive to discover the hidden possibilities for craft in our working lives.

If you would rather satisfy an urge to be *Homo faber* outside working hours, and really want craft to nourish your soul, you had best join the largest social movement in Western culture, which goes by the innocuous name of DIY. Its members gather regularly in superstores, where they buy nails, guttering and drills, in preparation for a vigorous weekend of doing it themselves. Under the guise of 'home improvement', DIY has educated millions of people in craft skills that have been disappearing for decades, helping a whole generation of men and women get in touch with their inner tool-user.

If this movement were to have its own personality cult, it would have to be centred on the American nature writer Henry David Thoreau, who was not only a master of simple living, but the first DIY sage of the modern age. In 1845, when he decided to live alone in the New England woods, he borrowed an axe, chopped down some pine trees and began hewing timbers for a hut. Thoreau's meticulous accounts show he spent under thirty dollars constructing his home, including $3.90 on nails and fourteen cents on hinges and screws. When he wrote that 'there is some of the same fitness in a man's building his own house that there is in a bird building its own nest', Thoreau had identified the essence of DIY.[32] There is an elemental satisfaction in creating the place you live in, giving it just the features you want, and gaining the pleasures of self-reliance and using your hands along the way.

Thoreau was consciously rejecting the machine age emerging around him, seeking a simpler way of life. I found a different, yet equally inspiring DIY model in Guatemala. Craft traditions remain strong amongst the indigenous Mayan population. In the villages of the Western Highlands you will see women wearing *huipiles*, elaborate hand-woven blouses which are coveted by the tourists, and men weaving bags and blankets on the back streets. Yet I was more struck by the DIY culture of the shanty towns surrounding Guatemala City. The hillside alleyways are filled with the brilliantly improvised architecture of the poorest city dwellers. Houses are built of any material available, from corrugated iron to stone blocks, wood panels, plastic sheeting and thatch. Where possible, the inhabitants have done their own plumbing and rigged up basic sinks and stoves, while creatively tapping into any electricity wires passing nearby. I don't wish to romanticise life in the slums as William Morris romanticised the lives of medieval craftworkers, but the self-built housing in Guatemala City and other shanty towns in developing countries displays craft skills that would be the envy of anybody in the West about to embark on a DIY adventure.

I once spent four months building a new kitchen in my home. I did so partly to save money – an off-the-shelf kitchen, including cupboards, appliances and full installation, was going to cost upwards of 10,000 dollars. I was able to complete ours for under a quarter that amount. Since I usually spent most of my days reading and writing, I also felt a need to get in touch with my neglected *Homo faber*. As I made silly mistakes screwing in hinges upside down, I imagined Thoreau gently chuckling at me from a perch in the corner. As I retrieved some old cupboards from a skip and fitted them into my design, I felt as resourceful as a Guatemalan shanty-town resident. As I became increasingly skilled at using a plane, and added rounded corners to the beech worktop, I was like a medieval apprentice honing his abilities. When I managed to incorporate my partner's old childhood toy cupboard into the breakfast bar, I knew I had made something that was both useful and beautiful.

DIY is not without dangers. It is tempting to be lured into its commercialism and spend a small fortune on designer paints or fancy drill bits that you rarely need. I imagine that Thoreau would avoid today's corporate superstores and shop instead at an independent hardware supplier, buying only the essentials. We should also be careful not to overemphasise the individualist aspects of DIY. This is because its self-sufficiency is suffused with a cooperative spirit – for instance when you borrow tools or seek advice and help from a neighbour – which echoes the shared learning and mutual aid of medieval craft culture. DIY should really be called DIWO, or do-it-with-others. Such caveats apart, joining the DIY movement remains the greatest opportunity in modern life to put into practice William Morris's belief that making things is good for you.

Following the two pathways towards creativity I have discussed – indulging in a daily dose of self-expression and nurturing ourselves as *Homo faber* – requires expanding the realm of creativity outside the traditional fine arts and sciences to include more ordinary pursuits like cooking dinner and putting up bookshelves. A third, more radical approach, is to relinquish the idea that creativity involves any defined activity and to treat it instead as a philosophy of living in its own right.

## Breaking conventions: in praise of nudist communist vegetarians

All artistic genres have their conventions, 'rules of the game' which shape subject matter, style and technique. Traditional Chinese painting contains no shadows and gives much greater prominence to natural landscape than Western art. Ancient Egyptian wall painting displayed virtually no innovations in visual representation for 3,000 years: the head and legs were invariably in profile, with the eyes and chest portrayed frontally. Classical Greek sculpture focused on the image of man, with scant interest shown in the female figure.[33]

Originality in art is a matter of breaking such deeply ingrained conventions. We revere those artists who discarded the old rules and established new standards of relevance, who took their imaginative freedom beyond the boundaries of conformity. On one level originality has involved shifting the subject or theme, as with the rise of non-religious painting in the Renaissance, or the nineteenth-century development of painting scenes of everyday city life. But it has also been about inventing new ways of seeing, which revolutionise the nature of perception. Two important moments of originality in Western art, which altered how the world was visualised, can help us think about how to live.

The first took place in 1425 when the Florentine architect Filippo Brunelleschi discovered – or 'rediscovered' – linear perspective. The ancient Greeks had known about foreshortening objects to make them appear more distant, but in one of the most mysterious disappearances in cultural history, the technique was lost for centuries. In medieval paintings, objects in the distance are typically out of proportion from the viewer's perspective, often appearing far too large. Brunelleschi's innovation was the 'vanishing point'. He demonstrated with mathematical precision how objects in a picture should be diminished in direct proportion to their distance from the viewer, creating the illusion of a three-dimensional space on a two-dimensional surface. Renaissance painters such as Uccello became obsessed with Brunelleschi's technique, and linear perspective was subsequently adopted as an artistic standard until the end of the nineteenth century.[34]

A second key moment occurred around 400 years later. This was the birth of cubism, which is often dated to the startling works created by Picasso and Braque from around 1907. The originality of the movement was in rejecting the single point of view that had become dominant through the convention of linear perspective. Instead, the cubists painted the same subject from several perspectives simultaneously. Perhaps their most formative influence was Cézanne, who on a single canvas depicted the variations of what he saw when he slightly changed his viewpoint.[35] In works such as *Trees by the Water* (1900–1904), writes the art critic John Berger, one tree becomes several possible trees:

> He observed that if he moved his head a little to the right he saw a different aspect of what was in front of him from what he would see if he moved his head a little to the left. Every child discovers this by lying in bed and closing each eye alternately. The difference was that Cézanne thought it mattered.[36]

The history of perspective in Western painting matters because of what it reveals for the art of living. Just as most artists conform to the stylistic conventions of the era into which they are born, we similarly conform to prevailing social conventions about how to live. These unwritten rules typically include getting married and having children, owning your own home and having a mortgage, shopping in supermarkets and driving a car, having a regular job and commuting to work, and flying abroad for holidays. For some people these are realities, for others they remain aspirations. It is common to feel social pressure to comply with them. At this point in Western history, they are amongst the dominant conventions that most of us have accepted with little questioning, much as Vermeer and other Dutch baroque painters of the seventeenth century accepted linear perspective without question. It is difficult to see beyond the limitations of the culture that has shaped our ways of looking at the world and at ourselves. We are trapped in the perspective of our own time.

Artists like Brunelleschi, Cézanne and Picasso were experimenters who broke the rules. If we wish to live truly creative and adventurous lives, we can take our inspiration from them and become experimenters who reject the social norms that bind us, discovering the freedom to develop our own perspective on

*Picasso's unfinished* Girl with a Mandolin *(1910), which demonstrated the new vision of cubism, with its multiple points of view.*

the art of living. This is not to say that conventions should be broken for their own sake – there is no reason to avoid having children just because others have them – only that we should become aware of their invisible presence, and consider defying those that might limit the possibilities for living a fulfilling life of our own choosing.

The short life of Mary Wollstonecraft displayed such creative originality. Her approach to living was as many-sided and shocking as an early cubist painting. She was the first modern woman, an eighteenth-century radical who valued her individuality above social convention.[37] 'Every obligation we receive from our fellow creatures is a new shackle, takes from our native freedom, and debases the mind,' she wrote. Wollstonecraft rejected the accepted social roles for women of her time and continually fought for her own independence. She embarked on a career as an author in an era when almost no women did so, then in 1792 wrote a famous feminist tract, *A Vindication of the Rights of Woman*, which marked her as a revolutionary thinker. She had a scandalous affair with the married artist Henry Fuseli, fell in love with a woman, and had a child out of wedlock while staying in Paris during the French Revolution. Following several suicide attempts after another unhappy relationship, she married the anarchist philosopher William Godwin, but true to their ideals they lived in two adjoining houses so they could maintain their independence. Wollstonecraft died following complications in childbirth in her late thirties, and for a century afterwards was pilloried by both men and women for her lack of morals and unorthodox lifestyle. Her reputation revived in the twentieth century and she eventually became a feminist icon. But she should also be celebrated as an icon for the art of living. 'Mary's life had been an experiment from the start,' concluded Virginia Woolf, 'an attempt to make human conventions conform more closely to human needs.'[38] It was a life of tragedy, but also a life of freedom.

Mary Wollstonecraft reminds me of my grandmother Naomi, who shocked 1930s Sydney with her bohemian radicalism. Born in Bessarabia – now Moldova – and the daughter of a rabbi, she fled to Manchuria as a young woman, then begged her way down to Shanghai, where she caught a slow boat to Australia. Naomi was not only a fervent member of the Communist Party, but also a nudist and a vegetarian. She lived in an abandoned tramcar, and married a man a decade younger than herself when she was already pregnant from another relationship. On weekends she drew the crowds by making political speeches on street corners, and was a rare female voice on national radio, giving talks on her favourite writers such as Leo Tolstoy and Anatole France. I don't know if she ever read Mary Wollstonecraft, but they were kindred spirits. When I find myself faced by a difficult decision, torn between social convention and individual freedom, I look at the photo of Naomi in my hallway and ask myself what she would have done in my shoes. She has been my guide to a more creative way of living, silently advising me to leave sensible jobs for nomadic travels, or to follow my passions even if they offer few financial rewards.

'To blossom forth,' said Picasso, 'a work of art must ignore or rather forget all the rules.' If we wish our lives to blossom, we should do the same, and transform creativity into a philosophy of personal independence, which shapes how we approach our work, our relationships, our beliefs and our ambitions.

Creativity remains one of the most mythologised aspects of human endeavour. The majority of people still believe it is the preserve of a minority who are born with a special gift – the talented painter, the visionary poet, the inventive physicist. Yet history tells us that creativity can become a more inclusive pursuit, whether it is through self-expression in the kitchen, by experiencing the joys of *Homo faber* or in breaking social conventions. Of course we are still faced with formidable barriers. Many people are trapped in jobs that are too specialised and mind-numbing to provide much scope for creative thinking. We can all easily be lured by passive forms of entertainment like television, which steals three to four hours a day from the average person – time that might otherwise be spent working with our hands or using our imaginations.[39] But at least we need not worry that we are not Michelangelos, blessed with innate brilliance by our deities. Creativity does not require the bestowal or inheritance of genius. Above all it requires the self-confidence to believe that we are capable of finding ways to express our uniqueness.

# 12

# Deathstyle

Death is more distant from the Western mind today than at any other point in history. This is partly due to the breathtaking increase in longevity across industrialised nations over the past century. If you had been born in England in the 1830s, you would have been likely to live, on average, to the age of around thirty-eight; within only 150 years, life expectancy had doubled. In the United States, a middle-aged woman in the 1950s had a 10 per cent chance of living to become a grand dame of ninety, a figure that has now risen to almost 30 per cent.[1] This huge leap in longevity may be the greatest social revolution in human history. In terms of changes to everyday life, nothing compares with the fact that our lives are decades longer than they once were – not the invention of the printing press, or the increase in living standards, or the extension of the right to vote, or the birth of the internet. Thanks to advances in medical knowledge and public health, we have defied millennia of evolution and granted ourselves an extra dose of the headiest drug known to humankind – existence itself.

This surge in lifespan, which remains absent in most of the developing world, has been accompanied by a radical decline in the public presence of death. The rise of a medicalised death in hospital, and the erosion of traditional funeral and mourning rituals, have made death largely invisible in modern society. We now almost never see dead bodies except in the gory fictions of horror films and war movies, and death has become the ultimate taboo topic of conversation, the perfect way to create an awkward silence at a dinner party. Like Oscar Wilde's creation Dorian Gray, whose dream was to stay forever young, we have managed to push death as far away as possible, into some almost unreal place in the future.

These changes call on us to rethink our attitudes towards death. While newspaper supplements encourage us to obsess about our lifestyle – whether we should take up ashtanga yoga or treat ourselves to a Mediterranean cruise – I believe we should engage much more deeply with the subject of *deathstyle*. By deathstyle I mean the art of growing old, facing our mortality and dying well. We can only master this art in a culture that talks about death openly and frankly. I would like to contribute to this conversation by exploring three historical perspectives on death: how the obsession with death during the Middle Ages created an intense appreciation of the value of life; the damage done by the gradual demise of death as a social event over the last century; and how different cultures have approached caring for elderly family members. These historical encounters may help to create the foundations of your own deathstyle philosophy.

## Dancing with death

It is almost impossible for us to imagine how much the sights, sounds and thoughts of death permeated the lives of medieval and Renaissance Europeans. This is not simply because high mortality rates meant you were likely to have siblings who had died in childhood, or because periodic outbreaks of plague led to bodies being piled in the streets, and priests were shouting at you about the fires of Hell. It was also because death itself was an integral part of public culture.

Just consider the social role of cemeteries. Today cemeteries are solemn and empty places typically located in the outer suburbs. While some retain an air of wildness, most are full of neatly clipped grass and polished headstones. But 600 years ago – partly due to their abundance of space and proximity to churches – they were the equivalent of city shopping malls. The cemeteries of medieval Paris, London and Rome were popular meeting places where you could find tradesmen selling wine, beer and linen, especially on saints days when pilgrims were passing through. People would stroll, socialise and make merry amongst the graves. Children played with human bones in the charnel houses by the church, where skeletons were stacked after being dug up to make space for new residents. The ancient tradition of dancing in cemeteries in communion with the dead was so widespread that the French Church repeatedly tried to ban it, though with little effect. In the Middle Ages, writes a historian of burial places, cemeteries were 'the noisiest, busiest, most boisterous, and most commercial place in the rural or urban community.'[2]

The iconography of death was as common and unavoidable as billboard advertising is today. In 1424 the first known dance of the dead, or *danse macabre*, was painted on a wall of the Cemetery of Saint Innocents in Paris (which was closed in the eighteenth century for sanitary reasons, and the human remains transferred to the city's catacombs – now a favourite tourist haunt). These paintings and frescoes, which became popular throughout Europe, depicted individuals of every social station, from popes to peasants, each dancing with a naked and rotting skeleton that had come to take them away from earthly life. The people often look stunned next to their ecstatically animated and bony partner, as they engage in a ghoulish waltz with their own mortality. The allegorical purpose was to remind the viewer not only that death was always close to them and could strike at any moment, but that everyone was equal in the face of it. These ideas were also symbolised by the figure of the Grim Reaper, a personification of death as a skeleton carrying a scythe and wearing a hooded cloak, which began appearing from the fifteenth century alongside the dance of the dead. The spread of this obsession with the macabre could be found in artworks showing 'transi', half-decomposed corpses often with the entrails spilling out, which became a common representation of death in Northern Europe in the late medieval period.

These gruesome creations were part of an artistic genre known as *memento mori* (Latin for 'remember you must die'), which later took the popular form of trinkets, brooches or rings showing a

*A* danse macabre *from a fifteenth-century French illuminated manuscript, in which an unlucky empress dances with a grinning Death, who is leading her away to her fate.*

skull or other symbol of death, and were casually worn just as we now wear a necklace or watch. Hans Holbein the Younger built his reputation on this deathly imagery: in 1538 his series of woodcuts on the *danse macabre* became a bestseller, while his portrait *The Ambassadors* in London's National Gallery shows Jean de Dinteville wearing a death's head *memento mori* on his hat and in the foreground floats the celebrated anamorphic skull, which is skewed so it can only be seen when viewed from a sharp angle.[3]

The morbid fascination with skulls and corpses that occupied the medieval mind is more than a historical curiosity: it contains a crucial message for us today. In the Middle Ages death was so prevalent that people had a heightened appreciation of the preciousness and fragility of life. Knowing that it could slip away from them at any time, they felt driven to live it with an intensity and passion that we no longer possess. That is why the historian Philippe Ariès, in his study of attitudes towards death over the last millennium, concluded, 'The truth is that probably at no time has man so loved life as he did at the end of the Middle Ages.'[4] When you are constantly reminded that death can snatch you away in an instant, when you grow up playing amongst human thigh bones and seeing skeletons dance on the walls, you are likely to realise that life exists to be lived to the full, that every moment must be cherished as a gift, that you should make the most of the few years granted to you. The very ubiquity of death propelled a whole age towards a state of radical aliveness.[5]

Death is no longer as imminent as it was in medieval times: we scarcely see its face or talk about it, and we imagine living long into our distant eighties or nineties. As a result our awareness of the rare value of existence has been diminished, and with it the ability to immerse ourselves in the present and suck all the marrow from life. We busy our brains with future plans and anxieties and find ourselves tolerating tedious jobs and watching hours of television. It is as if we are waiting around for the moment when our real lives will begin. The prospect of death no longer drives us to savour the human adventure.

There are two groups of people who are exceptions, both of whom have a medieval sense of the Grim Reaper looking intently over their shoulders. The first are those who have come close to death themselves. Amongst them is Jane Whiting, a counsellor and community artist I met while running a project collecting stories of turning points in people's lives. During a hiking trip in the Australian bush when in her thirties, Jane slipped while crossing a ferocious swollen river. She managed to cling onto a rock but the turbulent white water pushed her head under so she was unable to breathe. She couldn't let go as there was a waterfall just downstream with a 200-foot drop. Desperately gasping for air, Jane was sure she was going to die. But at the last moment she was pulled from the rock by one of her companions.

This near tragedy was a transformative moment, completely altering her worldview and ambitions. 'My whole life changed,' she said. 'After that experience, moving to a new town or even to a new country just didn't seem like a big deal. I nearly died but it was one of life's lessons that comes along and teaches you something.' Returning to England, she decided to give up her high-powered career as a consultant in London and move to a provincial town. She cut back her work to three days a week, having previously been swallowed up and stressed out by her job, and began spending the remaining two days doing art courses. 'I have a lot more time and space to do the kinds of things I want to do, which is brilliant,' she said. 'I've been able to have more time together with my sister, who I've got really close to, and with my parents, who are in their seventies. Now, for me, life is about getting balance instead of being an ambitious, big-city, coffee-fuelled person.'

There is a second group of people who, unlike Jane, make a conscious choice to dance with death. I am thinking of firefighters, humanitarian aid workers, cancer ward nurses and heart surgeons, whose front-line work regularly brings them into contact with the dying or puts their own lives at risk. For many of them, having close encounters with death offers a life-affirming experience and is a prime motivator for what they do. There may be no better example of this than the French high-wire artist Philippe Petit.

Born in 1949, Petit was a rebel from an early age, being expelled from five schools and running away from home at fifteen. He became interested in magic, then later trained himself as a tightrope walker, spurning work in circuses and formulaic performances to create his own way of crossing the wire. This led to his first spectacular feats in the early 1970s, walking without any safety equipment between the two towers of Notre Dame Cathedral, and then the pylons of the Sydney Harbour Bridge.

Petit was now prepared for the artistic crime of the century, which was to break into the Twin Towers in New York City and walk the forty-three metres of emptiness between their rooftops,

*Philippe Petit on his virtuoso walk between the Twin Towers, the subject of the startling documentary* Man on Wire.

more than a hundred storeys above the sidewalks of Manhattan. After years of planning, and assisted by a crack team, he defied the security guards, rigged his 450-pound cable with the help of a bow and arrow, and began his aerial crossing just after seven in the morning on 7 August 1974.

Petit is a born performer. So instead of making a single crossing, he went back and forth eight times, for a total of forty-five minutes. He also sat on the wire, lay down on it, and spoke to a seagull circling above his head.[6] A police officer dispatched to the site to arrest Petit reported what he saw:

> I observed the tightrope 'dancer' – because you couldn't call him a 'walker' – approximately halfway between the two towers. And upon seeing us he started to smile and laugh and he started going into a dancing routine on the high wire … And when he got to the building we asked him to get off the high wire but instead he turned around and ran back out into the middle … He was bouncing up and down. His feet were actually leaving the wire and then he would resettle

back on the wire again ... Unbelievable really ... Everyone
was spellbound in the watching of it.

Those observing from below, pausing in their morning rush
to work, were shocked at the fearlessness of the mid-air dancer,
but also entranced by the beauty of his act. It was a beauty
derived from the artist engaging in a dance with death. At any
second, with a gust of wind, it could have ended in tragedy. 'If
I die, what a beautiful death!' he said of his performance. For
many, the image of Petit amongst the clouds was a vision that
has stayed with them all their lives. It was a moment when the
city noises faded, everything went still and they glimpsed all the
possibilities of living – and dying – in Petit's ability to balance
with his pole. They glimpsed the preciousness and fragility of
human existence which was so well known in medieval times.

The high-wire walk was more than aesthetics or a bid for
fame; it was also the embodiment of a philosophy of life. As Petit
later explained:

> To me, it's really so simple, that life should be lived on the
> edge. You have to exercise rebellion. To refuse to tape your-
> self to the rules, to refuse your own success, to refuse to
> repeat yourself, to see every day, every year, every idea as a
> true challenge. Then you will live your life on the tightrope.

I am too risk-averse to seek the existential high of daredevil
pursuits like tightrope walking, bungee jumping or parachuting.
Similarly, I would rather avoid the near-death experience of Jane
Whiting even if it opened my mind to adventurous choices. And
I certainly have no nostalgia for the Middle Ages, knowing that
my partner might easily have died in childbirth, and our twins
along with her. But I do recognise that, as these examples reveal,
life and death are the most intimate of relations. We cannot know
one without meeting the other.

How can we bring this knowledge into everyday living? By
becoming aware that we are constantly surrounded by both life
and death, and that every moment or period of our lives deserves

special attention because it will pass into a little death of its own, a reflection of the impermanence of all things.[7] You can think of this as developing a new sense – the sense of transience. A flower opens its petals but is destined to fade, so smell the flower now. You will only be in your twenties once, so live them with a footloose passion before your twenty-something self disappears for ever. You will not always be fit and healthy enough to make that epic cycle ride with your partner around the coast, so pump up your tyres and get pedalling. Your daughter will never again be a toddler discovering language and exploring the world for the first time, so share these precious months with her rather than working over the weekends. Your parents are elderly and may not live much longer so make the effort to visit them more often; why live with the regret that you did not see them enough before they died? When I step onto the court for tennis practice, I often imagine that this is the last time I will ever be able to play, a thought that inspires me to revel in the spontaneity and beauty of the game. In the end, we may not survive to be four score and ten, or even two score and ten, so whatever your age, now is the moment for the fire of your life to burn brightly. Or as Philippe Petit might put it, take a deep breath and walk the wire.

You could even take the idea of a sense of transience a stage further, by ritually marking the end of significant periods in your life. When you change jobs, get married or move countries, hold an imaginary memorial party for the passing of the person you will no longer be, the life you will no longer live. When you hit your forties, you might conduct a funeral for your thirties, which have now died, never to return. Or you could create a 'tombstone book', in which you write epitaphs for each passing phase in your life, perhaps at the end of each season, year or decade. This will all serve to raise your awareness of those little deaths that constitute our lives, whose recognition can bring us closer to living with greater presence.

Our modern desire to keep death at a distance, to insulate ourselves from its shadowy presence, is a form of collective denial that diminishes our capacity to feel the fragility and fleetingness of our earthly being, and saps us of our life force. We need to breathe the air of death just as much as we need the air of life to flow through our bodies. We may savour the pleasures of existence when eating fine foods, making love or climbing a mountain, but recognising the true value of life means understanding that it could so easily be lost.

I recently visited a website which told me that, given my birth date, weight, height and medical condition, I was likely to die on Saturday, 1 October 2044. The apparent precision of this result was shocking, but also an incentive to seize the day, every day, and embrace the prospect of death.

## The community of death

My mother died from cancer when I was ten, but it was another twenty years before I visited her grave. When I arrived at the cemetery, which was in the northern suburbs of Sydney, I had to call on an attendant to help find her plot because she had no headstone. Her grave was an unmarked patch of grass. I sat down where she was buried, warming myself in the winter sun, feeling both a sense of connection with her and a terrible shame that it had taken me so long to make this pilgrimage. In most cultures the anonymity of her resting place, and my failure to visit it, would be considered both an insult to my mother's memory and a gross failure of family responsibility and love. I used to tell myself that my two decades of absence was because I had been living abroad for most of that time, and my occasional trips back to Sydney were always too brief. But gradually I recognised a deeper explanation, which was the veil of silence around her life and death. My father almost never spoke of her, nor did my stepmother, who had known her too. My mother's siblings rarely talked about her to me, nor did I have the curiosity or courage to ask them about the kind of person she was. Nobody ever mentioned her funeral – it was as if it had never happened. The only time I have ever seen my father cry was when I interviewed him about his life and we touched upon the subject of her death. He recollected the pain and traumas of her final years when she was ill and the hospital treatment was failing. He told me about their marriage, her laughter and intelligence, her zest for life, her love for her children. All the feelings were there, hidden beneath the surface. I too was in tears. The interview ended and the silence returned.

While one of the fundamental issues of deathstyle is how to expand our awareness of the fragility of life, a second concerns how we respond to the event of someone's death. Until the early twentieth century, the death of an individual was a major social occasion that altered the space and time of an entire community. This is no longer the case. We are losing the old rituals and traditions that help us make sense of death and keep the memories of the deceased in our lives. My mother's death is part of this new culture, which can so easily result in a void of silence and forgetting. We need to understand how this has happened, why it matters, and what can be done about it.

Death was once an accepted and familiar feature of everyday life, like the passing of the seasons. Elisabeth Kübler-Ross, a psychiatrist who wrote *On Death and Dying*, a famous study of how terminally ill patients confront their own deaths, remembered the last days of a farmer during her childhood in 1930s Switzerland:

> He fell from a tree and was not expected to live. He asked simply to die at home, a wish that was granted without questioning. He called his daughters into the bedroom and spoke with each one of them alone for a few minutes. He arranged his affairs quietly, though he was in great pain, and distributed his belongings and his land, none of which was to be split until his wife should follow him in death … He asked his friends to visit him once more, to bid good-bye to them. Although I was only a small child at the time, he did not exclude me or my siblings. We were allowed to share in the preparations of the family just as we were permitted to grieve with them until he died. When he did die, he was left in his own home, which he had built, and among his friends and neighbours who went to take a last look at him where he lay in the midst of flowers in the place he had lived in and loved so.[8]

A hundred years ago it was common to die, like the Swiss farmer, in your own home and in the presence of people who mattered to you. Death was a shared experience full of solemn farewells and involving children just as much as adults. It was quite usual to see the person slip away before your eyes, whereas today few of us have ever witnessed somebody die. Especially in rural areas, funerals were much more elaborate than those we have become accustomed to in recent decades – unless you were a pauper being tossed into an open pit. They were attended by the whole community and a long ecclesiastical procession carried the coffin from the house to the burial place, as my father recalled from his youth in pre-war Poland. In some countries it was even standard practice to bulk up the numbers by hiring strangers to act as professional mourners. The toll of church bells sent a message of sorrow into the distance for all to hear. The face of the deceased remained visible – as is still common amongst Catholics – but unlike today it would not have been so sanitised with cosmetics and manipulated into a pose of pretend sleep. The public presence of death appeared in the black clothing or armbands worn by family members for months, and sometimes years after the person had died.[9]

These customs have been disappearing in Europe and North America, and as a result death has taken on an almost secretive, shameful air. It is scarcely seen and barely discussed. One reason for this is the rise of a new medical phenomenon: the hospital death. Although 70 per cent of people say they would like to die at home, this is now rarely the case. Over half of us will take our last breath on an anonymous hospital ward, covered by tubes and sensors, hidden away from all but a few close relatives and friends, while another quarter will die in nursing homes and hospices.[10] A family member might squeeze our hand under the fluorescent lights as we inhale through a respirator, but they are likely to be displaced by doctors and nurses carrying out checks and attaching drips. Gone are the candlelight vigils and customary farewells by the bedside that Elisabeth Kübler-Ross recollected. Children are now normally kept away from relatives dying in hospital and not brought along to funerals. Protective parents believe it would be 'too much' for their kids to come face to face with mortality.[11]

The social presence of death has been further eroded by the demise of the community funeral, a casualty of fragmented urban living and increasing secularisation. When was the last time you saw a funeral procession go down your street, with neighbours joining in as it passes by? The funeral business also bears some responsibility for our growing distance from death, encouraging short and efficient funerals in the interests of time management and healthy profits.[12] While officiating at my aunt's recent funeral at a crematorium in Sydney, I was politely informed by the management that there would be a substantial fine if we exceeded our allotted forty-minute slot. How were we expected to celebrate seventy-seven years of vibrant life in under three-quarters of an hour – less than a minute per year? As soon as we finished (with ninety seconds to spare), we were all swiftly bundled out a side door so the next service could begin on time. The rising popularity of cremations has also helped to push death to the cultural sidelines. Between 1960 and 2008, the percentage of cremations in Britain more than doubled, from 35 per cent to 72 per cent, a trend that also exists in countries such as Australia and Sweden.[13] This has introduced a new finality to death, since not only does the body disappear from public view, but cremated remains are far less likely than interred bodies to be given a monument or to be visited regularly.

Once the corpse is in the ground or the ashes in a box, the flickering reminders of death can easily fade. The traditional cycles of masses that once took place in the months after a funeral are now rarely observed, while anybody who wears mourning clothes for a dead relative except on the day of the funeral itself is likely to be considered eccentric.[14]

The decline of communal rituals and traditions has robbed us of the social occasions and time we need for thinking about death, talking about it and eventually coming to terms with it. We have created silences where there need be none. Exorcising death from daily life has not only exacerbated our underlying fears of it, but has damaged our capacity to grieve.[15] There are now few opportunities to publicly express our feelings about the loss of a parent or dear friend, and we are left with the painful solitude of our own memories. Grieving has become a social embarrassment, so we make an effort not to cry in front of our work colleagues or on the bus home.[16] We are expected to get over someone's death quickly, to bite our quivering lip and put it all in the past, whereas coping with death may require a prolonged period of grieving, sometimes lasting years. Excluding children from hospitals and funerals, and telling them that Granny is now living in the sky or has gone on a long trip, might be necessary in some delicate cases, but shows little understanding of a child's need to grapple with bereavement just as much as an adult's.[17] I developed obsessive compulsive behaviour for several years after my mother died, but I wonder if this would have occurred in a culture that was more at ease with death and dying.

Death has not been completely eradicated from public life, as anybody who has attended a spirited, community-centred Irish funeral will know. But if we really want to appreciate how much has been lost, we should turn to those societies where death remains a significant part of the cultural landscape. Two places in the Americas are worth a visit on this leg of our deathstyle itinerary.

In *The Labyrinth of Solitude*, the Mexican poet and essayist Octavio Paz describes the essence of his country's national character:

> The word death is not pronounced in New York, in Paris, in London, because it burns the lips. The Mexican, in contrast, is familiar with death, jokes about it, caresses it, sleeps with it, celebrates it; it is one of his favourite toys and his most steadfast love. True, there is perhaps as much fear in his attitude as in that of others, but at least death is not hidden away: he looks at it face to face, with impatience, disdain or irony.[18]

These lines, written in the 1950s, express a view still popular today that Mexicans are not only obsessed by death but almost treat it as a welcome friend. Although an exaggeration of the reality – few welcome the tens of thousands of annual drug-related murders, and people weep at funerals like anywhere else – there is no doubt that Mexico displays an extraordinarily vibrant culture of death that verges on the medieval.[19] This is nowhere more visible than on their most popular holiday, the Day of the Dead, which takes place on All Saints' and All Souls' Days, 1 and 2 November respectively. During *El Día de los Muertos*, many parts of the country are enveloped in a macabre fiesta that has the atmosphere of carnival. Children play with toys in the shape of skulls, skeletons and coffins. Shops sell specially baked bread resembling human bones called *pan de muerto*, dead bread, as well as *calaveras de azúcar*, sugar skulls with people's names written across the forehead. Newspapers are peppered with cartoons depicting politicians as dancing skeletons, while dancing death figures and sculptures fill city parks. The cemeteries are overrun by people visiting their dead relatives, cleaning and decorating the graves, and maintaining all-night vigils in honour of the souls of the departed.[20]

The origins of the Day of the Dead lie in a hybrid history. It is partly rooted in the fascination with skulls and skeletons found in the Toltec and Aztec civilisations, which thrived in Mesoamerica between the ninth and sixteenth centuries. But the grisly humour and dancing figures are Spanish imports. In the sixteenth century, the conquistadors brought with them not only the Catholic commemoration of All Souls' Day, but the rather more exuberant dance of the dead. Early colonial churches, monasteries and coffins in Mexico are covered with the familiar medieval skeletons jiggling their bones and mocking the living person who is being summoned to die. These images helped create the Day of the Dead customs that are still celebrated today.[21] So when visitors pour out of tourist buses in early November, they are not only bearing witness to the legacy of Mexico's indigenous peoples, but also gazing upon the remnants of a lost European culture of death that has not been seen in its original environment for 500 years.

Travel further north and you might stumble upon a

traditional New Orleans jazz funeral in full swing. Distinct from the city's more famous Mardi Gras carnival, the funeral parades are held in working-class African-American communities, far off the tourist trail. They take place on most weekends and those for important local figures can bring together between 3,000 and 5,000 people. Many of them will be members of the deceased person's 'club' – benevolent societies with colourful names such as the Pigeon Town Steppers and Young Men Olympian. The clubs, which finance the funerals, have existed in the city since the late eighteenth century and form the centre of community life.

The street processions are divided into two sections. Up front is the 'first line', composed of a brass band and the club affiliates. Behind them is the 'second line', made up of friends, relatives, members of other clubs, neighbourhood residents and even passing strangers who join in the festivities, just as used to occur during funerals in Europe. The band traditionally begins playing sombre dirges but once the coffin enters the ground – a moment known as 'cutting the body loose' – the music explodes into an upbeat tempo with tunes like 'When the Saints Go Marching In'. Everyone then breaks into a party mood, dancing and clowning in their colourful costumes, twirling umbrellas and waving handkerchiefs.[22] Death in New Orleans has an unlikely air of celebration.

Stand back for a moment now. What does all this history tell us about how we should approach death? I think there are two lessons, one concerning ritual, the other related to the art of conversation. The decline of death as a community event with vibrant traditions offers a first lesson, which is that we should consider inventing our own rituals around death. Couples today get married on Ferris wheels and mountaintops, so why shouldn't funerals be just as imaginative? They are already moving in this direction, with many people personalising the service, specifying that they want everyone at their funeral to wear colourful clothes or that the Pink Panther theme tune should be played as their coffin is carried down the aisle. You might have in mind a New Orleans-style funeral with live music, dancing in the streets and an exhibition of your treasured bonsai tree collection. Maybe you'll even get people to dance in the cemetery around the grave, just as they did in medieval France. I know someone who plans to hold his funeral *before* he dies, so he can appreciate how lucky he is to still be alive, and also spend time with old friends who would otherwise turn up to his memorial service when he is hardly in a position to say hello.

There is always a place for sombre mourning, especially when someone's death has been unexpected, yet we should find ways for funerals not just to mark the passing of life, but also to celebrate it. We can be similarly inventive in our approach to traditions of remembrance. I can imagine once a year baking loaves of macabre 'dead bread', then eating them while staying up all night in the cemetery sitting by my mother's grave, telling my partner about my fondest memories of her as the candles burn on towards dawn. Such rituals are a form of communal therapy. They help us release our emotions, understand our feelings and move on to new stages in our lives.

The second lesson is that we should discover new ways of having conversations about death, both to help revive its social presence so we are better at confronting our fears and grief, and also to bring us closer to the lost medieval sense of the precariousness and preciousness of life. Death and dying are today's conversational unmentionables, the equivalent of discussing sex in Victorian England.[23] When you are at the pub after work, nobody is going to casually ask, 'So, how do you all feel about the prospect of dying?' But we can be thankful that the taboos are slowly beginning to lift. Illnesses like cancer are much less shameful than they once were. It is now rare to find cases like my grandmother who kept her stomach cancer a secret from us all for fifteen years, and obituaries no longer euphemistically describe cancer victims as dying from a 'very long illness'.[24] Doctors are more likely to tell dying patients about the realities of their illness than they were a generation ago, even if more could be done to ensure the issue is handled with sensitivity. The rise of the hospice movement and the invention of the 'living will' – in which you give instructions for your health care if you are no longer able to make decisions due to incapacity – have prompted a new generation of conversations about mortality, as have the debates around euthanasia and organ donation.[25]

Despite these openings, most people find it more difficult to talk about death than any other subject. When your neighbour tells you that her sister has just died, what are you supposed to say after muttering, 'I'm so sorry'? When you hear that a friend has cancer spreading through her body, how should you bring up her illness when you next meet? No set of techniques will tell you how to respond in these situations; using rehearsed phrases from a bereavement handbook is usually a route to stilted and artificial conversation. Yet there are some basic ingredients for a healthy conversation about death. It is unwise to pretend to the other person that nothing is wrong and that all will be well, with lines like 'don't worry, everything will be fine' or 'time will heal the pain'. As Florence Nightingale warned in 1860, 'there is scarcely a greater worry which invalids have to endure than the incurable hopes of their friends … I would appeal most seriously to all friends, visitors and attendants of the sick to leave off this practice of attempting to "cheer" the sick by making light of their danger and by exaggerating their probabilities of recovery.'[26] It is similarly unhelpful to offer advice for coping – unless it is asked for – whether it is the teachings of your religion or a mantra like 'think positively'. When the American social critic Barbara Ehrenreich discovered she had breast cancer, she encountered a cult of positive thinking advice which not only denied her fears and desire to be angry about her disease, but had the dangerous effect of giving people false hope.[27]

The most important conversational trait to develop is empathy. Although you will never know what it is really like to be in the other person's shoes, it is possible to be sensitive to how they might be thinking or feeling. You can listen carefully for hints that they want to talk about their illness or a relative who recently passed away, then offer them that opportunity. You can imagine what their fears might be, for instance how their son will cope if they were to die, and gently ask if they want to discuss them, respecting their right to remain silent. When my grandfather Ivan was dying of leukaemia, we all made an effort to respond to his greatest conversational comfort, which was recalling memories from his childhood in Poland.

Since the establishment of the modern nursing profession in the nineteenth century, nurses have – with some exceptions – shown themselves to be especially sensitive to the need for empathy in conversation with dying patients or grieving relatives. 'How little does anyone of good health fancy him or even herself into the life of a sick person!' exclaimed Florence Nightingale in her textbook on nursing, pointing out how often we fail to imagine ourselves in their shoes.[28] Cicely Saunders, a nurse who later trained as a doctor and founded the British hospice movement in the 1960s, once asked a man who knew he was dying what he needed above all from those who were caring for him. He replied, '[F]or someone to look as if they are trying to understand me.'[29] Empathy is the beginning of that understanding.

We also need courage. We spend so much of our lives hiding our emotions, wearing a mask. Talking about death requires finding the courage to take off your mask and be open with others about your thoughts and fears. You need courage to speak with friends about the worrying results of your latest blood test or diagnosis of prostate cancer. Courage will help you to have that awkward discussion with your parents about the care they might want if they become physically or mentally incapacitated. We should also discover the courage to make deathstyle a conversational habit: next time you have a meal with friends, you might discuss what music you'd all like played at your funerals, or whether you'd want the machine turned off if you were left in a vegetative state after a traffic accident. In all these scenarios, what is the worst thing that could happen if you reveal what is on your mind? So remove your mask, look other people in the eye and let the conversation begin.

We remain at the earliest stages of learning to talk about death, and are still surrounded by a culture of silence that needs to be broken. There is little to be lost, and much to be gained, from embracing death and letting it be heard upon our lips even if it leaves a burning sensation.

## How to care for the elderly

For fifty years my grandfather Leo lived south of Sydney on the edge of a vast national park. The house was little more than an extended shack. The doors didn't close properly, allowing possums to come scuttling down the hallway in the night. One morning he woke to find a kangaroo nibbling at his toes, which were sticking out of the end of the bed. The place was full of musty old books reflecting his eclectic tastes in socialist literature, Indian mysticism and Aboriginal culture. Leo spent his days sitting on the sofa tapping away at a decrepit typewriter, trying to finish a book he had been working on for three decades. Each year he threw a birthday party when the cherry tree blossomed, and family and friends gathered around it in the overgrown backyard listening to crackling jazz records and talking politics. The house was his spiritual home, an inseparable part of him. I felt sure that if he were forced to leave it, he would not live long.

Following his ninetieth birthday, Leo could no longer look after himself, even with regular day care. A family decision was made to put him into a nursing home. I remember visiting him there for the first time, having not seen him for over a year. The home was in an anonymous Sydney suburb devoid of trees, the opposite of the bushy wilderness where he had previously lived. I was directed to the common room, which was crammed with elderly people playing cards and watching cricket on a blaring television set. Nothing could be further from his old life: Leo's idea of leisure was reading poetry, not staring at TV sport. Eventually I found him in a corner on a reclining chair, covered with blankets. He was so thin and shrivelled, I hardly recognised him. He could no longer speak and didn't seem to know who I was. A carer came over and asked, 'Patrick, would you like a biscuit?' Patrick? Then I noticed the name tag around his wrist: Patrick Leo Kelly. He had been known as Leo all his life. My grandfather had lost everything – his old home, his friends and even his own name. He died in the nursing home six months later. I now wish he had shuffled off to Buffalo, as he used to put it, on the day of his ninetieth birthday under the branches of the cherry tree.

A consequence of the historical shift towards longer life is that caring for the elderly has become a major dilemma of our time. In 1950 around 8 per cent of Americans were over sixty-five; today that figure is 12 per cent, but by 2030 it will be close to 20 per cent.[30] Europe's and Japan's populations are ageing even more rapidly. As a result, welfare systems are being put under increasing strain and it is likely that social security for older people will be eroded in most countries over the coming decades. Living on a state pension will become a distant memory of the twentieth century. As your mother, father or favourite spinster aunt get older, who is going to look after them, and what kind of care do they deserve?

In the recent past it was usual for ageing parents to move in with their children: in the 1950s almost two-thirds of British people over sixty lived with their children or other relatives.[31] But this practice has been in rapid decline in the West over the last half-century, especially because the growing number of women entering the workplace means they are no longer con-fined to playing their traditional role as carers for the elderly. This development helps account for the phenomenal rise of the nursing home. Although nursing homes have existed for less than a hundred years, 20 to 30 per cent of people in the Western world now end their lives in a residential care home, and the figures are rising.[32]

Nursing homes are one of the greatest scandals of our 'civ-ilisation' and have come to resemble the ghettoes created for Jews in sixteenth-century Europe, becoming places where we put the elderly out of sight and out of mind. This is a serious charge, I know. There is no doubt that some care homes are excellent, offering luxury accommodation, expert medical ser-vices and a strong sense of community. Many elderly people want to live in them, favouring the prospect of continued independence over reliance on support from family. Unfortunately, they rarely provide the quality of life that is found in their glossy advertisements. According to a leading historian of the sector, ending your days in a nursing home 'is a formidable and desperate picture' and you are likely to experience 'a shameful form of dying'.[33] Apart from the exclusive care homes for the very wealthy, they are frequently understaffed and have poor medical and leisure facilities. Pervasive problems caused by neglect such as dehydration, malnutrition and bedsores have given rise to a new term, 'elder abuse'. Residents typically complain of loneliness, boredom, lack of privacy and being treated like children. Dignity diminishes as they become reliant on staff to help them wash and go to the toilet. Those whose minds remain active feel the oppression of being surrounded by others struggling with dementia, an epidemic illness that affects around half the population in residential care. 'I am only 62 but I feel 100,' revealed one resident in a study of US nursing homes. 'My children have left me and seem not to care whether I am alive or dead. I cannot bear Sundays, so on Saturday night I take some very strong tranquillisers which keep me dazed all day Sunday.' Nursing homes have become prisons of social and emotional isolation, where individuals are frequently stripped of their identities and languish in a limbo before their deaths.[34] As the Buddhist teacher Sogyal Rinpoche observes in *The Tibetan Book of Living and Dying* (2008):

> Our society is obsessed with youth, sex, and power, and we shun old age and decay. Isn't it terrifying that we discard old people when their working life is finished and they are no longer useful? Isn't it disturbing that we cast them into old people's homes, where they die lonely and abandoned?[35]

For all the criticisms, the modern nursing home is undoubtedly preferable to how elderly people were treated in many premodern societies, where they could be 'eliminated' once they became too much of a burden for the community to support. During the spring migration of the nomadic Bakhtiari people of Iran, one of the major obstacles is crossing the swollen Bazuft river with their sheep and goats. Until recently their custom was that if an old man or woman was too weak to make the crossing, they would be left behind to die.[36] A more extreme example comes from the Tiwi people of Bathurst and Melville Islands in northern Australia. In the 1920s the anthropologist Charles Hart encountered their tradition of 'covering up':

> The Tiwi, like many other hunting and gathering peoples, sometimes got rid of their ancient and decrepit females. The method was to dig a hole in the ground in some lonely place, put the old woman in the hole and fill it in with earth until only her head was showing. Everybody went away for a day or two and then went back to the hole to discover to their surprise that the old woman was dead, having been too feeble to raise her arms from the earth. Nobody had 'killed' her, her death in Tiwi eyes was a natural one.[37]

If we are looking for an alternative model of care to the nursing home, we should turn instead to the treatment of the elderly in China and Japan, which has long been based on the Confucian notion of filial piety. This is the idea that the primary obligation of sons and daughters is to serve and care for their parents.[38] The message has been reinforced for hundreds of years, for instance through the Chinese classic, *Twenty-Four Examples of Filial Piety*. Written in the fourteenth century, it contains extraordinary feats of devotion by children towards their parents, such as the story of the learned emperor Han Wendi, who spent three years constantly nursing his ailing mother, hardly closing his eyes by her bedside or changing his clothes, and spoon-feeding her with medicine he had first tasted himself to make sure it was neither too hot nor too weak.

Filial piety helps explain why, until the late twentieth century, it was the norm in China and Japan for ageing parents to live with one of their children. Although multigenerational households have been in decline for the past two decades, the sense of filial duty remains a significant cultural force. Around

40 per cent of Japanese over the age of sixty-five live with their children, while in parts of rural China co-residence can be more than 60 per cent. The equivalent figure in countries such as the United States, Germany and Britain is around 5 per cent.[39] When people say the Far East is exotic, they are usually referring to its food or art. But equally exotic is their traditional approach to parental care.

While most of us have not grown up in Confucian culture, the idea of filial piety may still speak to us. We can all think about what we owe to our parents. It was only after my twins were born that I realised the extent to which my mother and father had made sacrifices on my behalf. They changed my dirty nappies and cradled me when I cried in the night. For three months they stayed constantly by my hospital bedside after I had a near fatal accident as a toddler. They gave up their leisure time to care for me, and gave me unquestioning love and emotional support. For years their lives revolved around nurturing my own.

Given all they have done for us, we could follow the Chinese and Japanese example by considering how we can honour our parents or step-parents as they grow older. Perhaps you will be able to make the ultimate filial offering to a frail parent and invite them to live with you, sparing them some of the ignominies of a nursing home. Yet for most people this will not be a viable option. Not only may your parent prefer living independently in a care home, but work commitments might rule you out as an effective carer, and the personal strains of looking after an ageing parent can be enormous – particularly if they have an illness like Alzheimer's. But we can still tend to our parents with the grace and affection of Han Wendi. We can make an effort to visit them regularly, even when it is not convenient to us, helping them overcome any sense of isolation they may feel, or simply give them a quick daily phone call as we walk to work. We can bring our children into their lives, so they can benefit from the energising presence of the young. We might also experiment with more inventive forms of caring, such as taking them on travels they have always dreamed about, like a pilgrimage to their place of birth, or joining them on a life-drawing course. My own approach to filial caring, when my father retired, was to make a series of recordings of him talking about his life. It not only enabled him to leave a memento of his experiences for his family, but gave him an opportunity to reflect on what he had achieved and the personal journey he had taken. For me, it was a chance to bond with him in a unique way and be inspired by his humanity.

The relationship between a parent and child is the most elemental one we know and deserves a special kind of honouring. Our parents brought us into the world, and we can help them leave it with contentment and dignity, even if we have not always seen eye to eye. We must search for the most appropriate offerings and do our best to make the sacrifices required. What gifts might we bring to our parents' old age?

## Deathstyle culture

In Ingmar Bergman's film *The Seventh Seal* (1957), a medieval Swedish knight meets Death and challenges him to a game of chess. If the knight loses, Death will take him. The longer the game continues, the longer he can live, granting him the time he needs to perform a single act that will give his life a sense of meaning. The knight manages to outwit Death and achieve his ambition by helping a young couple and their child escape the plague, which is ravaging the land. Death then comes for the knight, leading him away in a macabre dance of death over the hilltops.

Unlike the knight, we no longer feel stalked by Death. Quite the opposite. The advent of dying in hospital, the decline of funeral rituals and our increasing lifespans have rendered death a distant, even imaginary event for most of us. The challenge we face today is to bring it closer to our lives in a way that deepens meaning without exacerbating our fears. We must embark, both as individuals and as a society, on an adventurous conversation about death that will create an invigorated deathstyle culture. The result may be a new world in which deathstyle becomes discussed just as much as lifestyle, and where there are *danse macabres* with jiggling skeletons painted on the walls of the subway stations.

# Epilogue

The German writer and natural scientist Johann Wolfgang von Goethe launched this odyssey into the last 3,000 years of human history, challenging us to find existential nourishment from past civilisations so that we are not condemned to living from hand to mouth. It is therefore fitting that a dramatic episode from his own life can help bring it to an end.

It was the late summer of 1786. Goethe had just celebrated his thirty-seventh birthday and was facing a mid-life crisis. He had achieved fame as a novelist and dramatist in his early twenties, but now his literary work was floundering and almost everything he started he failed to finish. He was bored with his job, having spent a decade as a top civil servant in the court of the Duke of Weimar. And he was suffering from unrequited love for a married woman seven years his senior. Goethe was on the verge of a breakdown.

So he decided to escape. A few days after his birthday, without telling anybody of his plans, he jumped on a mail coach at three in the morning, with no servant and only two small bags, and fled south to Italy under an assumed name.

It was the beginning of a trip that lasted almost two years, and which not only rejuvenated his spirit but gave him a new direction in life. He sketched ancient monuments in Rome, observed local customs in Verona, collected rock samples in Sicily and forged friendships amongst his bohemian fellow travellers. Goethe's aim was far more than to run away into anonymity or visit famous sites. 'My purpose in making this wonderful journey,' he wrote, 'is not to delude myself but to discover myself in the objects I see.' Invigorated by fresh surroundings, he emerged from his Italian adventure with a renewed self-confidence and recharged imagination that enabled him to write the greatest works of his career.[1]

This story has resonance today for anybody contemplating changes in their life, whether in the realm of work, love, money, belief or any of the other areas we have explored. No matter how clearly we recognise the troubles and challenges we face, or how many good ideas we have for transforming the way we live, it is always difficult to shift from the theory to the practice of change. Entrapped by our fears and habits, and reluctant to take risks or make mistakes, most of us baulk at the prospect of a step into the unknown – leaving an unfulfilling job, committing to walk down the aisle, or downsizing our consumer lifestyle. There is no pill we can pop to give us the courage and motivation to change.

What insights might we gain from Goethe's flight to Italy? His sudden departure looks like a reckless, even irresponsible act. You can't just abandon your job as first minister of a royal duchy without giving any notice. And it was folly for a literary genius to go gallivanting around Italy obsessively gathering mineral specimens when he should be sitting down quietly at home writing sublime verse. He left in secrecy, he said, because he knew his friends 'wouldn't have let me go if I hadn't'. Goethe's mode of travel displayed this same willingness to break social conventions. A titled gentleman of his public standing and financial means would be expected to have a private coach and a retinue of servants and letters of introduction, but instead he chose to make his way through Italy without hired help, and on any transport he could find, staying in tiny local inns and adopting casual dress so he would better blend in.[2] He was determined to follow his own route and avoid stifling rules of etiquette.

Like Mary Wollstonecraft, Henry David Thoreau and so many other pioneers of the art of living, Goethe realised that he would have to swim against the social tide. So too we must recognise that if we wish to incorporate the lessons of history into our own lives, we may have to defy cultural norms and risk standing out from the crowd. This could well happen if we choose to resign from a well-paid job to pursue a career that better reflects our values, or if we live in a home without a television set, or start talking about death at dinner parties. The price of being a pioneer is that we may be unable to keep up with the Joneses, or to receive their nods of approval. Yet at the same time we will be not only expanding our own horizons but also setting new standards for future generations, who will be able to look back at how we lived as a source of inspiration for their personal pursuits of radical aliveness.

Goethe's desire to 'discover myself in the objects I see' should matter to us just as much as his capacity for breaking conventions. He believed that excessive self-reflection and navel gazing could be harmful, leading to emotional confusion and paralysis. His approach to following Socrates' dictum 'know thyself' was not to ruminate about the state of his soul, but to launch himself into life, nurturing his curiosity about people, places, art and landscape. 'Man only knows himself insofar as he knows the world,' he wrote. This does not mean, though, that we should be filling our days with incessant activities, reducing ourselves from human beings to human doings. Rather, his point was that self-understanding comes not only from philosophical introspection but from experiential 'outrospection'.

The ultimate message from Goethe's journey, however, is that if we truly want to change how we live, there may come a point where we simply have to stop thinking and planning, and take action. This idea has, over the centuries, gone by many names, from *carpe diem* to a leap of faith to the slogan 'just do it'. It is about nothing less than choosing to make your life extraordinary, and living in such a way that your last years are not filled with regret for what you have not done. Although Goethe was in many ways a conservative person who sought a stable, secure life and domestic comforts, he knew that staying in Weimar was no solution to his problems. He had to shake himself up and break the pattern of his existence, even if he was unsure where his travels would lead him. If ever we feel trapped by life, or hesitant about how to move forward, we can always ask ourselves what bold move Goethe – or perhaps George Orwell or

Mary Kingsley – might make if they were in our shoes. What would they do to seize the day?

Goethe was universally admired – and often envied – for his artistic brilliance and worldly success, his cultured intellect and his scientific acumen. But we should not be overawed by his celebrity as a wide achiever. His life was full of sorrows and pains, just like anybody else's. One area in which he struggled was relationships. Throughout his life he was falling in and out of love, and getting himself into complex tangles with the women he desired, who might already be married, or decades younger than himself, or plain uninterested in his affections. His romantic flings and fantasies did little to bolster his own marriage, which failed to thrive after its early days. He knew, though, that passionate love, friendship and other kinds of relationships were vital ingredients of the good life. A few years after returning from Italy, where he had often felt great loneliness, he struck up a deep – and sometimes tense – friendship with the poet and philosopher Friedrich Schiller. When Schiller died after their decade of comradely *philia*, Goethe was devastated. 'I have now lost a friend and with him half my life,' he lamented.[3]

This cry of grief contains one of the golden threads that weaves its way through the history of how to live: that the mystery of existence is constituted by our relations with one another. While some people may discover meaning in God, nature, fighting for a cause or climbing a corporate ladder, it is through our relationships with other human beings that we are most likely to find fulfilment. Whether it is by forging an unexpected friendship like C. P. Ellis and Ann Atwater, nurturing varieties of love such as *pragma* and *ludus*, or breaking family silences with more open conversations, spiritual sustenance depends on creating bonds and sharing our lives with others. You can cook yourself the finest gourmet meals night after night, but you will eventually want somebody else sitting at the table with you, be they a lover, a friend or a stranger with a story to tell.

There is a second, life-enhancing thread to be found in history, which is that giving is good for you. Goethe understood this in theory, asking, 'What is my life if I am no longer useful to others?', but in practice he possessed a strong selfish streak, having a habit of discarding people who he no longer found interesting or useful for his personal ambitions. In doing so, he was denying himself one of the subtlest pleasures of human existence. Think back to John Woolman and Thomas Clarkson, who dedicated themselves to the struggle against slavery, or to Leo Tolstoy's famine relief work. For all of them, the meaning of their lives could be found in liberating themselves from egoistic concerns and acting on the behalf of others, honouring the ancient Greek ideal of *agape*. Giving may be our surest route to a life of purpose and fulfilment.

We might live our lives in a thousand different ways. And the civilisations of the past enable us to recognise that our habitual ways of loving, working, creating and dying are not the only options before us. We need only open the wonderbox of history and look inside to see new and surprising possibilities for the art of living. Let them spark our curiosity, captivate our imaginations and inspire our actions.

# Bibliography

Abbott, Mary (1993), *Family Ties: English Families 1540–1920* (London: Routledge).

Abrams, Rebecca (1999), *When Parents Die: Learning to Live with the Loss of a Parent* (London: Routledge).

Ackerman, Diane (1996), *A Natural History of the Senses* (London: Phoenix).

—— and Jeanne Mackin (eds.) (1998), *The Book of Love* (New York and London: Norton).

Anderson, Benedict (1991), *Imagined Communities: Reflections on the Origin and Spread of Nationalism* (London: Verso).

Ariès, Philippe (2008), *The Hour of Our Death* (New York: Vintage).

Armstrong, John (2003), *Conditions of Love: The Philosophy of Intimacy* (London: Penguin Books).

—— (2007), *Love, Life, Goethe: How to be Happy in an Imperfect World* (London: Penguin Books).

Armstrong, Karen (2007), *The Great Transformation: The World in the Time of Buddha, Socrates, Confucius and Jeremiah* (London: Atlantic Books).

Attlee, James (2011), *Nocturne: A Journey in Search of Moonlight* (London: Hamish Hamilton).

Baedeker, Karl (1870), *First Part: Northern Italy and Corsica* (Koblenz: Karl Baedeker).

—— (1909), *Baedeker's Central Italy and Rome* (Leipzig: Karl Baedeker).

Ballard, J. G. (2008), *Miracles of Life* (London: Fourth Estate).

Baron-Cohen, Simon (2011), *Zero Degrees of Empathy: A New Theory of Human Cruelty* (London: Allen Lane).

Bashō, Matsuo (1966), *The Narrow Road to the Deep North and Other Travel Sketches* (Harmondsworth: Penguin Books).

Batson, Charles D. (1991), *The Altruism Question: Toward A Social-Psychological Answer* (Hillsdale, N.J.: Lawrence Erlbaum Associates).

Beit-Hallahmi, Benjamin and Michael Argyle (1997), *The Psychology of Religious Behaviour, Belief and Experience* (London: Routledge).

Berg, Leila (1972), *Look at Kids* (Harmondsworth: Penguin Books).

Berger, John (1965), *Success and Failure of Picasso* (Harmondsworth: Penguin Books).

—— (1972), *Ways of Seeing* (London: BBC Books; and Harmondsworth: Penguin Books).

Berry, Mary Frances (1993), *The Politics of Parenthood: Child Care, Women's Rights, and the Myth of the Good Mother* (New York: Viking).

Boorstin, Daniel (1985), *The Discoverers: A History of Man's Search to Know His World and Himself* (New York: Vintage).

—— (1993), *The Creators: A History of Heroes of the Imagination* (New York: Vintage).

Boyle, Mark (2010), *The Moneyless Man: A Year of Freeconomic Living* (Oxford: Oneworld).

Bragg, Elizabeth Ann (1996), 'Towards Ecological Self: Deep Ecology Meets Constructionist Self-Theory', *Journal of Environmental Psychology*, Vol. 16: 93–108.

Brand, Stuart (1999), *The Clock of the Long Now: Time and Responsibility* (London: Phoenix).

Brandes, Stanley (2006), *Skulls to the Living, Bread to the Dead: The Day of the Dead in Mexico and Beyond* (Oxford: Blackwell).

Braudel, Fernand (1981), *Civilization and Capitalism 15th–18th Century, Volume 1: The Structures of Everyday Life* (London: Collins/Fontana).

—— (1982), *Civilization and Capitalism 15th–18th Century, Volume 2: The Wheels of Commerce* (London: Collins/Fontana).

Brendon, Piers (1991), *Thomas Cook: 150 Years of Popular Tourism* (London: Secker & Warburg).

Brillat-Savarin, Jean-Anthelme (1970), *The Philosopher in the Kitchen* (Harmondsworth: Penguin Books).

Broks, Paul (2003), *Into the Silent Land: Travels in Neuropsychology* (London: Atlantic Books).

Bronowski, Jacob (1976), *The Ascent of Man* (London: BBC Books).

Buchan, James (1998), *Frozen Desire: An Inquiry into the Meaning of Money* (London: Picador).

Burckhardt, Jacob (1945), *The Civilization of the Renaissance in Italy* (Oxford and London: Phaidon).

Burgess, Adrienne (1997), *Fatherhood Reclaimed: The Making of the Modern Father* (London: Vermillion).

Burton, Robert (1989), *The Anatomy of Melancholy, Vol. 1* (Oxford: Clarendon).

Buzzard, James (2002), 'The Grand Tour and After (1660–1840)', in Peter Hulme and Tim Youngs (eds.), *The Cambridge Companion to Travel Writing* (Cambridge: Cambridge University Press).

Cameron, Julia (1995), *The Artist's Way: A Course in Discovering and Recovering Your Creative Self* (London: Pan).

Cannadine, David (1983), 'The Context, Performance and Meaning of Ritual: The British Monarchy and the "Invention of Tradition", c.1820–1977', in Eric Hobsbawm and Terence Ranger (eds.), *The Invention of Tradition* (Cambridge: Cambridge University Press).

Carr, Deborah (2007), 'Death and Dying', in George Ritzer (ed.), *The Blackwell Encyclopedia of Sociology* (Oxford: Blackwell).

Chatwin, Bruce (1988), *The Songlines* (London: Picador).

Clark, Kenneth (1971), *Civilization* (London: BBC Books and John Murray).

Classen, Constance (1993), *Worlds of Sense: Exploring the Senses in History and Across Cultures* (London: Routledge).

Cobbett, William (1985), *Rural Rides* (Harmondsworth: Penguin Books).

Coleman, Simon and John Elsner (1995), *Pilgrimage Past and Present: Sacred Travel and Sacred Space in the World's Religions* (London: British Museum Press).

Coltrane, Scott (1996), *Family Man: Fatherhood, Housework, and Gender Equity* (New York: Oxford University Press).

Comfort, Alex (1996), *The Joy of Sex* (London: Quartet Books).

Corbin, Alain (1986), *The Foul and the Fragrant: Odour and the French Social Imagination* (Cambridge, Mass.: Harvard University Press).

Cowan, Ruth Schwartrz (1983), *More Work for Mother: The Ironies of Household Technology from the Open Hearth to the Microwave* (New York: Basic Books).

Crick, Bernard (1980), *George Orwell: A Life* (Harmondsworth: Penguin Books).

Darwin, Charles (1959), *The Voyage of the 'Beagle'* (London: Dent)

Davidson, Caroline (1982), *A Woman's Work is Never Done: A History of Housework in the British Isles 1650–1950* (London: Chatto & Windus).

Davidson, James (2007), *The Greeks and Greek Love: A Radical Reappraisal of Homosexuality in Ancient Greece* (London: Weidenfeld & Nicolson).

de Beauvoir, Simone (1972), *The Second Sex* (Harmondsworth: Penguin Books).

de Bono, Edward (1977), *Lateral Thinking: A Textbook for Creativity* (Harmondsworth: Penguin Books).

de Botton, Alain (2004) *Status Anxiety* (New York, Pantheon).

de Rougemont, Denis (1983), *Love in the Western World* (Princeton, N.J.: Princeton University Press).

de Waal, Frans (2006), *Primates and Philosophers: How Morality Evolved* (Princeton, N.J.: Princeton University Press).

Diamond, Jared (1998), *Guns, Germs and Steel: A Short History of Everybody for the Last 13,000 Years* (London: Vintage).

Dominguez, Joe and Robin, Vicki (1999), *Your Money or Your Life: Transforming Your Relationship with Money and Achieving Financial Independence* (New York: Penguin Books).

Donkin, Richard (2001), *Blood, Sweat and Tears: The Evolution of Work* (New York: Texere).

Dundes, Alan (1980), 'Seeing is Believing', in *Interpreting Folklore* (Bloomington: Indiana University Press).

Edwards, Betty (1994), *Drawing on the Right Side of the Brain* (London: BCA).

Edwards, John (1988), *The Roman Cookery of Apicius* (London: Rider Books).

Ehrenreich, Barbara (2009), *Smile or Die: How Positive Thinking Fooled America and the World* (London: Granta).

Elgin, Duane (1993), *Voluntary Simplicity: Toward a Way of Life that is Outwardly Simple, Inwardly Rich* (New York: Quill).

Elias, Norbert (2001), *The Loneliness of the Dying* (New York: Continuum).

Ellis, Richard J. (2005), *To The Flag: The Unlikely History of the Pledge of Allegiance* (Lawrence: University Press of Kansas).

Epstein, Edward Jay (February 1982), 'Have You Ever Tried to Sell a Diamond?', *Atlantic Monthly*.

*Fatherworld Magazine* (2005), Vol. 3 No. 2. (London: Fathers Direct).

Ferguson, Niall (2009), *The Ascent of Money: A Financial History of the World* (London: Penguin Books).

Fernley-Whittingstall, Jane (2003), *The Garden: An English Love Affair – One Thousand Years of Gardening* (London: Seven Dials).

Fernyhough, Charles (2008), *The Baby in the Mirror: A Child's World from Birth to Three* (London: Granta).

Feuerbach, Anselm von (1832), *Caspar Hauser* (Boston, Mass.: Allen and Ticknor).

Firth, Raymond (1973), *Symbols Public and Private* (London: George Allen & Unwin).

Fisher, M. F. K (1963), *The Art of Eating* (London: Faber and Faber).

Flacelière, Robert (1962), *Love in Ancient Greece* (London: Frederick Muller).

—— (2002), *Daily Life in Greece at the Time of Pericles* (London: Phoenix).

Forbes, Bruce David (2007), *Christmas: A Candid History* (Berkeley: University of California Press).

Frankl, Victor (1987), *Man's Search for Meaning: An Introduction to Logotherapy* (London: Hodder and Stoughton).

Frazer, James George (1978), *The Illustrated Golden Bough*, ed. Mary Douglas (London: Macmillan).

Fromm, Erich (1962), *The Art of Loving* (London: Unwin).

Galbraith, John Kenneth (1977), *The Age of Uncertainty* (London: BBC Books and André Deutsch).

Gandhi, Mahatma (1984), *An Autobiography, or The Story of My Experiments with Truth* (Ahmedabad: Navajivan Publishing House).

Gatenby, Reg (2004), 'Married Only At Weekends? A Study of the Amount of Time Spent Together by Spouses' (London: Office for National Statistics).

Geertz, Clifford (1993), 'Person, Time, and Conduct in Bali', in *The Interpretation of Cultures* (London: Fontana).

Giddens, Anthony (1992), *The Transformation of Intimacy: Sexuality, Love and Eroticism in Modern Societies* (Cambridge: Polity Press).

Gladwell, Malcolm (2005), *Blink: The Power of Thinking Without Thinking* (London: Penguin Books).

Goethe, Johann Wolfgang von (1970), *Italian Journey* (Harmondsworth: Penguin Books).

—— (1999), *The Flight to Italy: Diary and Selected Letters* (Oxford: Oxford University Press).

Goleman, Daniel (1996), *Emotional Intelligence: Why It Can Matter More Than IQ* (London: Bloomsbury).

—— (1999), *Working with Emotional Intelligence* (London: Bloomsbury).

Gombrich, E. H. (1950), *The Story of Art* (London: Phaidon).

Goody, Jack (1993), *The Culture of Flowers* (Cambridge: Cambridge University Press).

—— (1999), *Food and Love: Cultural History of East and West* (London: Verso).

Gosch, Stephen and Peter Stearns (eds.) (2008), *Pre-Modern Travel in World History* (New York and London: Routledge).

Gottlieb, Beatrice (1993), *The Family in the Western World from the Black Death to the Industrial Age* (New York: Oxford University Press).

Grayling, A. C. (2002), *The Meaning of Things: Applying Philosophy to Life* (London: Phoenix).

—— (2008), *Toward the Light: The Story of the Struggles for Liberty and Rights that Made the Modern West* (London: Bloomsbury).

Greenblatt, Stephen (2007), 'Stroking', *New York Review of Books*, 8 November.

Griffiths, Jay (2006), *Wild: An Elemental Journey* (New York: Jeremy P. Tarcher/Penguin Books).

Grinde, Bjorn and Grete Grindal Patil (2009), 'Biophilia: Does Visual Contact with Nature Impact on Health and Wellbeing?', *International Journal of Environmental Research and Public Health*, Vol. 6: 2332–43.

Halberstam, David (2008), *The Making of a Quagmire: America and Vietnam during the Kennedy Era* (Lanham, Md.: Rowman & Littlefield).

Hamilton, Jill (2005), *Thomas Cook: The Holiday-Maker* (Stroud: Sutton Publishing).

Hanh, Thich Nhat (1989), *Being Peace* (London: Rider).

Hazm, Ibn (1953), *The Ring of the Dove: A Treatise on the Art and Practice of Arab Love*, trans. A. J. Arberry (London: Luzac).

Herrigel, Eugene (1985), *Zen in the Art of Archery* (London: Arkana).

Hewlett, Barry (2000), 'Culture, History and Sex', *Marriage and Family Review*, Vol. 29, No. 2: 59–73.

Hite, Shere (1990), *The Hite Report on Male Sexuality* (London: Macdonald Optima).

Hobbes, Thomas (1996), *Leviathan*, ed. Richard Tuck (Cambridge: Cambridge University Press).

Hobsbawm, Eric (1983), 'Mass-Producing Traditions: Europe, 1870–1914', in Eric Hobsbawm and Terence Ranger (eds.), *The Invention of Tradition* (Cambridge: Cambridge University Press).

Hochschild, Adam (2006), *Bury the Chains: The British Struggle to Abolish Slavery* (London: Pan).

Hodgkinson, Tom (2005), *How to be Idle* (London: Penguin Books).

Hoffman, Martin (2000), *Empathy and Moral Development: Implications for Caring and Justice* (Cambridge: Cambridge University Press).

Honoré, Carl (2004), *In Praise of Slow: How a Worldwide Movement is Challenging the Cult of Speed* (San Francisco: HarperSanFrancisco).

House, Adrian (2000), *Francis of Assisi* (London: Chatto & Windus).

Howes, David (2005), 'Hyperesthesia, or, The Sensual Logic of Late Capitalism', in David Howes (ed), *Empire of the Senses: The Sensual Culture Reader* (Oxford: Berg).

—— (ed) (1991), *The Varieties of Sensory Experience: A Sourcebook in the Anthropology of the Senses* (Toronto: University of Toronto Press).

Hoyles, Martin (1991), *The Story of Gardening* (London: Journeyman Press).

Huizinga, Johan (1950), *Homo Ludens: A Study of the Play Element in Culture* (Boston, Mass.: Beacon Press).

—— (1965), *The Waning of the Middle Ages* (Harmondsworth: Penguin Books).

Hyde, Lewis (2006), *The Gift: How the Creative Spirit Transforms the World* (Edinburgh: Canongate).

Illich, Ivan (1975), *Medical Nemesis: The Expropriation of Health* (London: Calder & Boyars).

Illouz, Eva (1997), *Consuming the Romantic Utopia: Love and the Cultural Contradictions of Capitalism* (Berkeley: University of California Press).

Inglehart, Ronald (1997), *Modernization and Postmodernization: Cultural, Economic, and Political Change in 43 Societies* (Princeton, N.J.: Princeton University Press).

Jackson, Phillip, Eric Brunet, Andrew Meltzoff and Jean Decety (2006), 'Empathy Examined through the Neural Mechanisms Involved in Imagining How I Feel Versus How You Feel Pain', *Neuropsychologica*, Vol. 44, No. 5: 752–61.

James, Oliver (2007), *Affluenza: How to be Successful and Stay Sane* (London: Vermillion).

Jansen, William (1997), 'Gender Identity and the Rituals of Food in a Jordanian Community', *Food and Foodways*, Vol. 7, No. 2: 87–117.

Jaucourt, Louis, chevalier de (2005), 'Cuisine', in *The Encyclopedia of Diderot & d'Alembert*, trans. Sean Takats (Michigan: Scholarly Publishing Office of the University of Michigan).

Jenike, Brenda R. and John W. Traphagan (2009), 'Transforming the Cultural Scripts for Ageing and Elder Care in Japan', in Jay Sokolovsky (ed.), *The Cultural Context of Ageing: Worldwide Perspectives* (Westport, Conn.: Praeger): 240–58.

Judt, Tony (2010), 'The Glory of the Rails', *New York Review of Books*, 23 December.

Jung, Carl (1978), *Man and His Symbols* (London: Picador).

Kellehear, Allan (2007), *A Social History of Dying* (Cambridge: Cambridge University Press).

Keller, Helen (1958), *The Story of My Life* (London: Hodder and Stoughton).

—— (2003), *The World I Live In* (New York: New York Review Books).

Kellert, Stephen R. and Edward O. Wilson (eds.) (1993), *The Biophilia Hypothesis* (Washington, DC: Island Press and Shearwater Books).

Kelley, Jonathan and Nan Dirk de Graaf (1997), 'National Context, Parental Socialization, and Religious Belief: Results from 15 Nations', *American Sociological Review*, Vol. 62: 639–59.

Kemp, Simon and Garth Fletcher (1993), 'The Medieval Theory of the Inner Senses', *American Journal of Psychology*, Vol. 106, No. 4: 559–76.

Kerber, Linda K. (1988), 'Separate Spheres, Female Worlds, Woman's Place: The Rhetoric of Women's History', *Journal of American History*, Vol. 75, No. 1: 9–39.

King, Ross (2006), *Michelangelo and the Pope's Ceiling* (London: Pimlico).

Koestler, Arthur (1964), *The Act of Creation* (London: Pan).

Kohn, Alfie (1990), *The Brighter Side of Human Nature: Empathy and Altruism in Everyday Life* (New York: Basic Books).

Koshar, Rudy (2000), *German Travel Cultures* (Oxford: Berg).

Krakauer, Jon (2007), *Into the Wild* (London: Pan).

Kropotkin, Peter (1974), *Fields, Factories and Workshops of Tomorrow*, ed. Colin Ward (London: George Allen & Unwin).

—— (1998), *Mutual Aid: A Factor of Evolution* (London: Freedom Press).

Krznaric, Roman (2007), 'For God's Sake Do Something! How Religions Can Find Unexpected Unity Around Climate Change', Human Development Report Office Occasional Paper 2007/29 (New York: United Nations Development Programme).

—— (2008), 'You Are Therefore I Am: How Empathy Education Can Create Social Change', Oxfam Research Report (Oxford: Oxfam).

—— (2010), 'Five Lessons for the Climate Crisis: What the History of Resource Scarcity in the United States and Japan Can Teach Us', in Mark Levene, Rob Johnson and Penny Roberts (eds.), *History at the End of the World? History, Climate Change and the Possibility of Closure* (Penrith: Humanities Ebooks).

Kübler-Ross, Elisabeth (1973), *On Death and Dying* (London: Tavistock Publications).

Kumar, Satish (2000), *No Destination: An Autobiography* (Totnes: Green Books).

Lader, Deborah, Sandra Short and Jonathan Gershuny (2006), 'The Time Use Survey, 2005: How We Spend Our Time' (London: Office for National Statistics).

Lakoff, George (2005), *Don't Think of an Elephant: Know Your Values and Frame the Debate* (Melbourne: Scribe Short Books).

—— and Mark Johnson (1981), *Metaphors We Live By* (Chicago: University of Chicago Press).

Lamb, Michael (2000), 'The History of Research on Father Involvement', *Marriage and Family Review*, Vol. 29, No. 2: 23–42.

Lancaster, Bill (1995), *The Department Store: A Social History* (London: Leicester University Press).

Lane, Eric (1987), 'Introduction' to *The Sorrows of Young Werther* by Johann Wolfgang von Goethe (London and New York: Dedalus/ Hippocrene).

Layard, Richard (2005), *Happiness: Lessons from a New Science* (London: Allen Lane).

—— (2007), 'Happiness and the Teaching of Values', *CentrePiece*, Summer: 18–23.

Leach, William (1993), *Land of Desire: Merchants, Power, and the Rise of a New American Culture* (New York: Pantheon Books).

Lee, John Alan (1998), 'Ideologies of Lovestyle and Sexstyle', in Victor C. de Munck (ed.), *Romantic Love and Sexual Behaviour: Perspectives from the Social Sciences* (Westport, Conn.: Praeger), 33–76.

Lee, Laurie (1971), *As I Walked Out One Midsummer Morning* (Harmondsworth: Penguin Books).

Lewis, Clive Staples (1958), *The Allegory of Love: A Study in Medieval Traditions* (Oxford: Oxford University Press).

—— (2002), *The Four Loves* (London: HarperCollins).

Lewis, Milton J. (2007), *Medicine and Care of the Dying: A Modern History* (Oxford: Oxford University Press).

Lindqvist, Sven (1997a), *'Exterminate All the Brutes'* (London: Granta).

—— (1997b) *The Skull Measurer's Mistake* (New York: New Press).

Louv, Richard (2005), *Last Child in the Woods: Saving Our Children from Nature-Deficit Disorder* (London: Atlantic Books).

Lowe, Donald (1982), *History of Bourgeois Perception* (Brighton: Harvester Press).

Mabey, Richard (2006), *Nature Cure* (London: Pimlico).

MacClancy, Jeremy (1992), *Consuming Culture* (London: Chapmans).

Macfarlane, Robert (2007), *The Wild Places* (London: Granta).

McIntosh, Alex (1999), 'The Family Meal and Its Significance in Global Times', in Raymond Grew (ed.), *Food in Global History* (Boulder, Colo.: Westview Press).

McKibben, Bill (2003), *The End of Nature: Humanity, Climate Change and the Natural World* (London: Bloomsbury).

—— (2009), *Deep Economy: Economics as if the World Mattered* (Oxford: Oneworld).

McMahon, Darrin (2006), *Happiness: A History* (New York: Grove Press).

Maitland, Sara (2008), *A Book of Silence* (London: Granta).

Mandela, Nelson (1995), *Long Walk to Freedom* (London: Abacus).

Mander, Jerry (1978), *Four Arguments for the Elimination of Television* (New York: Quill).

Marshall, George (2007), *Carbon Detox: Your Step-By-Step Guide to Getting Real about Climate Change* (London: Gaia).

Marx, Karl (1982), *The Marxist Reader*, ed. Emile Burns (New York: Avenel Books).

Mayhew, Henry (1949), *Mayhew's London: Selections from London Labour and the London Poor*, ed. Peter Quennell (London: Spring Books).

Mendelson, Edward (1985), 'Baedeker's Universe', *Yale Review*, Vol. 74: 386–403.

Miles, Rosalind (1989), *The Women's History of the World* (London: Paladin).

Mill, John Stuart (1989), *Autobiography* (London: Penguin Books).

Miller, Daniel (ed.) (1993), *Unwrapping Christmas* (Oxford: Clarendon Press).

Miller, Michael B. (1981), *The Bon Marché: Bourgeois Culture and the Department Store, 1869–1920* (London: George Allen & Unwin).

Miller, Stephen (2006), *Conversation: A History of a Declining Art* (New Haven, Conn.: Yale University Press).

Mitchell, Lynette G. (1997), *Greeks Bearing Gifts: The Public Use of Private Relationships in the Greek World, 435–323 BC* (Cambridge: Cambridge University Press).

Mitford, Jessica (1998), *The American Way of Death Revisited* (London: Virago).

Morley, David (1986), *Family Television: Cultural Power and Domestic Leisure* (London: Comedia).

Morris, William (1979), *The Political Writings of William Morris* (London: Lawrence & Wishart).

Mukherjee, Rudranshu (ed.) (1993), *The Penguin Gandhi Reader* (New Delhi: Penguin Books).

Mumford, Lewis (1938), *The Culture of Cities* (New York: Harcourt, Brace and Company).

—— (1955), 'The Monastery and the Clock' in *The Human Prospect* (Boston, Mass.: Beacon Press).

Murcott, Anne (1997), 'Family Meals – A Thing of the Past?', in Pat Caplan (ed.), *Food, Health and Identity* (London: Routledge).

Myers, Scott (1996), 'An Interactive Model of Religiosity Inheritance: The Importance of Family Context', *American Sociological Review*, Vol. 61: 858–66.

Nash, Roderick Frazier (2001), *Wilderness and the American Mind* (New Haven, Conn.: Yale University Press).

New Economics Foundation (2009), *The Great Transition* (London: New Economics Foundation).

Newby, Eric (1986), *A Book of Travellers' Tales* (London: Picador).

Nicholl, Charles (2005), *Leonardo da Vinci: The Flights of the Mind* (London: Penguin Books).

Nicholson, Virginia (2002), *Among the Bohemians: Experiments in Living 1900–1939* (London: Viking).

Nightingale, Florence (2007), *Notes on Nursing* (Stroud: Tempus).

Nussbaum, Martha (2003), *Upheavals of Thought: The Intelligence of Emotions* (New York: Cambridge University Press).

Office for National Statistics (July 2006), *The Time Use Survey, 2005: How We Spend Our Time* (London: Office for National Statistics).

Ong, Walter (1970), *The Presence of the Word: Some Prolegomena for Cultural and Religious History* (New York: Clarion).

Onyx, Jenny and Rosemary Leonard (2005), 'Australian Grey Nomads and American Snowbirds: Similarities and Differences', *Journal of Tourism Studies*, Vol. 16, No. 1.

OPP Unlocking Potential, 'Dream Job or Career Nightmare?', July 2007, http://www.opp.eu.com/uploadedFiles/dream-research.pdf.

Orme, Nicholas (2003), *Medieval Children* (New Haven, Conn., and London: Yale University Press).

Oruch, Jack B. (1981), 'St. Valentine, Chaucer, and Spring in February', *Speculum*, Vol. 56, No. 3: 534–65.

Orwell, George (1962), *The Road to Wigan Pier* (Harmondsworth: Penguin Books).

—— (1974), *Down and Out in Paris and London* (Harmondsworth: Penguin Books).

—— (2002), 'Pleasure Spots' in *Essays* (London: Everyman).

Paz, Octavio (1967), *The Labyrinth of Solitude: Life and Thought in Mexico* (London: Allen Lane).

—— (1996), *The Double Flame: Love and Eroticism* (London: Harvill Press).

Peck, M. Scott (1978), *The Road Less Travelled: A New Psychology of Love, Traditional Values and Spiritual Growth* (London: Rider).

Petit, Philippe (2003), *To Reach the Clouds: My Hire-Wire Walk Between the Twin Towers* (London: Faber and Faber).

Phillips, Adam and Barbara Taylor (2009), *On Kindness* (London: Hamish Hamilton).

Pittenger, David J. (2005), 'Cautionary Comments Regarding the Myers-Briggs Type Indicator', *Consulting Psychology Journal: Practice and Research*, Vol. 57, No. 3: 210–21.

Plato (1991), *Symposium* (London: Folio Society).

Pollock, Linda (1987), *A Lasting Relationship: Parents and Children over Three Centuries* (Hanover, N.H.: University Press of New England).

Pope, Rob (2005), *Creativity: History, Theory, Practice* (London and New York: Routledge).

Porter, Roy (1997), *The Greatest Benefit to Mankind: A Medical History of Humanity from Antiquity to the Present* (London: HarperCollins).

Read, Herbert (1934), *Art and Industry* (London: Faber and Faber).

Regis, Helen A. (1999), 'Second Lines, Minstrelsy, and the Contested Landscapes of New Orelans Afro-Creole Festivals', *Cultural Anthropology*, Vol. 14, No. 4: 472–504.

Rifkin, Jeremy (2009), *The Empathic Civilization: The Race to Global Consciousness in a World in Crisis* (Cambridge: Polity).

Rinpoche, Sogyal (1998), *The Tibetan Book of Living and Dying* (London: Rider).

Roach, Joseph (1996), *Cities of the Dead: Circum-Atlantic Performance* (New York: Columbia University Press).

Robb, Graham (2008), *The Discovery of France* (London: Picador).

Roberts, David (ed.) (2002), *Signals and Perception: The Fundamentals of Human Sensations* (Basingstoke: Palgrave Macmillan).

Robinson, Jane (1995), *Unsuitable for Ladies: An Anthology of Women Travellers* (Oxford: Oxford University Press).

Rogers, Carl and Barry Stevens (1973), *Person to Person: The Problem of Being Human* (London: Souvenir Press).

Roszak, Theodore (1995), 'Where Psyche Meets Gaia', in Theodore Roszak, Mary E. Gomes and Allen D. Kanner (eds.), *Ecopsychology: Restoring the Earth, Healing the Mind* (San Francisco: Sierra Club Books).

Ruggles, Steven (1987), *Prolonged Connections: The Rise of the Extended Family in Nineteenth-Century England and America* (Madison: University of Wisconsin Press).

Ruskin, John (1907), *The Stones of Venice* (London: New Universal Library).

Russell, Bertrand (1976), 'Romantic Love' in *Marriage and Morals* (London: Unwin).

Sabatos, Terri (2007), 'Father as Mother: The Image of the Widower with Children in Victorian Art', in Trev Lynn Broughton and Helen Rogers (eds.), *Gender and Fatherhood in the Nineteenth Century* (Basingstoke: Palgrave Macmillan).

Sahlins, Marshall (1972), *Stone Age Economics* (New York: Aldine de Gruyter).

Sajavaara, Kari and Jaakko Lehtonen (1997), 'The Silent Finn Revisited', in Adam Jaworski (ed.), *Silence: Interdisciplinary Perspectives* (The Hague: Mouton de Gruyter).

Saul, John Ralston (1992), *Voltaire's Bastards: The Dictatorship of Reason in the West* (London: Sinclair Stevenson).

Schama, Simon (1988), *The Embarrassment of Riches: An Interpretation of Dutch Culture in the Golden Age* (London: Fontana).

—— (1996), *Landscape and Memory* (London: Fontana).

Schlosser, Eric (2002), *Fast Food Nation: What the All-American Meal is Doing to the World* (London: Penguin Books).

Schmidt, Leigh Eric (1993), 'The Fashioning of a Modern Holiday: St. Valentine's Day, 1840–1870', *Winterthur Portfolio*, Vol. 28, No. 4: 209–45.

Schweitzer, Albert (1949), *On the Edge of the Primeval Forest* (London: Readers Union).

Seaton, Beverly (1989), 'Towards a Historical Semiotics of Literary Flower Personification', *Poetics Today*, Vol. 10, No. 4: 679–701.

Seligman, Martin (2002), *Authentic Happiness* (London: Nicholas Brealey).

Sennett, Richard (2003), *Respect: The Formation of Character in an Age of Inequality* (London: Allen Lane).

—— (2009), *The Craftsman* (London: Penguin Books).

Shi, David E. (1985), *The Simple Life: Plain Living and High Thinking in American Culture* (New York: Oxford University Press).

Singer, Peter (1997), *How Are We to Live? Ethics in an Age of Self-interest* (Oxford: Oxford University Press).

Smith, Adam (1898), *The Wealth of Nations* (London: George Routledge and Son).

—— (1976), *The Theory of Moral Sentiments* (Indianapolis, Ind.: Liberty Classics).

Smith, Tom. W. (1988), 'Counting Flocks and Lost Sheep: Trends in Religious Preference Since World War II', General Social Survey Report No. 26 (revised 1991), National Opinion Research Center, University of Chicago.

Sokolovsky, Jay (ed.) (2009), *The Cultural Context of Ageing: Worldwide Perspectives* (Westport, Conn.: Praeger).

Sontag, Susan (1991), *Illness as Metaphor, AIDS and Its Metaphors* (London: Penguin Books).

Sprawson, Charles (1992), *Haunts of the Black Masseur: The Swimmer as Hero* (London: Vintage).

Sullivan, Sheila (2000), *Falling in Love: A History of Torment and Enchantment* (Basingstoke and London: Papermac).

Süskind, Patrick (2008), *Perfume: The Story of a Murderer* (London: Penguin Books).

Suzuki, Daisetz Teitaro (1986), *Living By Zen* (London: Rider).

Swinglehurst, Edmund (1982), *Cook's Tours: The Story of Popular Travel* (Poole: Blandford Press).

Symons, Michael (2001), *A History of Cooks and Cooking* (Totnes: Prospect Books).

Synnott, Anthony (1991), 'Puzzling over the Senses: From Plato to Marx', in David Howes (ed.), *The Varieties of Sensory Experience: A Sourcebook in the Anthropology of the Senses* (Toronto: University of Toronto Press).

Tabori, Paul (1966), *A Pictorial History of Love* (London: Spring Books).

Tannen, Deborah (1985), 'Silence: Anything But', in Deborah Tannen and Muriel Saville-Troike (eds.), *Perspectives on Silence* (Norwood, N.J.: Ablex).

—— (1999), 'Women and Men in Conversation', in Rebecca S. Wheeler (ed.), *The Workings of Language: From Prescriptions to Perspectives* (Westport, Conn.: Praeger).

Tatarkiewicz, Wladyslaw (1980), *A History of Six Ideas: An Essay on Aesthetics* (The Hague, Boston, Conn., and London: Martinus Nijhoff; Warsaw: PWN, Polish Scientific Publishers).

Tawney, Richard (1938), *Religion and the Rise of Capitalism* (Harmondsworth: Penguin Books).

Terkel, Studs (1982), *American Dreams: Lost and Found* (London: Paladin Granada).

—— (1993), *Race* (London: Minerva).

—— (2002), *Will the Circle Be Unbroken? Reflections on Death and Dignity* (London: Granta).

Thomas, Keith (1985), *Man and the Natural World: Changing Attitudes in England 1500–1800* (London: Penguin Books).

—— (ed.) (1999), *The Oxford Book of Work* (Oxford: Oxford University Press).

—— (2009), *The Ends of Life: Roads to Fulfilment in Early Modern England* (Oxford: Oxford University Press).

Thompson, Edward P. (1967), 'Time, Work Discipline and Industrial Capitalism', *Past and Present*, Vol. 38.

Thoreau, Henry David (1986), *Walden and Civil Disobedience* (New York: Penguin Books).

Thornton, Bruce S. (1997), *Eros: The Myth of Ancient Greek Sexuality* (Boulder, Colo.: Westview Press).

Thucydides (1989), *The Peloponnesian War*, The Complete Hobbes Translation, with notes and a new introduction by David Grene (Chicago: University of Chicago Press).

Todd, Janet (2001), *Mary Wollstonecraft: A Revolutionary Life* (London: Phoenix).

Tolstoy, Leo (2008), *A Confession* (London: Penguin Books).

Totman, Conrad (1989), *The Green Archipelago: Forestry in Pre-Industrial Japan* (Athens: Ohio University Press).

Towner, John (1985), 'The Grand Tour: A Key Phase in the History of Tourism', *Annals of Tourism Research*, Vol. 12, No. 3: 297–333.

Townsend, Peter (1957), *The Family Life of Old People: An Inquiry in East London* (London: Routledge & Keagan Paul).

Troyat, Henri (1967), *Tolstoy* (Garden City, N.Y.: Doubleday).

Ulrich, Roger S. (1984), 'View Through a Window May Influence Recovery from Surgery', *Science*, New Series, Vol. 224, Issue 4647, 27 April: 420–21.

Vasari, Georgio (2008), *The Lives of the Artists*, trans. Julia Conaway Bondanella and Peter Bondanella (Oxford: Oxford University Press).

Vehling, Joseph Dommers (1977), *Apicius: Cooking and Dining in Imperial Rome* (New York: Dover).

Vernon, Mark (2005), *The Philosophy of Friendship* (Basingstoke: Palgrave Macmillan).

Vernon, P. E. (ed.) (1970), *Creativity: Selected Readings* (Harmondsworth: Penguin Education).

Vinge, Louise (1975), *The Five Senses: Studies in a Literary Tradition* (Lund: Royal Society of Letters).

Visser, Margaret (1993), *The Rituals of Dinner: The Origins, Evolution, Eccentricities, and Meaning of Table Manners* (London: Penguin Books).

Wang, Robin W. (2003), 'The Principled Benevolence: A Synthesis of Kantian and Confucian Moral Judgment', in Bo Mou (ed.), *Comparative Approaches to Chinese Philosophy* (Aldershot: Ashgate), 122–43.

Ward, Colin (1995), *Talking Schools* (London: Freedom Press).

—— and Dennis Hardy (1986), *Goodnight Campers! The History of the British Holiday Camp* (London and New York: Mansell).

Weber, Max (1958), *The Protestant Ethic and the Spirit of Capitalism* (New York: Charles Scribner's Sons).

Westwood, Andy (2002), 'Is New Work Good Work', The Work Foundation, http://www.theworkfoundation.com/Assets/PDFs/newwork_goodwork.pdf.

White, Lynn Jr. (1967), 'The Historical Roots of Our Ecological Crisis', *Science*, Vol. 155, No. 3767, 10 March: 1203–7.

Wilson, A. N. (1989), *Tolstoy* (Harmondsworth: Penguin Books).

Wilson, Edward O. (1984), *Biophilia: The Human Bond with Other Species* (Cambridge, Mass.: Harvard University Press).

Woodcock, George (1986), 'The Tyranny of the Clock', in George Woodcock (ed.), *The Anarchist Reader* (London: Fontana).

—— (2004), *Anarchism: A History of Libertarian Ideas and Movements* (Ontario: Broadview Press).

Woolf, Virginia (1932), *The Common Reader, Second Series* (London: Hogarth Press).

Zeldin, Theodore (1984), *The French* (London: Vintage).

—— (1995), *An Intimate History of Humanity* (London: Minerva).

—— (1999a), *Conversation* (London: Harvill Press).

—— (1999b), *The Future of Work*, http://www.oxfordmuse. com/?q=the-future-of-work.

Zhang, Hong (2009), 'The New Realities of Ageing in Contemporary China: Coping with the Decline of Family Care', in Jay Sokolovsky (ed.), *The Cultural Context of Ageing: Worldwide Perspectives* (Westport, Conn.: Praeger), 196–215.

# Notes

## Preface

1. Thucydides 1989: xxi.

## 1. Love

1. Oruch 1981: 535, 538, 556–8; Schmidt 1993: 210–13, 233; http://www.businessinsider.com/valentines-day-spending-2011–2?slop=1#.
2. de Rougemont 1983: 173.
3. de Rougemont 1983: 5; Davidson 2007: 11; Sullivan 2000: 24.
4. Thornton 1997: 17, 23; Davidson 2007: 14–24.
5. Davidson 2007: 31.
6. Flacelière 2002 : 73–4.
7. Tabori 1966: 35.
8. Flacelière 1962: 11.
9. McMahon 2006: 27–9; Flacelière 1962: 106.
10. Mitchell 1997: 1–21; Davidson 2007: 32–4; Vernon 2005: 12–13; Flacelière 1962: 155.
11. Lee 1998: 37; Grayling 2002: 64; Sullivan 2000: 26.
12. Tabori 1966: 218–30.
13. Huizinga 1950: 77.
14. http://www.psychologytoday.com/articles/199907/the-power-play.
15. Flacelière 1962: 66, 95, 99.
16. Grayling 2002: 64.
17. Fromm 1962: 11, 22.
18. http://www.guardian.co.uk/society/2008/mar/28/socialtrends; http://www.divorcerate.org/
19. Lee 1998: 38.

20.  Lewis 2002: 141–70; Davidson 2007: 12; de Rougemont 1983: 67–9.
21.  Wang 2003: 127–8.
22.  Fromm 1962: 45.
23.  Peck 1978: 70.
24.  http://www.virginia.edu/marriageproject/pdfs/SOOU2001.
      pdf; Peck 1978, 79.
25.  http://www.wollamshram.ca/1001/Vol_2/v012.htm.
26.  Zeldin 1995: 83; Sullivan 2000: 37.
27.  Zeldin 1995: 78, 83; de Rougemont 1983: 106–7.
28.  Hazm 1953.
29.  Ackerman and Mackin 1998: 604.
30.  de Rougemont 1983: 73–4, 106–7; Paz 1996: 71, 72; Lewis 1958: 2.
31.  de Rougemont 1983: 90.
32.  Paz 1996: 30, 67; Russell 1976: 51; Sullivan 2000: 36.
33.  Tabori 1966: 139; Lewis 1958: 13.
34.  Huizinga 1965: 67, 76, 79; Russell 1976: 49.
35.  Lewis 1958: 3–4; Tabori 1966: 207–11.
36.  Huizinga 1965: 104.
37.  de Rougement 1983: 50–51.
38.  Schama 1988: 414, 421.
39.  Schama 1988: 185–6, 377, 422, 424, 521.
40.  Schama 1988: 423–7.
41.  Thomas 2009: 214–18.
42.  de Rougemont 1983: 218; Armstrong 2003: 3.
43.  Lane 1987: 7.
44.  Goody 1999: 98, 106–9, 121; Sullivan 2000: 17; Giddens 1992: 41.
45.  Epstein 1982.
46.  Illouz 1997: 6–16.
47.  http://www.surgery.org/sites/default/files/Stats2010_1.pdf.
48.  Fromm 1962: 10.
49.  Fromm 1962: 9, 22.
50.  Comfort 1996: 7, 201.
51.  Hite 1990: 339.
52.  Russell 1976: 55.

## 2. Family

1.  Ballard 2008: 182–6, 199, 206, 227; http://www.jgballard.ca/
     interviews/sunday_times_1988interview.html.
2.  http://careerplanning.about.com/cs/altoptgen1/a/stay_home_
     dads.htm; http://www.stayathomedads.co.uk/news.html.

3. Gatenby 2004.
4. Lader, Short and Gershuny 2006: 3, 11, 63.
5. http://www.mumsnet.com/Talk/relationships/1067969-It-has-just-dawned-on-me-that-my-husband-has.
6. http://news.bbc.co.uk/1/hi/uk/7638056.stm.
7. Burgess 1997: 87–8; Hewlett 2000: 63.
8. Coltrane 1996: 176–85; Burgess 1997: 86; Hewlett 2000.
9. Burgess 1997: 74–83.
10. Coltrane 1996: 38; Cowan 1983: 16–18.
11. Cowan 1983: 17–31; Lamb 2000: 27; Miles 1989: 187.
12. Burgess 1997: 44; Abbott 1993: 169.
13. Berry 1993: 42.
14. Burgess 1997: 46–8; Sabatos 2007.
15. Pollock 1987: 12; Ruggles 1987: 4–5; Burgess 1997: 43; Schama 1988: 386–7; Gottlieb 1993: 3–23.
16. Townsend 1957: 31.
17. Miles 1989: 150–51.
18. Kerber 1988: 11, 29–30; Coltrane 1996: 35; Miles 1989: 187.
19. http://www.gutenberg.org/cache/epub/10136/pg10136.txt.
20. Coltrane 1996: 183; Lamb 2000.
21. Cowan 1983: 44–68; Coltrane 1996: 37–8.
22. William Dodds quoted in Davidson 1982: 187; Miles 1989: 188–95; de Beauvoir 1972: 144–7.
23. Burgess 1997: 60–61.
24. Burgess 1997: 121, 127.
25. *Fatherworld Magazine* 2005: 7.
26. Tannen 1999: 211.
27. Murcott 1997: 32, 45.
28. Plato 1991: 58.
29. Flacelière 2002: 55, 173–5.
30. Gottlieb quoted in McIntosh 1999: 221.
31. McIntosh 1999: 221; Visser 1993: 275–80; Murcott 1997: 43.
32. MacClancy 1992: 101; McIntosh 1999: 228; Zeldin 1999a: 37; Jansen 1997: 104.
33. Honoré 2004: 55; http://www.gallup.com/poll/10336/empty-seats-fewer-families-eat-together.aspx.
34. McIntosh 1999: 220.
35. Gottleib 1993: 43; Zeldin 1999a: 37; Zeldin 1995: 32; McIntosh 1999: 221; Visser 1993: 264.
36. Maitland 2008: 142–3.
37. Sajavaara and Lehtonen 1997: 270.

38. Miller 2006: 72–8, 91–125.
39. Miller 2006: 186.
40. Mill 1989: 58.
41. Mill 1989: 113.
42. Tannen 1985: 96.
43. Orwell 2002: 988.
44. Mander 1978: 24.
45. http://www.csun.edu/science/health/docs/tv&health.html;
    http://www.mediaweek.co.uk/news/668085/
    Average-TV-viewing-rises-last-decade/.
46. Morley 1986: 18–39.
47. Mander 1978: 24.
48. http://www.kff.org/entmedia/mh012010pkg.cfm: Miller 2006:
    298.
49. Zeldin 1999a: 39–41.

## 3. Empathy

1. House 2000: 56–8.
2. Kohn 1990: 99–101, 114–16; Goleman 1996: 98–9; Rogers
   and Stevens 1973: 92–4; Hoffman 2000; Batson 1991: 128–48;
   Nussbaum 2003: 334–5; Krznaric 2008.
3. http://www.guardian.co.uk/world/2001/sep/15/september11.
   politicsphilosophyandsociety2.
4. Layard 2007: 20; 2005: 234; Goleman 1999: 137–8; Kohn 1990;
   Mukherjee 1993: 91.
5. Armstrong 2007: xiv, 390.
6. Hobbes 1996: ix–xii.
7. Rifkin 2009: 43.
8. Smith 1976: 499–502.
9. Smith 1976: 502.
10. Phillips and Taylor 2009: 27.
11. Kohn 1990: 102–3; Fernyhough 2008: 63–6; Hoffman 2000.
12. de Waal 2006: 6, 27, 33; see also my interview with de Waal at
    www.outrospection.org.
13. Jackson et al. 2006; Broks 2003: 4–5; Goleman 1996: 102–4.
14. Baron-Cohen 2011; Rifkin 2009: 82–3.
15. Terkel 1982; 1993.
16. http://www.oxfordmuse.com/?=node/81.
17. Orwell 1962: 129–30.
18. Crick 1980: 217–18.

19. Orwell 1974: 189.
20. Hochschild 2006: 5, 222, 366; Krznaric 2008.

## 4. Work

1. Donkin 2001: 31–3; Thomas 1999: 106.
2. Marx 1982: 273–4; Mayhew 1949: 119, 306.
3. de Botton 2004: 60.
4. http://www.statistics.gov.uk/articles/labour_market_trends/jobmobility_nov03.pdf, p. 543.
5. Pittenger 2005.
6. Westwood 2002: 29; OPP Unlocking Potential 2007: 3.
7. Smith 1898: 3–4.
8. Smith 1898: 613.
9. Zeldin 1999b.
10. Inglehart 1997.
11. Seligman 2002: 177.
12. Schweitzer 1949: 3.
13. Porter 1997: 113.
14. Tawney 1938: 1999.
15. Thomas 2009: 86–7.
16. Frankl 1987: 35, 76, 79, 107, 110.
17. Sennett 2003.
18. Hoyles 1991: 48.
19. Saul 1992: 466–98.
20. Zeldin 1999a: 54.
21. Boorstin 1993: 389–90.
22. Nicholl 2005: 7, 241.
23. Emerson's journal, 11 November 1842, http://www.archive.org/stream/heartofemersonsj008022mbp/djvu.txt/.

## 5. Time

1. http://pewsocialtrends.org/2006/02/28/whos-feeling-rushed/; Honoré 2004, 7–8; http://news.bbc.co.uk/1/hi/talking_point/3898025.stm.
2. Boorstin 1985: 5–12.
3. Boorstin 1985: 28–53: Honoré 2004: 22.
4. Boorstin 1985: 47; Thompson 1967.
5. Boorstin 1985: 587.

6.  Thompson 1967.
7.  Woodcock 1986; Thompson 1967.
8.  Donkin 2001: 147–52.
9.  Mumford 1955: 5; Woodcock 1986.
10. Judt 2010.
11. Brand 1999: 16.
12. Schlosser 2002: 18–21; Honoré 2004: 55.
13. Honoré 2004: 59.
14. Lakoff and Johnson 1981: 4–9; Lakoff 2005: 3–4.
15. Robb 2008: 75–77; http://www.nytimes.com/2007/11/25/
    opinion/25robb.html.
16. Quoted in Hodgkinson 2005: 85.
17. Geertz 1993.
18. Hanh 1987: 109.
19. Herrigel 1985; Suzuki 1986.
20. Brand 1999: 2, 48, 144.

## 6. Money

1.  Schama 1988: 306.
2.  Buchan 1998.
3.  http://basildonrecorder.co.uk/news/4657635_2_5m_lottery_
    winner_still_delivers_catalogues/.
4.  http://www.statistics.gov.uk/cci/nugget.asp?id=1659;
    http://econpapers.repec.org/article/ucpjconrs/
    v_3a35_3ay_3a2008_3ai_3a4_3ap_3a622–639.htm.
5.  *Sunday Times*, 26 December 2010, p. 21.
6.  Thomas 2009: 138.
7.  Leach 1993: xiii.
8.  Thomas 2009: 110–46.
9.  Quoted in Thomas 2009: 146.
10. Weber 1958; Tawney 1938; Thomas 2009: 142–44.
11. Thomas 2009: 65–76, 118–32, 142–6, 155–6; Braudel 1981: 316;
    Braudel 1982: 60–75.
12. Miller 1981: 168.
13. Miller 1981: 165–89; Lancaster 1995: 16–41.
14. Leach 1993: xv.
15. Berger 1972: 131.
16. de Botton 2004: 182.

17. Layard 2005: 32–3; for more recent research, see
    http://www.pnas.org/content/107/38/16489.full.
    pdf+html?sid=aac48a0b-d009–4ce6–8c14–7f97c5310e15.

18. James 2007: 52.

19. Quoted in Thomas 2009: 146.

20. Thoreau 1986: 73.

21. Sahlins 1972: 14.

22. Honoré 2004: 189.

23. http://www.statistics.gov.uk/articles/labour_market_trends/
    Working_time_patterns.pdf.

24. http://www.statcom.gc.ca/pub/11-008-x/2007001/pdf/9629-
    eng.pdf.

25. Nicholson 2002: 3.

26. Quoted in Shi 1985: 33.

27. Shi 1985: 39.

28. *The Journal of John Woolman*, http://www.strecorsoc.org/
    jwoolman/w03.html.

29. Quoted in Shi 1985: 41; *The Journal of John Woolman*, http://www.
    strecorsoc.org/jwoolman/w04.html.

30. Quoted in Shi 1985: 44.

31. Shi 1985: 47.

32. Galbraith 1977: 29–30.

33. Elgin 1993; Dominguez and Robin 1999.

34. Several of these ideas can be found in Boyle 2010.

35. Ferguson 2009: 233.

36. McKibben 2009: 102.

## 7. Senses

1. Ackerman 1996: 9, 73, 290.

2. Classen 1993: 126–31.

3. Classen 1993: 2–3; Vinge 1975: 15–21.

4. Kemp and Fletcher 1993; Burton 1989: 150–53; Classen 1993: 3.

5. Classen 1993: 4; Synnott 1991: 70.

6. Roberts 2002; http://www.nature.com/nature/journal/v301/
   n5895/abs/301078a0.html.

7. Classen 1993: 15.

8. Howes 1991: 4; Classen 1993: 9.

9. Dundes 1980: 89; Howes 1991: 4, 169; Howes 2005; Classen 1993:
   5–6.

10. Classen 1993: 17–20.

11. Corbin 1986: 4.
12. Quoted in Howes 1991: 144.
13. Lowe 1982: 3–4.
14. Quoted in Howes 1991: 167, 171; Ong 1970: 1–9.
15. Quoted in Synnott 1991: 68.
16. Classen 1993: 28; Greenblatt 2007.
17. Classen 1993: 6, 27.
18. Berger 1972: 108; Lowe 1982.
19. Classen 1993: 17–29.
20. Seaton 1989: 686, 694; Goody 1993: 425.
21. Fernley-Whittingstall 2003: 244–5; Hoyles 1991: 227.
22. Seaton 1989: 697.
23. Classen 1993: 16; Howes 1991: 4.
24. Feuerbach 1832: 119, 125–38; Classen 1993: 40–46.
25. Classen 1993: 45.
26. Keller 1958: 26, 210.
27. Keller 2003: 11.
28. Keller 2003: 30, 56.

# 8. Travel

1. Hamilton 2005: vii.
2. Hamilton 2005: 4, 58–65, 83, 129, 136, 158–9, 174, 191, 207; Brenden 1991: 5–37; Swinglehurst 1982.
3. Boorstin 1985: 116, 121; Gosch and Stearns 2008: 42.
4. Bashō 1966: 51.
5. Coleman and Elsner 1995: 187.
6. Coleman and Elsner 1995: 188; Attlee 2011: 119.
7. Coleman and Elsner 1995: 181–90.
8. Kumar 2000: 79–81, 95, 110–11.
9. Quoted in Buzzard 2002: 40.
10. Mendelson 1985; Buzzard 2002: 40; Towner 1985.
11. Buzzard 2002: 47.
12. Baedeker 1909: lix.
13. Mendelson 1985.
14. Baedeker 1909: 29–30.
15. Baedeker 1909: 23.
16. Baedeker 1870: 185, 208; http://www.archive.org/stream/mrsrthelifeofele002126mbp/mrsrthelifeofele002126mbp_djvu.txt.
17. Mendelson 1985.
18. Zeldin 1984: 7.

19. Bronowski 1976: 59–68.
20. Quoted in Chatwin 1988: 218.
21. Ward and Hardy 1986: 2–3.
22. Ward and Hardy 1986: 1–8.
23. Onyx and Leonard 2005.
24. Darwin 1959: 203, 209; Lindqvist 1997a: 122–41.
25. Robinson 1995: 216–7.
26. Quoted in Newby 1986: 84.
27. Lindqvist 1997b, 140–45.
28. Ferguson 2009: 20–24.
29. Cobbett 1985: 309.
30. Cobbett 1985: 19.
31. Cobbett 1985: 19–20, 317–8.
32. Lee 1971: 11–12, 178.

## 9. Nature

1. Nash 2001: 141–3, 154–60.
2. Nash 2001: 11–17; Thomas 1985: 194.
3. http://www.britishmuseum.org/explore/highlights/
   highlight_objects/pd/h/hans_holbein_the_younger,_a_wi.aspx.
4. Thomas 1985: 194, 258–61; Nash 2001: 21; Clark 1971: 271, 283;
   Sprawson 1992: 201–13; Schama 1996: 103.
5. Nash 2001: 84–7; Thomas 1985: 216, 261.
6. Hoyles 1991: 37.
7. Thomas 1985: 193–4; Nash 2001, 49.
8. Clark 1971: 271.
9. Griffiths 2006: 2.
10. Krakauer 2007.
11. Wilson 1984: 1.
12. Kellert and Wilson 1993.
13. Nash 2001: 103.
14. Thomas 1985: 238.
15. Ulrich 1984; Grinde and Grindal Patil 2009; Kellert and Wilson
    1993; Wilson 1984; Bragg 1996; Louv 2005; Mabey 2006.
16. Roszak 1995: 5.
17. http://www.acu.edu.au/__data/assets/pdf_file/0005/158315/
    Henriks-and-Hall_Indigenous_Mysticism.pdf.
18. Data from Millennium Ecosystem Assessment (2005), http://
    www.greenfacts.org/en/biodiversity/figtableboxes/1035-bird-
    density-map-rates.htm.

19. Based on 2004 data, http://www.oxfam.org.uk/resources/policy/climate_change/downloads/bp117_climatewrongs.pdf.
20. Thomas 1985: 17, 26, 30–33.
21. Thomas 1985: 18–23; McKibben 2003: 79; White 1967: 1205; Krznaric 2007.
22. Braudel 1981: 369.
23. Smith 1898: Book 1, Chapter 6.
24. Schama 1996: 173; Thomas 1985: 197.
25. Totman 1989: 25, 171; Krznaric 2010.
26. New Economics Foundation 2009: 20.
27. McKibben 2003: xiv, 48, 60–61.
28. Marshall 2007: 162–3.
29. Macfarlane 2007: 10–11.

## 10. Belief

1. Halberstam 2008: 128.
2. Beit-Hallahmi and Argyle 1997: 24–5, 242.
3. Myers 1996.
4. Smith 1988: 24–5, 63–4; Beit-Hallahmi and Argyle 1997: 106.
5. Beit-Hallahmi and Argyle 1997: 100.
6. Kelley and de Graaf 1997.
7. Beit-Hallahmi and Argyle 1997: 25, 96, 242.
8. Forbes 2007: 7–10, 17–21, 25–32. See also Miller 1993: 8–11, 18; Frazer 1978: 189–91, 221–2.
9. Anderson 1991: 7.
10. Anderson 1991: 114; Ward 1995: 12.
11. Ellis 2005: 69, 80, 216; Firth 1973: 352.
12. http://www.sfmuseum.org/hist10/lange2.html.
13. Ellis 2005: 74–80, 164–9.
14. Hobsbawm 1983: 280; Ellis 2005: 218.
15. http://news.bbc.co.uk/1/hi/uk/7162649.stm.
16. Quoted in Cannadine 1983: 102.
17. Hobsbawm 1983: 1.
18. Cannadine 1983: 109–19.
19. Hobsbawm 1983: 282; Cannadine 1983: 122.
20. Cannadine 1983: 131–6.
21. Gladwell 2005: 84–6; http://asr.sagepub.com/content/74/5/777.
22. Boorstin 1985: 302, 323.
23. Boorstin 1985: 314–27; Bronowski 1976: 196–218; Grayling 2008: 88–97.

24. Woodcock 2004: 185–98; Wilson 1989: 108, 115–16; Tolstoy 2008: 12–13.
25. Wilson 1989: 6, 173, 275, 346, 400–01; Woodcock 2004: 196–218; Troyat 1967: 519–20.
26. Troyat 1967: 517.
27. Tolstoy 2008: 17–18, 62, 87–8, 92.
28. Troyat 1967: 512–16.
29. ftp://sunsite.unc.edu/pub/docs/books/gutenberg/etexts99/resur10.txt.
30. http://www.jkrishnamwti.org/about-krishnamurti/dissolution-speech.php.
31. Gandhi 1984: 135, 177, 274.
32. Mandela 1995: 749.
33. Singer 1997: 255.

## 11. Creativity

1. Burckhardt 1945: 81.
2. Boorstin 1993: 407–8.
3. Tatarkiewicz 1980: 247, 254–7; Pope 2005: 37.
4. Boorstin 1993: 407–19; Gombrich 1950: 220–9.
5. Vasari 2008: 425.
6. Boorstin 1993: 417.
7. John R. Taylor (Studio Art Centers International, Florence), personal communication, 31 August 2010; King 2006.
8. Boorstin 1993: 448–9.
9. Vernon 1970: 55.
10. Koestler 1964: 114–16; Jung 1978: 25.
11. http://www-history.mcs.st-andrews.ac.uk/Biographies/Wiles.html.
12. Sennett 2009: 172; http://edition.cnn.com/2009/BUSINESS/11/26/innovation.tips.index.html.
13. de Bono 1977: 86.
14. Edwards 1994: 98–113; Cameron 1995: 9–18.
15. Pope 2005: 40.
16. Office for National Statistics, July 2006: 11.
17. Quoted in Jaucourt 2005; Symons 2001: 110.
18. Edwards 1988; Fisher 1963: 33.
19. Vehling 1977: 268.
20. Hyde 2006: xiv, 58.
21. Brillat-Savarin 1970: 13.

22. Koestler 1964: 103, 269.
23. http://news-nationalgeographic.com/news/2004/10/1006_
    041006_chimps.html; Diamond 1998: 36; Bronowski 1976: 40–46;
    Sennett 2009: 6.
24. Sennett 2009: 8, 23.
25. Morris 1979: 33, 68–9.
26. Kropotkin 1998: 129–79; Mumford 1938: 29–35; Orme 2003: 312.
27. Read 1934: 12.
28. Sennett 2009: 86–7.
29. Kropotkin 1974: 169.
30. Ruskin 1907, Vol. 2: Chapter 6, Sections 14–16.
31. Sennett 2009: 289–90.
32. Thoreau 1986: 88.
33. Koestler 1964: 336, 379; Boorstin 1993: 425.
34. Boorstin 1993: 393–7; Gombrich 1950: 163–5.
35. Boorstin 1993: 729; Berger 1965: 59.
36. Berger 1965: 54.
37. Todd 2001: ix.
38. Woolf 1932.
39. http://www.csun.edu/science/health/docs/tv&health.html;
    http://www.mediaweek.co.uk/news/668085/Average-TV-
    viewing-rises-last-decade/.

## 12. Deathstyle

1. Porter 1997: 1; Sokolovsky 2009: xvii; http://web.ukonline.
   co.uk/thursday.handleigh/demography/life-death/life.htm.
2. Auguste Bernard quoted in Ariès 2008: 64; Ariès 2008: 59–60,
   64–9; Illich 1975: 124; Orme 2003: 118.
3. Ariès 2008 : 113–16, 330; Illich 1975: 122–31; Elias 2001: 14.
4. Ariès 2008: 132.
5. Ariès 2008: 128–9; Illich 1975: 122–4, 142.
6. Petit 2003: 185–8.
7. Rinpoche 1998: 27.
8. Kübler-Ross 1973: 5.
9. Ariès 2008: 165–6, 559–60.
10. Kellehear 2007: 207; Ariès 2008: 563; Kübler-Ross 1973: 6–8; Lewis
    2007: 4, 123.
11. Kübler-Ross 1973: 6–7.
12. Mitford 1998.

13. http://www.srgw.demon.co.uk/CremSoc4/Stats/
    National/2008/StatsNat.html.

14. Ariès 2008: 178.

15. Kübler-Ross 1973: 2.

16. Terkel 2002: xxiii.

17. Berg 1972: 78–81; Abrams 1999: 16.

18. Paz 1967: 49.

19. Brandes 2006: 181–6.

20. Brandes 2006: 3–10.

21. Brandes 2006: 51–60.

22. Regis 1999: 472–504; Roach 1996: 14–15, 61–2, 277–9.

23. http://www.aviva.co.uk/media-centre/story/1236/
    dying-conversation-death-remains-a-taboo-subject-a/.

24. Sontag 1991: 100.

25. Brandes 2006: 184; Carr 2007: 973.

26. Nightingale 2007: 109–10.

27. Ehrenreich 2009: 28–33, 41–2.

28. Nightingale 2007: 113.

29. Rinpoche 1998: 176.

30. http://www.aoa.gov/AoARoot/Aging_Statistics/index.aspx.

31. Townsend 1957: 21.

32. Kellehear 2007: 207, 213.

33. Kellehear 2007: 208, 215.

34. Kellehear 2007: 203–23; Elias 2001: 74; http://www.elderabuse.
    org.uk/; http://www.iqnursinghomes.com/.

35. Rinpoche 1998: 9.

36. Bronowski 1976: 64.

37. Quoted in Sokolovsky 2009: xxviii.

38. Zhang 2009: 215, n. 18; Jenike and Traphagan 2009: 246.

39. Zhang 2009: 204; Jenike and Traphagan 2009: 243–5, 249; http://
    www.jrf.org.uk/sites/files/jrf/sc100.pdf.

# Epilogue

1. Goethe 1970: 14, 57, 151; Goethe 1999: ix, xxiv.

2. Goethe 1999: xi, 28–9.

3. Armstrong 2007: 241–60, 330, 352, 432–42.

# Illustration Credits

p19.   *The Grand Duke Ferdinand II of Tuscany and his Wife (c.* 1660) by Justus Sustermans.

p19.   *Married Couple in a Garden* (Isaac Massa and Beatrix van der Laen) by Frans Hals (*c.* 1622) © Corbis.

p26.   *The Kiss* by Constantin Brancusi © Getty Images.

p44.   *The Family Meal* (oil on canvas) by Le Nain Brothers, (seventeenth century) (after) Musee des Beaux-Arts, Lille, France/Giraudon/The Bridgeman Art Library Nationality/ copyright status: French/out of copyright.

p64.   C. P. Ellis and Ann Atwater © Press Association.

p74.   Navy press gang at work (*c.* 1780) © Mary Evans.

p83.   £20 note, reproduced with kind permission from the Bank of England.

p86.   Albert Schweitzer, one of Europe's greatest organists © Mary Evans/IMAGNO/Photoarchiv Setzer-Tschiedel.

p86.   Albert Schweitzer at the hospital he opened in Africa © Mary Evans.

p105.  *The United States of North America* (1861) by Yoshikazu © Freer Gallery of Art.

p108.  Henry Ford's first moving assembly line, installed in 1913 © Getty Images.

p132.  The main staircase of Bon Marché (*c.*1880) © Mary Evans.

p139.  *Book Illustration of the Quakers Meeting Engraving After Maarteen Van Heemskerck* © Corbis.

p155.  *Margarita philosophica* (1503) © Getty Images.

p164.  *Mr and Mrs Andrews* by Thomas Gainsborough (1750) © Mary Evans/Interfoto Agentur.

p173.  Helen Keller (*c.* 1907) with kind permission from the Library of Congress.

p181.  *Since the crescent moon I have been waiting for tonight* © Asian Art & Archaeology, Inc./Corbis.

p188.  Eleanor Roosevelt taking a gondola ride during her honeymoon in Venice in 1905 © Bettmann/Corbis.

p205.  Joseph Knowles in *Naked in the Woods,* with thanks to Jim Motavilli.

p207.  *A wild man brandishing an uprooted tree trunk, a drawing* by Hans Holbein the Younger (1528) © the trustees of the British Museum.

p221.  *The Mountains at Lauteraar* (1776) by Caspar Wolf © Bridgeman Art Library.

p230.  *Buddhist monk Thich Quang Duc* (1963) by Malcolm Browne © Press Association

p238.  *American schoolchildren of Japanese descent pledging allegiance to the US flag in San Francisco's Little Tokyo district* (1942) © Dorothea Lange Estate.

p247.  *Tolstoy Ploughing* (*c.* 1889) by Ilya Repin © Bridgeman Art Library.

p257.  *Pietà* by Michaelangelo (1499) © Bridgeman Art Libary.

p264.  *Apicius* (1709) here subtitled *The Art of Cooking*.

p276.  *Girl with a Mandolin* by Pablo Picasso (1910) © Bridgeman and DACS.

p283.  *Danse macabre of the Empress with a skeleton, an allegory of death and life* © Mary Evans/Rue des Archives/Tallandier.

p286.  Philippe Petit (1972) in *Man on Wire.*

# Acknowledgements

Daniel Crewe at Profile Books has been the most wonderful editor, offering inspiring ideas and wise advice throughout the process of creating this book. Ruth Killick, Penny Daniel and Caroline Pretty at Profile Books have been a joy to work with too. *The Wonderbox* would not exist without the vision of my superb agent, Margaret Hanbury, who recognised its potential and has been enormously supportive and encouraging. Thanks also to Stuart Rushworth and Henry de Rougemont from the Hanbury Agency.

I have been lucky to have so many friends share their insights on the art of living, and give so much time and thought to making comments on early drafts of the text. They include Andrew Ray, Annalise Moser, Darwin Franks, Eka Morgan, Ellen Bassani, Eric Lonergan, Flora Gathorne-Hardy, Flutra Qatja, Forrest Metz, George Marshall, Hillary Norris, Hugh Griffith, Hugh Warwick, Ian Lyon, Jane Whiting, Jenny Carter, Jenny Raworth, Jo Lonergan, John Taylor, Lisa Gormley, Marcelo Goulart, Quentin Spender, Richard Gipps, Richard Raworth, Rob Archer, Robert Kelsey, Sarah Edington, Sophie Howarth, Tim Healing, Vera Ryhajlo and my parents, Anna and Peter Krznaric. Special thanks to everyone at The School of Life, especially Caroline Brimmer, Harriet Warden, Morgwn Rimel and Angharad Davies, and to all those who have attended my talks and workshops on the topics of this book.

Three historians have had a major impact on how I think about the past and helped me understand its relevance to how we live today: Theodore Zeldin, Michael Wood and the late Colin Ward. Their innovative historical thinking has been a constant source of inspiration, both through their books and in conversation.

I have been accompanied from beginning to end by my partner, Kate Raworth. More than anyone else, she is responsible for nurturing both the book and its writer. And thank you to my children, Siri and Casimir, for reminding me that life itself is a wonderbox of possibilities.

# About the author

Roman Krznaric is a cultural thinker and founding faculty member of The School of Life in London, which offers instruction and inspiration on the important questions of everyday life. He advises organisations including Oxfam and the United Nations on using empathy and conversation to create social change, and has been named by the *Observer* as one of Britain's leading lifestyle philosophers.

After growing up in Sydney and Hong Kong, he studied at the universities of Oxford, London and Essex, where he gained his PhD. He has taught sociology and politics at Cambridge University and City University, London, and has done human rights work in Central America with refugees and indigenous people. For several years he was Project Director at The Oxford Muse, the avant-garde foundation that aims to stimulate courage and invention in personal, professional and cultural life. He regularly speaks at public events on topics such as empathy, the history of love, the future of work, and the art of living. Recent appearances include the Edinburgh International Festival, the Latitude Arts Festival and the London Design Festival.

He is the author of *How to Find Fulfilling Work*, part of The School of Life's practical philosophy series edited by Alain de Botton. He has also written a book on what sport can teach us about life, *The First Beautiful Game: Stories of Obsession in Real Tennis* and, with the historian Theodore Zeldin, edited *Guide to an Unknown University*. His work has been translated into over a dozen languages and his blog dedicated to empathy, www.outrospection.org, has been featured in the media around the world.

Roman is a fanatical real tennis player, has worked as a gardener and has a passion for furniture making. For further details see his website www.romankrznaric.com.

# Index

**A**

Aborigines, Australian 135–6
Achilles 7
Adams, Henry 110
*agape* 9–10, 13, 16, 24, 25, 27, 310
Aka Pygmies 32–4, 39, 41, 52
Alberti, Leon Battista 96–7
Alcibiades 42
Alexander the Great 97
All Souls' Day 294
Allen, Woody 22, 219
*Alone in the Wilderness* (Knowles)
  205
*Ambassadors, The* (Holbein) 283
Amnesty International 88, 250
*Anatomy of Abuses* (Stubbes) 163
*Anatomy of Melancholy, The*
  (Burton) 154
Al-Andalus 14–15
Anderson, Benedict 236
animals 33, 58, 157, 160, 220
*Anna Karenina* (Tolstoy) 41, 246
Anthony, St 137
Antiochus Epiphanes, King of
  Syria 159
*Apicius* 263, 264
Aquinas, Thomas 163
*Arabian Nights, The* 13–14
Arapesh people 32
Ariès, Philippe 284
Aristophanes 43

Aristotle
  on five senses 153, 154, 157
  on human rationality 220
  on love 7, 11
  on pursuit of money 124
  on social bonds 146
  teaching career 97
art 254–8, 274–7
Arts and Crafts movement 267
*As I Walked Out One Midsummer
  Morning* (Lee) 201
Aspasia 6
Athens, classical 5–6, 42–3, 159
attention span 120–1
Atwater, Ann 62–4, 66, 309
aural culture 161–2
Austen, Jane 20
Avicenna 154, 156

**B**

Baden-Powell, Robert 195
Baedeker, Karl 186–90
Bakairi people 44
Bakhtiari people 301–2
Balinese time 118–19
Ballard, J. G. 28–30, 33
Barnardo's homes 87
Baron-Cohen, Simon 59
Barton, Clara 87
Bashō, Matsuo 179–80, 181, 183,
  184, 201

*Beagle*, HMS 196
Beck, Harry 98
beliefs 230–1
  monarchist 239–41
  nationalist 235–8
  religious 233–5
  transcendent cause 252
Bell, Alexander Graham 170
Bellamy, Francis 237
Beltane 209
Benedictine Rule 45
*Beowulf* 206
Berger, John 132–3, 164, 275
Bergman, Ingmar 304
Berry, Mary Frances 35
biodiversity loss 219
biophilia 216–19
Black Elk 218
*Bohème, La* (Puccini) 138
Bon Marché 128–32
Boone, Daniel 213
Borrow, George 194
*Boston Post* 204
Boucicaut, Aristide 128–30, 134
bourgeois culture 130–1, 164,
  186–7
Boy Scouts 195
Bradford, William 207–8
brain
  left and right 261
  structure 59
  in a vat 231–2
  ventricles 154–5
Brancusi, Constantin 25, 26
Brand, Stuart 122
Braque, Georges 275
Brillat-Savarin, Jean-Anthelme
  266
British monarchy 239–41
Browne, Malcolm 230
Brunelleschi, Filippo 274, 275

Bucchō 179
Buchwald, Art 147
Buddhism
  meditation 119–20, 179
  pilgrimage 179
  self-immolation of monk
    229–30
  sense of mindful awareness
    262
  silence 45
  Theravāda 10
  Zen 118, 119–20, 179
Burckhardt, Jacob 255
Burton, Sir Richard 13
Burton, Robert 154
Byron, Lord 210

**C**

calendars 103, 118, 130
*Call of the Wild, The* (London) 214
Calvin, John 11, 88
Calvinism 17
Cameron, Julia 261
camping 194–6
Capability Brown 93, 166
capitalism
  attitude to time 57, 58
  consumer 129, 131, 138
  division of labour 82
  eighteenth-century 57, 58, 127
  environmental impact 220, 221
  love 21, 22, 23
  nineteenth-century 129, 199
  seventeenth-century economic
    thought 127
  wage slavery 268
carbon emissions 219, 224–6
CARE USA 88
career
  choices 79–81
  'portfolio' 97–8

Caroline, Queen 239
Cavafy, Constantine 184
cemeteries 281–2, 289
Cézanne, Paul 275, 277
chair making 269–71
*Chapters in the Life of a Dundee Factory Boy* 106–7
charities 87–8
charity shops 144, 145
Chatwin, Bruce 192
Chaucer, Geoffrey 3, 4
Child, Julia 265
childcare 30, 32–3, 35–7, 40, 80, 162
China
care of parents 302–3
gardens 166
painting 274
Christianity 9–10, 220–1, 234–5, 247
Christmas 125, 234–5
Church of England 71
Churchill, Winston 117
Clark, Kenneth 208
Clarkson, Thomas 71–2, 75, 310
Classen, Constance 163, 170
climate change 219, 224, 225
climbing 212–13, 215
Clock of the Long Now 122
clocks 103–4, 116–17
coal 38, 210, 221
Cobbett, William 35, 199–200, 202
coffee houses 46
Coleridge, Samuel Taylor 209, 210
Cologne, clock 104
Columbus, Christopher 196, 198
Comfort, Alex 23
common sense 154, 231
communication 110–11

community life 146–7
computer age 270
*Confession, A* (Tolstoy) 245
Confucianism 10, 302
conservation movement 222–3
Constantine, Emperor 178, 234
consumer culture 125–8
conventions 275–8, 307–8
conversation
adventurous 50, 305
art of 41, 45, 295
about death 296–9
empathic 56, 60–1, 297–8
family 28, 30, 41–52, 309
history of 42, 46–9
love and 5, 11, 17, 27
origins 42
Cook, John Mason 177
Cook, Thomas 176–7, 186, 198
cooking 262–6
Copernicus 242–3
Cortés, Hernán 84
courage 298
Cranmer, Thomas 249
creativity 253–4, 258–62, 278–9
cremation 292
Crimean War 110, 183, 245
Crisp, Quentin 145
Crusaders 160
cubism 274–5, 276
Cupid 5, 25

**D**
dance of the dead (*danse macabre*) 282–3, 305
Daniel, Arnaut 15
Dante 97, 124, 185, 256
Darwin, Charles 59, 196–7
Daumer, Dr Georg Friedrich 168
David, Elizabeth 265
*David* (Michelangelo) 256

Day of the Dead 294
De Beers 21–2
de Bono, Edward 260
de Botton, Alain 133
*De Revolutionibus* (Copernicus)
    242
de Waal, Frans 59
Dean, James 37
death, attitudes to 280–1, 284,
    296–7
deathstyle 281, 298
Defoe, Daniel 127
della Rovere, Vittoria 19
department store 128–9
Descartes, René 96, 156, 220
diamonds 21–2
diaries 109, 117, 162, 214, 255
Dickens, Charles 106
Diem, Ngo Dinh 229
Diogenes 137
Disraeli, Benjamin 240
*Divine Comedy* (Dante) 124
division of labour 82–3, 85, 95,
    99
divorce 9, 24, 30, 39, 41
DIY 271–2
Donne, John 160
*Down and Out in Paris and London*
    (Orwell) 68–9
Drake, Francis 196
Druids 208, 209, 212
Dunlop, Fuchsia 265
Dutch Golden Age 17–18

**E**
Eden Project 223
Edison, Thomas 260
education system 236–7
Edward VII, King 240–1
Edwards, John Menlove 215
Egyptian wall painting 274

Ehrenreich, Barbara 297
Eiffel, Gustave 129
Einstein, Albert 231
El Dorado 84
elderly people 299–304
Elgar, Edward 82
Ellington, Duke 151
Ellis, C. P. 61–4, 65–6, 309
Emerson, Ralph Waldo 100,
    141–2, 209
empathy
    cognitive 54
    conversational 297–8
    cultivating 75
    deficit 55, 66
    definition 54, 55
    expanding 60, 66, 68
    experiential 69–70
    human capacity for 57–60
    importance of 54–6
    mass empathy and social
        change 70–5
*Empire of the Sun* (Ballard) 29
enclosure movement
    209–10
Enlightenment 155, 163, 258
Eno, Brian 122
Epstein, Jacob 174
equilibrioception 157
Eros 5
*eros*
    courtly love 15
    idea of 5–7
    marriage 17–18
    power of 6
    relationships 25, 26, 27
    romantic love 13–15, 20, 24
Escoffier, Auguste 265
Europa 6
Everest 212
exploration 196–202

**F**

Facebook 8
factories 106–7, 269
family life 34–6
*Family Meal, The* (Le Nain brothers) 44
fantasy 154
fast food 111–12
fathers 30–5
Ferdinand II of Tuscany 19
Fermat's Last Theorem 259
Feuerbach, Anselm von 169
Fiennes, Celia 208
Finland 46
Flaubert, Gustave 116
flight emissions 225
Fonda, Jane 48
Forbes, Bruce 235
Ford, Henry 93–4, 107, 108, 111
forests 206–7, 208–10, 221–2
Forster, E. M. 188–9
France, Anatole 278
Francis of Assisi, St 53–4, 69–70, 221
Frankl, Victor 89–90
Franklin, Benjamin 107
Freecycle 145
French Revolution 87
Freud, Sigmund 11
friends 7–8, 63–4, 309
Fromm, Erich 22
funerals 291, 292, 295–6
Fuseli, Henry 277

**G**

Gaia 218
Gainsborough, Thomas 164
Galatea 6
Galen, Claudius 154
Galileo 104, 242–5, 248

Gandhi, Mahatma
  grave 182
  hand-spinning 268
  simple living 138, 146, 250–1
  on slow living 114
  Talisman 54–5
  Tolstoy Farm 247
gap-year students 200
gardening 92–3, 165–7
George IV, King 239–40
George and the Dragon 16
Gershwin, George 265
Gilbert, W. S. 51
Gilbreth, Frank and Lillian 107
Girl Guides 147, 195
*Girl with a Mandolin* (Picasso) 276
Gladstone, William 240
Godwin, William 277
Goethe, Johann Wolfgang von
  xii, 20, 208, 210, 306–10
Golden Rule 55
Gottlieb, Beatrice 43, 45
Graceland 178
Grand Tour 185–6, 187, 189–90
graves 282, 289
Gray, Thomas 208
Greece, ancient
  five senses 153, 157
  sculpture 274
  segregation of women 43, 52
  *symposium* 42–3, 46
  types of love 4, 5–12, 15, 23, 24, 25
  view of work 88
Green Men 209
grieving 292–3
Griffiths, Jay 212
Guatemala
  author's studies 66, 95
  author's travels 69, 115, 192, 200, 249

DIY culture 272–3
pace of life 115
Gutenberg, Johannes 162

## H

Halberstam, David 229
Hall, Edward 161
Hals, Franz 19
Hammond, Samuel 216
Hampton Court Palace 160
*Hard Times* (Dickens) 106
Hardy, Dennis 194
Hart, Charles 302
Hauser, Kaspar 168–70, 172
hearing 153, 158
Helena, St 178
Herrigel, Eugene 120
Herzen, Alexander 246
hibernation 117
Hildegard of Bingen 97, 102
Hite, Shere 24
Hobbes, Thomas x, 56–7
Hochschild, Adam 71, 72–3
Holbein, Hans the Younger 107,
   283
Homer 7
*Homo erectus* 266
*Homo faber* 267–71, 273, 278
*Homo Ludens* (Huizinga) 8
*Homo sapiens* 266–7
homosexuality 5–6
Hopkins, Gerard Manley 208–9
Horace 177
hospices 147, 291, 296, 298
hospitals 86–7, 291–2
househusband 29, 31–2, 34–5,
   39–40
housewife 34, 37
housework 28, 30, 35, 37–40
Howes, David 158
Huizinga, Johan 8

Human, Alan 64–5
human library movement 192
Human Rights Watch 250
Hume, David 60
hunter-gatherers 135–6
*Husbands and Wives* (film) 22
Hyde, Lewis 265

## I

IBM 94
Ibn Battuta 178
Ibn Hazm 14–15
Ibn Khaldun 193
imagination 154
individualism 255–6
Innocent 94
Inquisition 244
instinct 154
*Into the Wild* (Krakauer) 214–15
Ivan (author's grandfather) 298

## J

J. Walter Thompson 21
Japan
   Bashō's pilgrimage 179–80,
      181
   care of parents 302–3
   deforestation 222
Jekyll, Gertrude 167
Jencks, Charles 167
Jerusalem 178
Jesus 137, 234–5
Johnson, Dr Samuel 46–7, 186
Joshua 242
*Joy of Sex, The* (Comfort) 23

## K

Keller, Helen 170–4
Kennedy, John F. 171
Keynes, John Maynard 136,
   241–2

kinaesthesia 157
King, Martin Luther 62, 75, 182
Kingsley, Mary 197–8, 199, 309
Kinsey, Alfred 48
Kipling, Rudyard 197
*Kiss, The* (Brancusi) 25, 26
kissing 15, 25
Knights of St John of Jerusalem 86
Knights Templar 86
Knowles, Joseph 204–5
Köhler, Wolfgang 266
Krakauer, Jon 214–15
*Kramer versus Kramer* (film) 39
Krishnamurti, Jiddu 249–50
Kroc, Ray 111
Kropotkin, Prince Peter 246
Ku Klux Klan (KKK) 56, 61–2, 64
Kübler-Ross, Elisabeth 290, 291
Kumar, Satish 180–3
!Kung people 135–6

**L**

La Rochefoucauld, François de 4
*Labyrinth of Solitude, The* (Paz) 293
Lake District 208, 210
Lancelot and Guinevere 16
landscape gardening 93, 166
landscape painting 164, 211, 274
Lange, Dorothea 238
lateral thinking 260
Latimer, Hugh 249
Lawrence, T. E. 157
Layard, Richard 54
Lazarus (Epstein sculpture) 174
Le Nain brothers 44
Leach, William 126, 131
Leda 6
Lee, Laurie 200–2, 249
Lent 119

Leo (author's grandfather) 299–300
Leonardo da Vinci 97, 98–9, 102, 154, 256
*Leviathan* (Hobbes) 57
Libanius 234
life expectancy 280
Livy 263
Local Exchange Trading Schemes 147
London 127, 180, 282
London, Jack 214
*Long Walk to Freedom* (Mandela) 251
lotteries 123–4
Loudon, John 92
Louis XV, King 269
Louv, Richard 217
love
    courtly 15–16
    erotic 5–7
    at first sight 14
    friendship 7–8
    ludic 8–9
    mature 9
    romantic 12–13
    selfless 9–10
    self-love 10–11
*ludus* 8, 12, 13, 23–5, 27, 309
Luther, Martin 88, 89
luxury 148

**M**

McCandless, Chris 213–16, 224
McDonald's 111–12
McEwan, Ian 54
McKibben, Bill 146, 223–4
McLuhan, Marshall 162
*Madame Bovary* (Flaubert) 116
Madrid 127
Magellan, Ferdinand 196

magnetic fields 169
magnetoreception 157
Mallory, George 212–13
Mandela, Nelson 251
Mander, Jerry 50
Manetti, Giannozzo 256
*Man on Wire* 286
*Man's Search for Meaning* (Frankl) 89–90
Marie Antoinette, Queen 137–8
Marie de Champagne, Countess 15
Markham, Gervase 220
marriage 9, 15, 17–19, 25
*Married Couple in a Garden* (Franz Hals) 19
Marshall, George 226
Marx, Karl 79, 97
May Day 209, 212
*Mayflower* 208
Mbuti people 32
Mecca 178
Médecins Sans Frontières 88
meditation 119–20, 179
*memento mori* 282–3
memory 154, 162
Menon, Prabhakar 180–2
*Mettā* 10
Mexico, attitudes to death 293–4
Michelangelo Buonaroti 97, 255, 256–8, 259
Microsoft 145
Midas, King 124
Middle Ages
    DIY 269
    kissing 15
    spices and perfumes 160
    spoken word 162
    view of creation 256
    view of death 281–4
    view of forests 206, 217
view of work 88
views of the senses 153–4, 163
Mill, John Stuart 47–8, 51
Miller, Michael 129
*Miracle Worker, The* (film) 171
monarchy 239–41
Mondrian 264
money 84–5, 123–5
Monopoly 146
Monroe, Marilyn 21
Morning Pages 261
Morris, William 267–8, 270, 271, 272
Morse, Samuel 110
Moscow 180, 182
mountains 208, 210–11, 212–13
*Mountains at Lauteraar, The* (Wolf) 211
Mozart, Wolfgang Amadeus 258
*Mr and Mrs Andrews* (Gainsborough) 164
*Mrs Beeton's Book of Household Management* 37
Muir, John 223
Mumford, Lewis 108
Mumsnet 31
Murger, Henri 138
Murray, John 187
music 172, 255
Musil, Robert 116
Muslim communities 44–5

**N**
N. W. Ayer 21
Naomi (author's grandmother) 278
Napoleon 80
Narcissus 10, 75
*Narrow Road to the Deep North, The* (Bashō) 179
Nash, Roderick 215

nationalism 235–41
*Natural History* (Pliny) 165
nature
    end of 224, 226
    Western perception of 208–9
Nero, Emperor 160
Netherlands 17–18
New Orleans, funeral parades 295
Newton, Isaac 259, 264
Nhat Hanh, Thich 119
Nietzsche, Friedrich 65, 90
Nightingale, Florence 87, 183, 297, 298
Nobel Peace Prize 85
nociception 157
nomadism 192–6
'now' 121–2
Nuer people 44
nursing homes 300–1

O
Obama, Barack 55
old age 299–304
*On Death and Dying* (Kübler-Ross) 290
Ongee people 151, 158
Orthodox Church 247
Orwell, George 49, 66–70, 199, 249, 308
Ovid 8
Owen, Robert 141
Owen, Wilfred 236
Oxfam 88, 253
Oxford, sensory tourist trail 174–5

P
Pan 206
Pankhurst, Emmeline 75
parents, care of 302–4

Paris 127, 180, 182, 185, 282
Pascal, Blaise 192
patriarchy 37
Patroclus 7
Pawukon calendar 118
Paz, Octavio 293
Penn, William 139–40
*Perfume* (Süsskind) 160–1
*Perfumed Garden, The* 15
perfumes 159–60
Pericles 6
Perkins, William 89
Persia 13–14, 166
perspective, linear 274–5
Petit, Philippe 285–7, 288
Petrini, Carlo 112
PhD 95
*philauteo* 10–11, 13, 23, 24
*philia* 7–8, 12–13, 18, 23–7, 309
Philo of Alexandria 153
Piaget, Jean 58–9
Picasso, Pablo 254–5, 275, 276, 277, 278
*Pietà* (Michelangelo) 256, 257
pilgrimage 179, 178–84
Pilgrimage for Peace 180–3
pin factory 82–3, 84, 95
Pizarro, Francisco 198–9
Plato 42, 153, 156
play 8–9
Pliny the Elder 165
Poincaré, Henri 259
Pollock, Jackson 265
Polo, Marco 178
Polyphemus 6
Popul Vuh 218
Potosí silver mines 198–9
poverty 67–9, 136, 141, 199–200
*pragma* 9, 13, 17–18, 24, 25, 27, 309
Prague, clock 104

Presley, Elvis 178
press gangs 73, 74
*Pride and Prejudice* (Austen) 20, 47
printing 162
Prodicus 5
proprioception 157
Protestant ethic 88–9, 115, 127
Protestant Reformation 88, 163
Proudhon, Pierre-Joseph 246
Proust, Marcel 156
Ptolemy 97, 242, 243
Puccini, Giacomo 138
Puritans 138, 139

**Q**

Quakers 45, 71, 138–40, 142, 143, 199
Quang Duc, Thich 229–30, 249

**R**

*Rain, Steam, and Speed* (Turner) 109
Ramadan 119
rationality 220
*Rebel Without a Cause* (film) 37
*ren* 10
Renaissance
    gardens 19, 165, 166
    idea of creative genius 254, 255, 256–8, 259, 260, 262, 263
    idea of individuality 255–6
    ideal of the generalist 96–7, 99
    painting and sculpture 112, 186, 208, 274–5
    view of common sense 154
    view of death 281
Repin, Ilya 247
respect 92–4
*Resurrection* (Tolstoy) 248
Ridley, Nicholas 249

Rimsky-Korsakov, Nikolai 151
*Ring of the Dove, The* (Ibn Hazm) 14–15
rituals, religious 119
*Robbers, The* (Schiller) 194
Roman Catholic Church 243–4
*Romance of the Rose, The* 15
Romantic movement 20, 47, 208–12, 222
Rome
    ancient 160, 234–5, 263
    cemeteries 282
    St Peter's 178, 185, 256–7
Romeo and Juliet 16
*Room With a View* (film) 118
Roosevelt, Eleanor 188
roses 165–6
Roszak, Theodore 218
Rousseau, Jean-Jacques 210, 215
Royal Navy 73, 221–2
*Rural Rides* (Cobbett) 199–200
Ruskin, John 270
Russell, Bertrand 180, 182

**S**

Sabbath 119
Sahlins, Marshall 135–6
Sappho 6
Sartre, Jean–Paul 68
Saturnalia 234
Saunders, Cicely 298
Schama, Simon 17
Scheherazade 13
Schiller, Friedrich 194, 309
Schopenhauer, Arthur 247
Schumacher, E. F. 144
Schweitzer, Albert 85–6, 88
*Scientific Management* (Taylor) 107
scientific method 163–4

*Scouting for Boys* (Baden-Powell) 195

*Self Help* (Smiles) 74

senses 151–2
  Christian distrust of 163
  five 153, 156
  inner 154–6
  outer 154
  ten 156–7

*Seventh Seal, The* (film) 304–5

sex 15, 21, 23–4, 25, 48–9

Shahryar 13

Shaker communities 269

Shakespeare, William 165

Shaw, George Bernard 55, 235

shopping
  Bon Marché story 128–32
  consumer culture 125–6, 132–5
  rise of 127–8

Siena 187–8

Sierra Club 223

sight 151–2, 153, 158–9, 167–8

silence 45–6

Singer, Peter 252

Sistine Chapel 185, 256–7, 258

slavery, campaign against 71–2, 73–4, 140–1

Slow Food movement 112

slowing down 114–15

*Small Is Beautiful* (Schumacher) 144

smell
  Greek view 153
  importance of 151
  perfumes 159–60
  Puritan view 163
  sensitivity to 158, 169–70, 172
  stench of the past 160–1

Smiles, Samuel 74

Smith, Adam
  on division of labour 82–3, 95
  on empathy 57–8, 60
  *Wealth of Nations* 57, 82–3, 127, 134, 221

Socrates 42–3, 75, 102, 249, 308

Sogyal Rinpoche 301

Sol Invictus 234–5

Solomon, King 242

*Songlines, The* (Chatwin) 192

*Sorrows of Young Werther, The* (Goethe) 20

Soulmates 13

Spanish Civil War 201–2, 249

specialisation 95–6

*Spectator* 197–8

speech 153, 162

spice trade 160

status 91–2

steam trains 109–10

Stephen, Sir Leslie 47

Stevens, Wallace 253–4

Stone, Lawrence 20

Stonehenge 212

storytelling 162

Stubbes, Phillip 163

Suffragettes 250

Sullivan, Annie 170–1

Sultan (chimpanzee) 266

Supertramp, Alexander 213

Süsskind, Patrick 160–1

Sustermans, Justus 19

Suzuki, Daisetz Teitaro 120

symbolism 166, 167

synaesthesia 151

**T**

Tahiti 32

taste 153, 163

Tawney, R. H. 88

Taylor, Frederick 107, 108, 112

telegraph 110

telescope 163, 243–4

television 49–51, 279
Terkel, Studs 61
Tewa Indians 121
*Theory of Moral Sentiments, The*
57–8
Theosophy movement 249–50
thermoception 156–7
Thesiger, Wilfred 190
Thomas, Keith 128, 222
Thonet, Michael 269
Thoreau, Henry David
on cost of shopping 135
publication of work 205
simple living 142–4, 145,
146–7, 215, 271–3, 307
view of nature 209, 211, 226
*Tibetan Book of Living and Dying,*
*The* (Sogyal Rinpoche) 301
time-and-motion studies 107–8
time management 112–13
'time off' 113–14
*Times, The* 239
Tiwi people 302
Tolstoy, Leo
beliefs 242, 245–7, 249, 250
on family life 29, 41
lifestyle 215, 246–8, 310
*Tolstoy Ploughing* (Repin) 247
tool making 266–7
tortilla 263–5
touch 151, 153, 162
tourism 185–92
Transcendalists 141–2, 209, 223
transport 109–10
travel agents 176–7
trees 208–9, 221–2
*Trees by the Water* (Cézanne)
275
Tristan and Isolde 16
Turner, J. M. W. 109
Twain, Mark 83, 171

*Twenty-Four Examples of Filial*
*Piety* 302
Twitter 7

**U**
Uccello, Paolo 274
United States
national reserves 222–3
Pledge of Allegiance 237–8
*United States of North America,*
*The* (Yoshikazu) 105

**V**
Valentine, St 3–4
Van Gogh, Vincent 90–1
Vanuatu 44
Vasari, Georgio 257–8
Vaucanson, Jacques de 269
Venice 127–8
ventricles of the brain 154–5
Vermeer, Johannes 275
Victoria, Queen 240
*Vindication of the Rights of*
*Woman, A* (Wollstonecraft) 277
visual culture 161–2
Voltaire 269

**W**
*Walden* (Thoreau) 142–3
Walpurgis Night 209
Ward, Colin 194
Washington 180
watches 101–2, 104–6, 116
*Ways of Seeing* (Berger) 132–3
*Wealth of Nations, The* (Smith) 57,
82–3, 127, 221
Wedgwood, Josiah 106, 113
WEEE man 223
Wei, Han Emperor 166
Wendi, Han Emperor 302, 303
Wertherism 20

White, Lynn 221
Whiting, Jane 284–5, 287
Wilberforce, William 71
*Wild* (Griffiths) 211–12
Wild Men 206, 207, 208
Wilde, Oscar 281
wilderness
    attitudes to 208, 221–2
    Knowles's story 204–5
    McCandless's story 213–15,
        224
    recreation experiences 217–18
    Romantic vision 211–12, 215
    Thoreau's adventure 143–4
Wiles, Andrew 259
Wilson, Edward 216
Wolf, Caspar 211
Wollstonecraft, Mary 277–8, 307
Woodcraft Folk 195

woodland 208–10
Woolf, Virginia 47, 278
Woolman, John 140–1, 146, 310
Wordsworth, William 208, 211,
    217
Work Foundation 81
working hours 136–7
Wren, Christopher 264

Y
Yoshikazu 105

Z
Zeldin, Theodore 51, 96
*Zen in the Art of Archery* (Suzuki)
    120
Zeus 6
Zola, Émile 116, 129